WordPress 2.7 Cookbook

100 simple but incredibly useful recipes to take control
of your WordPress blog layout, themes, widgets, plugins,
security, and SEO

Jean-Baptiste Jung

BIRMINGHAM - MUMBAI

WordPress 2.7 Cookbook

First published: July 2009

Production Reference: 2100709

Published by Packt Publishing Ltd.
32 Lincoln Road
Olton
Birmingham, B27 6PA, UK.

ISBN 978-1-847197-38-2

www.packtpub.com

Cover Image by Vinayak Chittar (vinayak.chittar@gmail.com)

Credits

Author

Jean-Baptiste Jung

Reviewers

Alan Doucette

Narayan Bhat

Paul Thewlis

Acquisition Editor

David Barnes

Development Editors

Amey Kanse

Nikhil Bangera

Technical Editors

Mehul Shetty

Rakesh Shejwal

Copy Editor

Leonard D'Silva

Editorial Team Leader

Akshara Aware

Project Team Leader

Lata Basantani

Project Coordinator

Joel Goveya

Proofreader

Jeff Orloff

Indexer

Monica Ajmera

Production Coordinator

Shantanu Zagade

Adline Swetha Jesuthas

Cover Work

Shantanu Zagade

About the Author

Jean-Baptiste Jung is a Web developer, Web designer, and blogger born in Paris, France and now living in Wallonia (French-speaking part of Belgium) with his wife and cat.

Jean unearthed the World Wide Web in 1998 and started creating web sites three years later. In 2006, while working as a freelance Web developer for a well known French TV channel, Jean started to work with blogs and WordPress. A few months later, he created his first blog.

He became immensely passionate about WordPress and launched a blog dedicated to WordPress hacks, http://www.wprecipes.com/, which quickly managed to become one of the most popular WP-related web sites over the Internet. Meanwhile, Jean is also an author on some prestigious blogs, such as WpHacks, ProBlogDesign, and Smashing Magazine.

When he's not blogging or tweaking web sites, Jean enjoys travelling and spending time with his wife and cat. He has a strong love for animals and always stands up to defend animal rights.

I'd like to thank my wife Emmanuelle as well as our cute cat for being here with me. They mean so much to me.

About the Reviewers

Alan Doucette is a partner of KOI (`www.koitech.net`), a web development company. He is passionate about PHP and Open Source software. His constantly changing blog can be found at `http://alanio.net`.

Thanks go to the awesome WordPress community for all their daily hard work creating great Open Source software. I would also like to thank Brandi & Jack Lee (`www.pandria.com`) for their support and dealing with me while I constantly put time into Open Source projects.

Narayan Bhat is an avid user of Blogger, Twitter, and other useful web applications. He is a top contributor to the Blogger Help Group with more than 50,000 posts to date. Get Blogger tips and tricks and hacks at his blog `http://www.blogdoctor.me`.

He has also worked on the following books:

- *Blogger Beyond the Basics* by Lee Jordon.
- *WordPress for Business Bloggers* by Paul Thewlis.

Paul Thewlis has worked as a Web communications professional in public and private sectors. He is currently E-Communications Manager for a multinational transport company based in the UK. He began his Web career as a Technical Editor, working on web design books for a well-known publisher. He has extensive experience of many Content Management Systems and blogging platforms. He is an expert in the use of social media within corporate communications, and blogs about that subject, as well as WordPress and the Web in general, at http://blog.paulthewlis.com. He also runs the popular Twitter trivia quiz, Twrivia (http://twrivia.com), and the email reminder service, Urge-Me (http://urge-me.com).

Paul is the author of *WordPress For Business Bloggers*, published by Packt.

Table of Contents

Preface

About 120,000 blogs are created every day. Most of them quickly die, but a few stay, grow up, and then become well known and respected places on the Web. If you are seriously interested in being in the top league, you will need to learn all the tricks of the trade. WordPress 2.7 Cookbook focuses on providing solutions to common WordPress problems, to help make sure that your blog will be one of the ones that stay.

The author's experience with WordPress enables him to share insights on using WordPress effectively, in a clear and friendly way, giving practical hands-on solutions to WordPress problems, questions, and common tasks—from themes to widgets and from SEO to security.

Are you feeling limited with WordPress, or are you wondering how popular blogs do a certain kind of thing that you can't? With this cookbook, you will learn many WordPress secrets and techniques with step-by-step, useful recipes dedicated to achieving a particular goal or solving a particular problem. You'll learn the secret of expensive premium themes, how to optimize your blog for SEO and online profits, and how to supercharge WordPress with killer functions used by the most popular blogs over the Internet.

What this book covers

Chapter 1 introduces you to WordPress. It introduces you to some basic—but often forgotten—built-in tools to make your blogger life easier.

Chapter 2 discusses the various WordPress themes and provides you with the location where to find professional—but free—themes. It also teaches you how to install and customize these themes.

Chapter 3 teaches you how to customize any existing WordPress theme and make it fit your taste and need.

Chapter 4 describes an easy procedure to install plugins. It shows what different plugins can do for you in particular situations. It also teaches you how to download and install widgets and how to make a WordPress theme widget-ready.

Chapter 5 describes the procedure to display posts and to retrieve post information from WordPress.

Chapter 6 teaches you to manage a multi-author blog and integrate powerful functions for creating an author page template.

Chapter 7 educates you about hacks, plugins, and tips and tricks to secure your database and your WordPress blog.

Chapter 8 teaches you—by providing you with tips and tricks—the art of getting traffic from search engines to your blog.

Chapter 9 discusses the monetization solution that can be used in a WordPress blog. It will also provide you with many tips and tricks to make money while blogging.

Chapter 10 helps you make your blog easy and functional for your visitors.

Chapter 11 provides you with tips and hacks to make your blog better than your competitor's blog.

What you need for this book

You'll need a working installation of WordPress on a server, or on your local machine (using MAMP, WampServer, EasyPHP, and so on). WordPress can be downloaded from the link, `http://wordpress.org/download/`.

You need to have minimal knowledge of XHTML and CSS, PHP and JavaScript.

You also need an FTP client for uploading files. I recommend Cyberduck (`http://cyberduck.ch/`) for Mac and Filezilla (`http://filezilla-project.org/`) for both GNU/Linux and Windows platforms.

Who this book is for

This book is for anyone who wants to enhance their WordPress blog to make it more engaging and feature-rich. It is not specifically for developers or programmers, rather it can be used by anyone who wants to get more out of their WordPress blog by following step-by-step instructions. A basic knowledge of PHP, XHTML, CSS, and WordPress is desirable, but not necessary.

Conventions

In this book, you will find a number of styles of text that distinguish between different kinds of information. Here are some examples of these styles, and an explanation of their meaning.

Code words in text are shown as follows: "We can include other contexts through the use of the `include` directive."

A block of code is set as follows:

```php
<?php
if (current_user_can('level_10')){ ?>
    <a href="<?php bloginfo('wpurl');?>/wp-admin/edit.php?p=
    <?php the_ID(); ?>">Edit Post</a>
<?php } ?>
```

New terms and **important words** are shown in bold. Words that you see on the screen, in menus or dialog boxes for example, appear in the text like this: "Scroll down until you see a **Page template** link".

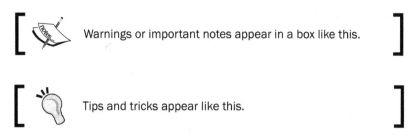

Warnings or important notes appear in a box like this.

Tips and tricks appear like this.

Reader feedback

Feedback from our readers is always welcome. Let us know what you think about this book—what you liked or may have disliked. Reader feedback is important for us to develop titles that you really get the most out of.

To send us general feedback, simply send an email to feedback@packtpub.com, and mention the book title via the subject of your message.

If there is a book that you need and would like to see us publish, please send us a note in the **SUGGEST A TITLE** form on www.packtpub.com or email suggest@packtpub.com.

If there is a topic that you have expertise in and you are interested in either writing or contributing to a book on, see our author guide on www.packtpub.com/authors.

Customer support

Now that you are the proud owner of a Packt book, we have a number of things to help you to get the most from your purchase.

Downloading the example code for the book

Visit `http://www.packtpub.com/files/code/7382_Code.zip` to directly download the example code.

The downloadable files contain instructions on how to use them.

Errata

Although we have taken every care to ensure the accuracy of our content, mistakes do happen. If you find a mistake in one of our books—maybe a mistake in the text or the code—we would be grateful if you would report this to us. By doing so, you can save other readers from frustration, and help us to improve subsequent versions of this book. If you find any errata, please report them by visiting `http://www.packtpub.com/support`, selecting your book, clicking on the **let us know** link, and entering the details of your errata. Once your errata are verified, your submission will be accepted and the errata added to any list of existing errata. Any existing errata can be viewed by selecting your title from `http://www.packtpub.com/support`.

Piracy

Piracy of copyright material on the Internet is an ongoing problem across all media. At Packt, we take the protection of our copyright and licenses very seriously. If you come across any illegal copies of our works, in any form, on the Internet, please provide us with the location address or website name immediately so that we can pursue a remedy.

Please contact us at `copyright@packtpub.com` with a link to the suspected pirated material.

We appreciate your help in protecting our authors, and our ability to bring you valuable content.

Questions

You can contact us at `questions@packtpub.com` if you are having a problem with any aspect of the book, and we will do our best to address it.

1
Getting Ready to Cook with WordPress

Back in 2003, when blogs weren't as popular as they are nowadays, an average 2000 users used a blogging platform created by Michel Valdrighi known as **b2**.

This year, two b2 users, Matt Mullenweg and Mike Little, decided to create a fork of b2 and named it as WordPress.

Due to the growing popularity of the blogging platform, several core members of WordPress development team decided to create a company devoted to promote and enhance WordPress, called **Automattic**. The team also started to provide a hosted service at www.wordpress.com.

Today, WordPress is used by many people and companies. While there's a lot of personal blogs, with people simply willing to stay tuned with their friends, some very well-known companies, such as CNN, use WordPress to share their content on the web.

With its Open Source code, dynamic community, and passionate individuals WordPress can be used by everyone and easily make it fit to their own needs.

Even if understanding the working of WordPress isn't that difficult, it may take some time for a novice or a non-developer to get accustomed to it. The WordPress Cookbook can be read chapter wise, as a way to understand the working of WordPress and explore new things using it.

On the other hand, it is possible to keep the WordPress Cookbook on your desk and refer to it in case an issue arises. WordPress Cookbook features many **recipes** that can be read in no particular order.

In this chapter, you will learn:

- ▶ Managing media files with the Media Library
- ▶ Live editing themes with the built-in Theme Editor
- ▶ Editing plugins with the WordPress built-in Plugin Editor
- ▶ Managing authors and users with the User Manager
- ▶ Importing and Exporting content with the Import and Export tool

By default, WordPress provides some useful tools for the bloggers that make your blogging life easier. The following are the tools provided by WordPress:

- ▶ Media Library
- ▶ Theme Editor
- ▶ Plugin Editor
- ▶ User Manager
- ▶ Import/Export Manager

Managing media files with the Media Library

The Media Library allows you to manage all the media files (images, videos, and so on) in one place. The Media Library allows you to add, delete, and edit media files for further integration on your blog posts.

Getting ready

To access WordPress Media Library, log in to your WordPress **Dashboard** and go to **Media | Library**, located to the right of the screen.

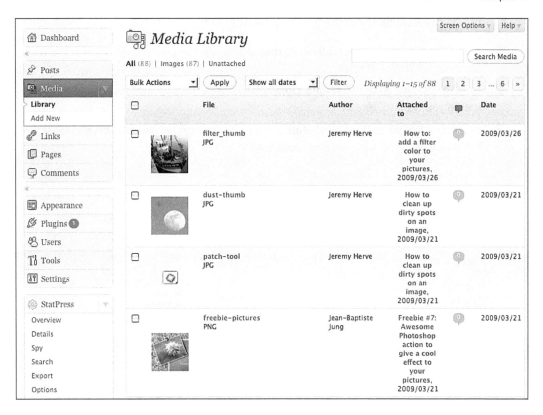

How to do it...

1. To add a new media file on the Media Library, click the **Media** option, in WordPress admin menu, and then click on **Add new**. A **Select files** button will be displayed. Simply click on it and select the media files from your hard drive.

2. There are two uploaders available: the Flash uploader (which uses Adobe Flash technology) and the Browser uploader (which uses a good old input file HTML field). The Flash uploader allows you to select multiple files at once, while the browser uploader allows you to upload only one file at a time. With WordPress 2.6, the Flash uploader wasn't working on Mac OS and GNU/Linux platforms. This has been fixed with WordPress 2.7. However, if you have any issues with Flash uploader, the Browser uploader will always work.

To delete the media, carry out the following steps:

1. Deleting media is an easy process. On the Media Library, simply hover an item and the **Edit**, **Delete**, and **Views** buttons will be displayed.

2. Click on **Delete** and the media will be deleted for good.

For bulk media deletion, carry out the following steps:

1. If you need to delete around 5 or 10 media files, WordPress allows you to erase all the undesired files at once.

2. To do so, simply go to the **Media Library** and check the checkboxes related to the media you want to delete.

3. Select the **Delete** option in the **Bulk Actions** drop-down list (located on the top left of the page) and then click on the **Apply** button.

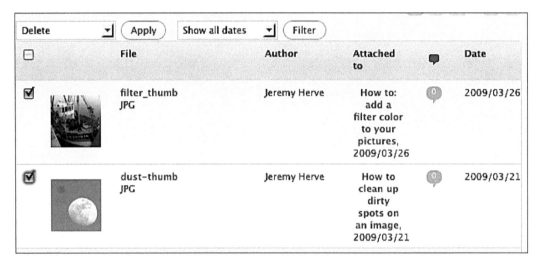

All media files can be edited. You can change its title and add a caption or description. Carry out the following steps to do so:

1. Go to the **Media Library**.

2. Hover the mouse over the item you'd like to edit and click on the **Edit** link which appears.

3. A new page opens, allowing you to define the file settings.

4. Click on the **Apply** button when you're done editing the file settings.

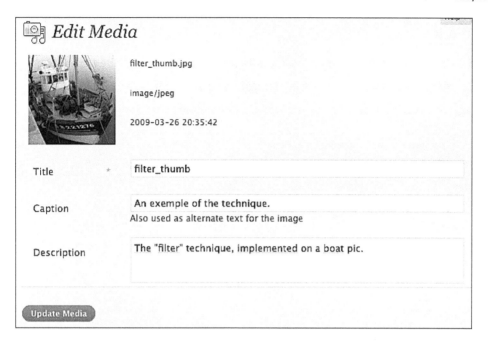

How it works...

The **Media Library** allows you to manage, upload, and delete media files. Unlike adding or deleting media files directly on your server by using a FTP program, the **Media Library** ensures that database entries related to media are updated or deleted, depending on the action you have taken.

Live editing themes with the built-in Theme Editor

Among other tools, WordPress features the Theme Editor, which allows you to edit your theme files without downloading or uploading the files. Chapter 3 covers WordPress themes in detail.

Getting ready

To access the **Theme Editor**, log in to your WordPress **Dashboard**, and go to **Appearance | Editor** located at the top of the screen. To select a theme for editing, use the drop-down list located at the top right of the screen. By default, you'll be editing the theme being used currently by your blog.

How to do it...

1. You can access the templates in the **Theme Files**, located on the right of the screen.

2. Simply click on one of the files to begin editing that particular file.

3. When you're done, click on the **Update File** button to save your modifications.

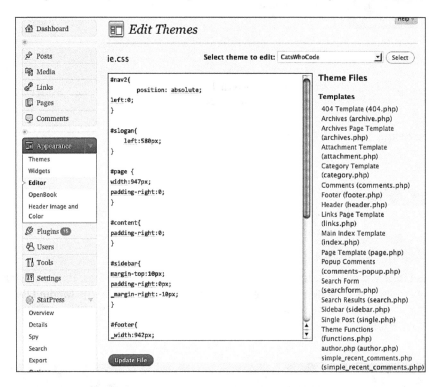

How it works...

While editing a theme file in WordPress theme editor, you're actually editing the real file on the server. Once you press the **Update File** button, the file is saved and the previous version is erased.

There's more...

Although the Theme Editor is probably my favorite built-in tool from WordPress, you have to be careful with it.

▶ It is safe to always have a backup of your theme before editing. The Theme Editor does not save revisions. If you have made a modification and later would like to undo the modification, you need to have a backup of the previous version of the file.

- ▶ Use the Theme Editor only if you're sure about what you're doing. If you're editing your current theme and make a programming error (for example, a PHP syntax error), it is possible that your blog will stop functioning.

- ▶ Sometimes, a programming mistake can result in you losing access over the Theme Editor. While this is quite a rare case (it mostly happens when you make a code mistake in the `functions.php` file), the problem can be important enough for you to always be sure to have a proper backup of your theme, as well as a valid FTP connection to your blog server, before editing any files.

- ▶ In case you are not able to access the editor after editing a file on it, use a FTP program to transfer a backup version of the file you've just edited to your WordPress server.

Editing plugins with the WordPress built-in Plugin Editor

As WordPress features an editor allowing you to live edit your theme, it also provides another editor for editing plugins. Chapter 4 covers plugins in detail.

Getting ready

To access the Plugin Editor, log in to your WordPress **Dashboard** and go to **Plugins | Editor** located at the top of the screen. Then, select the plugin to edit from the list located on the right of the screen.

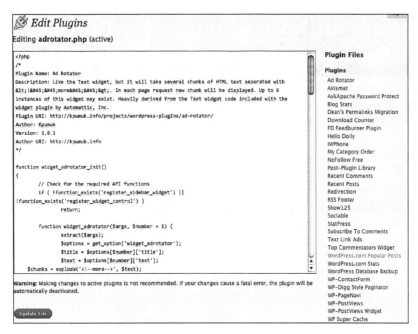

How to do it...

1. Once you have selected the plugin to edit, make the desired changes.

2. Finally, click on the **Update File** button when you are done. The file will be saved.

How it works...

The built-in Plugin Editor works in exactly the same way as the theme editor. When a file is modified and saved, the modifications are written directly in the source file—there's no copy or backup.

There's more...

Similar to the Theme Editor, even the Plugin Editor is a very useful tool. However, it also can raise problems in the case of a mistake in the code.

▶ Unless you're very sure about what you're doing, always deactivate the plugin before editing it.

▶ Always have a backup of the plugin you're editing, as the Plugin Editor does not save any revisions.

▶ If—after editing a plugin—your blog is messed up, deactivate the plugin, and upload your plugin files backup to your `wp-content/plugins/yourplugin` directory.

Managing authors and users with the User Manager

Among other built-in tools, WordPress features the User Manager, which is useful for multi-author blogs or blogs with open registration. If you have a personal blog, you'll not need the User Manager, except in rare instances; for example, to change your password or email ID.

Getting ready

To access the User Manager, log in to your WordPress **Dashboard**, and then click on the **Users** option on the WordPress menu.

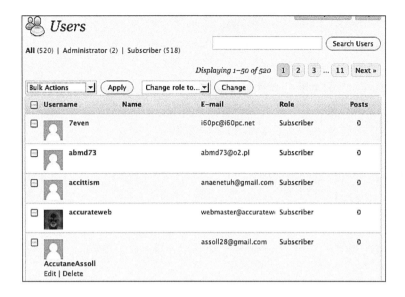

How to do it...

WordPress User Manager allows you to edit or delete user or author accounts. Let's learn How to do it, in detail.

In order to delete users, carry out the following steps:

1. Deleting users is an easy process. To do so, simply find the user you'd like to delete (a mini search engine is included on the top right of the page) and place the mouse cursor over his or her name. The **Edit** and **Delete** button will appear.

2. Once you click on the **Delete** button, you'll have to choose between deleting the user and all the content which he has provided (posts, comments, and so on) or deleting the user but transferring the content to another author.

3. It is also possible to bulk delete users, simply check the checkbox related to the users you'd like to delete.

4. Once done, click on the **Bulk Actions** drop-down and select the **Delete** option. Finally, click on the **Apply** button.

In order to delete users, carry out the following steps:

1. Of course, it is also possible to edit the user details. All users can edit their own information, while the administrators can edit the details of any user.

2. To edit user details, find his or her name in the list and hover the mouse point over it. The **Edit** and **Delete** buttons will be displayed.

3. Click on the **Edit** button.

4. On the next page, you can edit the following information about the user:

   ❑ Enable/Disable Visual Editor

   ❑ Admin color scheme

   ❑ Enable/Disable keyboard shortcuts

   ❑ User Role

   ❑ First name, Last name, and Nickname

   ❑ How the user name should be publicly displayed

   ❑ Contact info

   ❑ User bio

   ❑ Password

5. Simply fill out the required fields, scroll the page down, and click on the **Update User** button to save your modifications.

How it works...

The User Manager doesn't use any advanced process. It simply gets your changes and saves it on WordPress database.

User management will be discussed, in detail, in Chapter 6.

Importing and exporting content with the Import and Export tool

WordPress features a very useful script to import your posts, comments, and links from another platform to WordPress. Of course, it is possible to export your current blog content.

Getting ready

To access the Import tool, log in to your WordPress **Dashboard** and click on **Tools | Import** located at the top of the screen. To access the Export tool, go to **Tools | Export**.

How to do it...

Let's see in detail how to use both the Import and Export tools.

WordPress is able to import your previous blog content and automatically create post with it, as shown in the upcoming screenshot. WordPress can import content from Dotclear, TypePad/ Movable Type, LiveJournal, Greymatter, Textpattern, Blogware, and Blogger.

It is also possible to import tags from tagging plugins, such as Jerome's keywords, Simple Tagging, or Ultimate Tag Warrior.

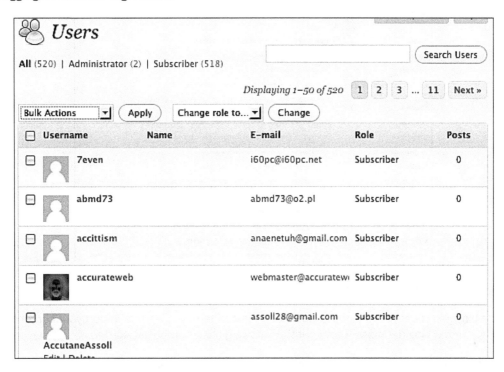

To import your content from another blogging platform, you have to follow a platform specific procedure.

To import content from an export file, carry out the following steps:

The blogging clients, namely, LiveJournal, MovableType/Typepad, Blogware, and WordPress allow you to export your content into an XML, OPML, or TXT file. Follow this procedure to import your content from one of these blogging platforms:

1. Connect to your old blog and export your content. Save the file on your hard drive.

2. Log in to your WordPress **Dashboard**, then go to **Tools | Import**.

3. Select the blogging platform from where you're importing the content.

4. On the next page, click on the **Browse** button to select the exported file located in your hard drive.

5. Once done, click on the **Upload file and import** button.

6. You're done! Please note that depending on your exported file size, this procedure can take a while.

🍴 *Import*	

If you have posts or comments in another system, WordPress can import those into this blog. To get started, choose a system to import from below:

Blogger	Import posts, comments, and users from a Blogger blog.
Blogroll	Import links in OPML format.
Blogware	Import posts from Blogware.
Bunny's Technorati Tags	Import Bunny's Technorati Tags into WordPress tags.
Categories and Tags Converter	Convert existing categories to tags or tags to categories, selectively.
DotClear	Import categories, users, posts, comments, and links from a DotClear blog.
GreyMatter	Import users, posts, and comments from a Greymatter blog.
Jerome's Keywords	Import Jerome's Keywords into WordPress tags.
LiveJournal	Import posts from a LiveJournal XML export file.
Movable Type and TypePad	Import posts and comments from a Movable Type or Typepad blog.
RSS	Import posts from an RSS feed.
Simple Tagging	Import Simple Tagging tags into WordPress tags.
Textpattern	Import categories, users, posts, comments, and links from a Textpattern blog.
Ultimate Tag Warrior	Import Ultimate Tag Warrior tags into WordPress tags.
WordPress	Import **posts, pages, comments, custom fields, categories, and tags** from a WordPress export file.

To import content from the database, carry out the following steps:

If the blogging client you're using is Dotclear or Textpattern, you have to import your content using your old blog database. Carry out the following procedure to get started:

1. Log in to your WordPress **Dashboard**, and then go to **Tools | Import**.

2. Select the blogging platform you're using.

3. On the next page, fill out the form to let WordPress know about your old blog server, database name, password, and so on.

4. When you're done, click on the **Import** button.

5. Your content will now be imported. Note that the process can take a while depending of your database size.

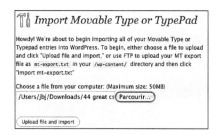

To import content from Blogger, carry out the following steps:

Blogger is a very popular blogging platform—owned by Internet giant, Google. If you wish to move your Blogger blog into WordPress, carry out the following simple steps:

1. Make sure you have a Google account and an upgraded (New, was Beta) blog hosted on `www.blogspot.com`.

2. Log in to your WordPress **Dashboard**, then go to **Tools | Import**.

3. Select the **Blogger** option.

4. On the next page, you have to authorize WordPress to access your Blogger account. To do so, click on the **Authorize** button.

5. You will be redirected to a Google page, where you'll see your Blogger blog listed. Click on the **Allow access** button to authorize WordPress to access your old blog.

6. Once done, you'll be taken back to your WordPress **Dashboard**, where you'll see your Blogger blog's name. Click on the **Import** button to start importing your content.

Blogger Blogs

Blog Name	Blog URL	Posts	Comments	The Magic Button
Techblog	techblog-admin.blogspot.com	0/4	0/1	Import

7. After you have finished the import process, you can clear the account information that has been stored into WordPress database during the content import. Simply click on the **Clear account information** button to get rid of your old account information. This will not affect any of your posts or comments.

For some reasons—such as, moving to another blogging platform, re-using your posts on another blog, and so on—you may want to export your content into a file that can be imported on another blogging platform or a different WordPress blog.

Exporting content is a very easy process, simply carry out the following steps:

1. Log in to your WordPress **Dashboard**, then go to **Tools | Export**.

2. Select an author to export if you want to get the posts from a specific author only, otherwise select the **All Authors** option.

3. Click on the **Download Export File** button.

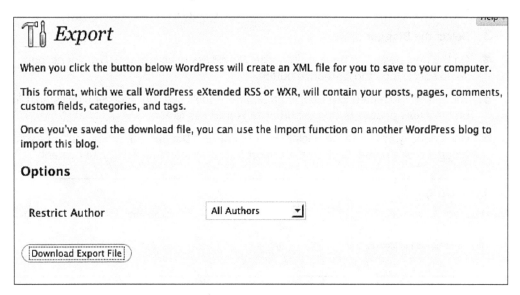

How it works...

After having a look at the Import and Export tools, let's have look at how they work:

When the **Download Export File** is clicked, WordPress generates an XML file and prompts you to download it. This file—often referred to, as **WXR** (**WordPress Extended RSS**)—will contain your posts, pages, comments, custom fields, categories, and tags. It can be imported on any WordPress install by using the Import Tool.

Depending from which platform you're importing content, the WordPress Import Tool functions accordingly. For some content, you just have to submit a file (for example, suppose you want to import posts from a previous WordPress installation), whereas in some other cases (for example, importing from Dotclear blogs) you have to connect to the old blog database in order to import the content into WordPress.

2
Finding and Installing Themes

Themes are probably—after content, of course—one of the most important parts of a WordPress blog. Many people still use the two basic themes that come with WordPress by default. These themes aren't that bad, but too many people use them.

If you want to make your blog stand out, then the first step is to have a stunning and unique design. It doesn't matter if you have the ability to create your own blog theme or not, because the existing themes can be your source of inspiration or the choice for your blog design.

I have compiled a list of themes that are very simple and complete. Above all, it's free, as well as premium.

In this chapter, you will learn:

- ▸ Installing a theme

Installing a theme

Let's go ahead and learn how to download and install a WordPress theme.

Getting ready

Installing a theme is easy. You only need to browse through one of the theme galleries that are listed from page 4 to 11, and carry out the following simple steps:

How to do it...

1. Visit the WordPress Theme Directory web site at: `http://wordpress.org/extend/themes/`.

2. You might find a theme that you like right on the homepage, so just scroll up and down and see what catches your eye. However, don't forget that a theme may look great as a thumbnail but might not be right for your type of content or audience.

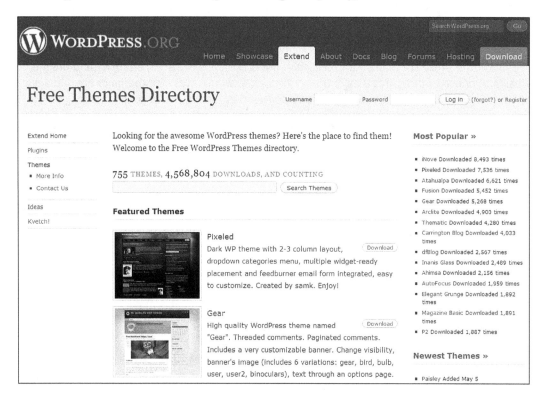

3. You can also browse through the web site for themes based on popularity, tags, or by searching the descriptions (and tags) for words that fit your needs.

4. Once you've found a theme of your choice, click on its name for more information; as shown in the following screenshot:

5. You can see how the theme will look in a live blog by clicking on the **Preview** button. This is a great way to eliminate themes before you download them. The following screenshot shows the preview of a theme:

6. If you like the theme, then click on the close (**X**) button, and then click on the
Download button. This will save the theme in a `zip` format. Make sure you remember
where you have saved it because you will need to locate it when it comes to installing
the custom theme. Otherwise, keep browsing until you see a theme that you like. You
don't have to make your final choice yet. Download a few themes. Don't make your
final choice until you see how it looks with your content.

There's more...

This section is about finding free and premium themes online.

Your theme will be your blog's visual identity. Therefore, using the right theme is a very
important factor to be considered. To help you make your choice, I have compiled a list of very
good looking themes. Don't hesitate to try as many themes as you want and see how they fit
your content.

Classic themes

Let us start with browsing through a few classic themes. Themes that I call **classic** are simple
and do what you expect from a blog. They display entries on the homepage in chronological
order. The classic layouts are the most popular, mainly because they don't need extra or
manual configuration, and because they're visually stunning.

Agregado theme

Agregado is a very beautiful free theme, which is brought to you by Darren Hoyt and
the Smashing Magazine. Agregado features fancy CSS or JavaScript effects (drop-down
menu, search bar, and so on) and a life stream displaying your entries from Twitter, Flickr,
Magnolia, and many other web sites. Visit the following web site for more information on the
Agregado theme:

```
http://www.smashingmagazine.com/2008/09/08/agregado-a-free-wordpress-
theme/
```

The Agregado theme will appear as shown in the following screenshot:

This is one of my favorite free themes ever!

Leopress theme

If you love Mac OS X (as I do) you'll probably enjoy the Leopress theme! Leopress mimics the look of the Mac OS X Leopard desktop with a **Finder** window displaying your posts. Visit the following web site for more information on the Leopress Theme:

`http://www.7graus.com/tech/wordpress/leopress/`

The Leopress theme will appear as shown in the following screenshot:

Rio theme

The Rio theme is very simple in terms of code, but has a very beautiful design. It is also extremely easy to customize. You can transform it into your very own theme in less than 20 minutes. If you're looking to create a photoblog, then this theme is just perfect. Visit the following web site for more information on the Rio theme:

```
http://www.amypink.com/downloads/rio-theme-wordpress-theme/
```

The Rio theme will appear as shown in the following screenshot:

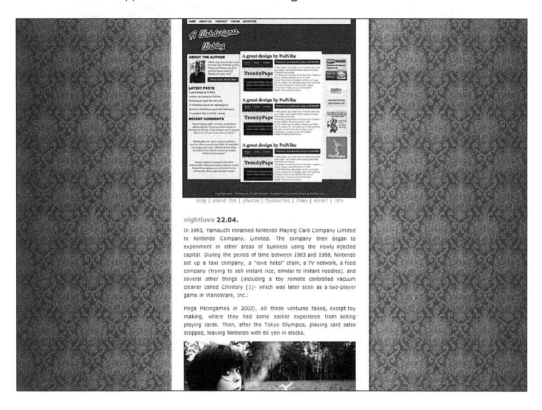

WP Imagination theme

The WP Imagination theme, created by ThemeLab, is perfect for a design or a company blog and includes a nice image gallery on its footer. Visit the following web site for more information on the WP Imagination theme:

`http://www.themelab.com/2008/03/05/free-release-18-wp-imagination/`

The WP Imagination theme will appear as shown in the following screenshot:

WP CODA theme

Inspired by the well known Coda web site, WP CODA is a delicious mix of WordPress and JQuery. Even if this theme may not be suitable for every blog, if you're looking for a stunning design and functionality, then you should give WP CODA a try. Visit the following web site for more information on the WP CODA theme:

```
http://bustatheme.com/wordpress/wp-coda/
```

The WP CODA theme will appear as shown in the following screenshot:

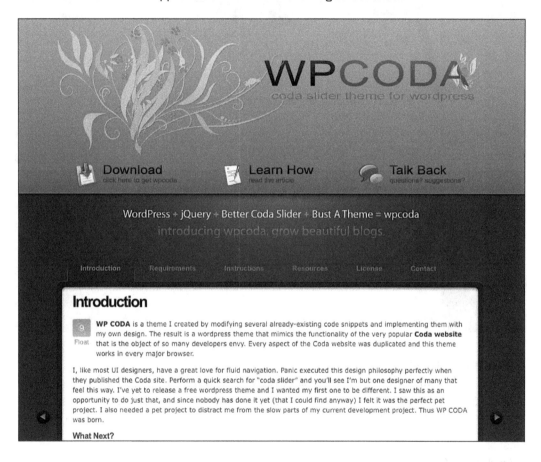

Outdoorsy

The Outdoorsy theme is a very unique theme with its nature design. I would recommend this theme to anyone who wants to stands out of the crowd of white, grey, or blue themes. Visit the following web site for more information on the Outdoorsy theme:

```
http://wefunction.com/2008/07/free-theme-outdoorsy/
```

The Outdoorsy theme will appear as shown in the following screenshot:

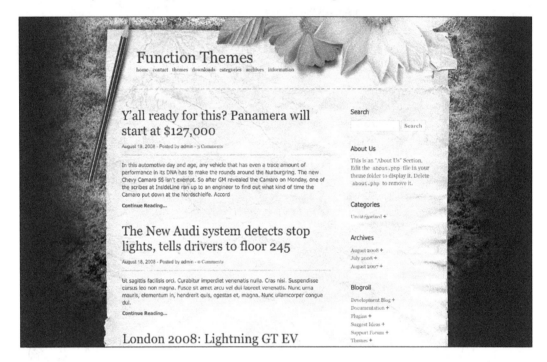

Advanced themes

Now that I have introduced you to a few of my favorite classic themes, let's have a look at the advanced themes. The advanced themes are usually referred to as **Magazine** themes due to their online magazine-like layouts.

Most of the advanced themes need some extra configuration to be added to the custom admin page or by directly editing the source code. Refer to the theme web site for more details.

Mimbo 2

The most popular free magazine theme, Mimbo 2, has been downloaded by thousands of users and was a huge source of inspiration for many theme designers (including me).

Mimbo 2 is a must download theme for everyone who want to create a magazine theme. A few features of the Mimbo 2 are:

- ▶ It is very easy to customize
- ▶ It can be the base of your own magazine theme
- ▶ You can use its clean source code to learn many **secrets** of premium WordPress themes

Visit the following web site for more information on the Mimbo 2 theme:

```
http://www.darrenhoyt.com/2007/08/05/wordpress-magazine-theme-released/
```

The Mimbo 2 theme will appear as shown in the following screenshot:

OpenBook

OpenBook was one of the first WordPress themes that I created, and it has been downloaded more than 5000 times since its release in May 2008. OpenBook features a drop-down menu for your categories, a JavaScript gallery to visually enhance your best posts, fancy color, and a three column homepage. Moreover, one of the most important features of OpenBook is its embedded control panel, which allows the user to set theme options without having to manually edit the code. Visit the following web site for more information on the OpenBook theme:

```
http://www.catswhocode.com/blog/featured/wordpress-openbook-premium-
theme-available-for-download-20
```

The OpenBook theme will appear as shown in the following screenshot:

Brightness

Brightness is a very beautiful magazine theme; even if it's less popular than the Mimbo and the Revolution theme. Just like OpenBook, Brightness features its own control panel where you can set up the theme options without editing any files. It is a nice theme with an original light brown and orange color scheme. Visit the following web site for more information on the Brightness theme:

```
http://www.dailywp.com/brightness-wordpress-theme/
```

The Brightness theme will appear as shown in the following screenshot:

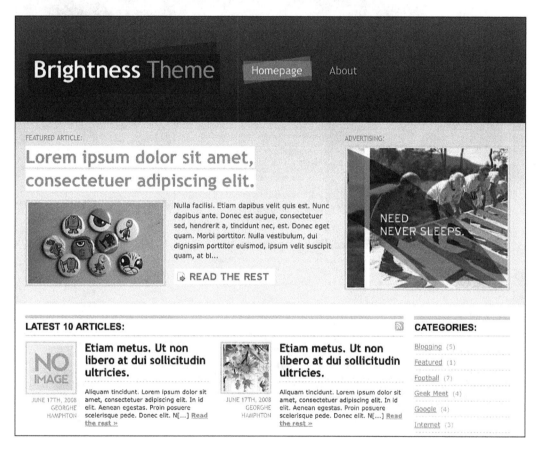

Rebel Magazine

The Rebel Magazine is a free magazine theme with an easy to customize layout, a video integration system, a featured post, and a two column layout. This will prove to be a good choice if you need a simple and clean magazine theme and want to transform it to fit your needs. Visit the following web site for more information on the Rebel Magazine theme:

```
http://www.wpthemedesigner.com/2008/05/07/rebel-magazine-theme/
```

The Rebel Magazine theme will appear as shown in the following screenshot:

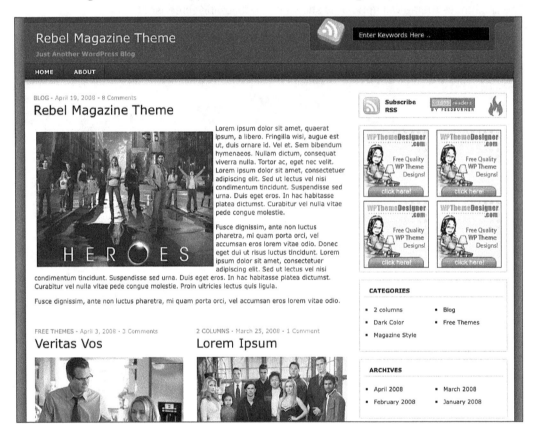

Revolution 2

Brian Gardner is one of the world most famous WordPress theme designers. After successfully launching the Revolution series themes back in 2007, Brian is back with the Revolution 2 series, which is even more beautiful than the first one. Visit the following web site for more information on the Revolution 2 theme:

```
http://www.revolutiontwo.com
```

The Revolution 2 theme will appear as shown in the following screenshot:

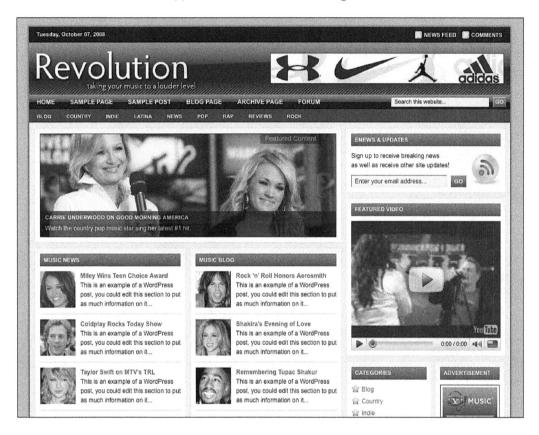

Arthemia

Arthemia is the perfect theme for an online magazine or a blog, with lots of content. Arthemia features thumbnails images in posts, category browsing, featured section, and a very professional menu. This theme is also very easy to customize and I have seen many great personalization of it. Visit the following web site for more information on the Arthemia theme:

```
http://michaelhutagalung.com/2008/08/arthemia-20-released-the-updates/
```

The Arthemia theme will appear as shown in the following screenshot:

Premium themes

We have already learned about the Classic and the Advanced WordPress themes. Let's now learn more about a few premium WordPress themes.

Mimbo Pro

If you liked Mimbo 2, then there are strong chances that you'll love Mimbo Pro. It is more colorful than the free version. This premium theme provides drop-down menus, JavaScript slideshow, and colors per category. A good choice if you're looking for a complete but clean magazine theme. Visit the following web site for more information on the Mimbo Pro theme:

```
http://www.darrenhoyt.com/2008/03/12/mimbo-pro-magazine-theme-
released/
```

The Mimbo Pro theme will appear as shown in the following screenshot:

WP Vybe

With ten different color schemes and two different layouts (two or three columns) the WP Vybe theme is actually one of the most advanced premium WordPress themes available. Another good point is that you'll get the PSD files along with the purchase of this theme, so its customization will be a lot easier! Visit the following web site for more information on the WP Vybe theme:

```
http://www.solostream.com/category/wordpress-blog-themes/
```

The WP Vybe theme will appear as shown in the following screenshot:

Open Air

With its frozen color scheme and very clean layout, the Open Air theme is the most original theme in comparison to most of the WordPress magazine themes. Curiously, I have never seen it being used on a blog. It is a good purchase if you want to be original. Visit the following web site for more information on the Open Air theme:

```
http://www.woothemes.com/amember/go.php?r=402&i=b0
```

The Open Air theme will appear as shown in the following screenshot:

Citrus theme

Citrus is an original premium WordPress theme that is slightly different from most paid themes. Available in 6 different color schemes and two layouts (Blog style and News style), Citrus also features a very complete control panel which will allow you to change many settings without editing a single line of code. Visit the following web site for more information on the Citrus theme:

```
http://www.citrustheme.com/
```

The Citrus theme will appear as shown in the following screenshot:

Fresh News

One thing I really like about the Fresh News theme is that it comes with a lot of different styles and color schemes. Therefore, I feel that this theme will be suitable for almost every blogging project. It doesn't matter whether your blog is about gardening, about music, or about your company. Visit the following web site for more information on the Fresh News theme:

```
http://www.woothemes.com/amember/go.php?r=402&i=b0
```

The Fresh News theme will appear as shown in the following screenshot:

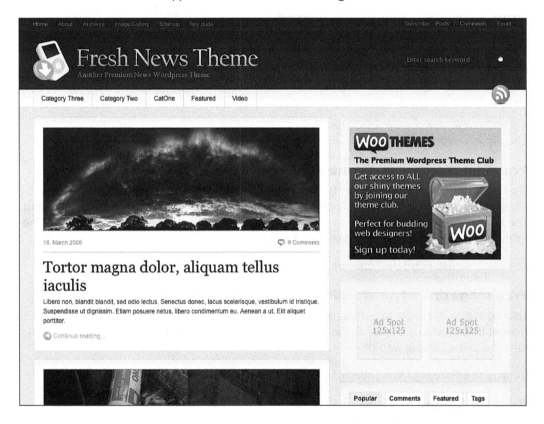

Lists of themes

Here's a list of web sites where you can select, and download, a WordPress theme of your choice.

WordPress.org theme gallery

There are actually 500+ themes in this web site. All of them are free to download and use. Most of them are very nice. The following link will take you to the `WordPress.org` theme gallery:

`http://wordpress.org/extend/themes/`

100 excellent WordPress themes

At this site you will find 100 WordPress themes, organized by style. This page has been a good resource for me while I was looking for some inspiration. The following link will take you to the desired web site:

`http://www.smashingmagazine.com/2008/01/08/100-excellent-free-high-quality-wordpress-themes/`

Premium WordPress themes gallery

If you're looking for a premium (paid) theme, then this page is one of the most complete web sites that I was able to find on the Internet. All the themes listed here feature an online demo. The list is updated frequently so you won't have to worry about old, unsupported themes. The following link will take you to the desired web site:

`http://hackwordpress.com/best-premium-wordpress-themes-gallery/`

Free magazine style WordPress theme gallery

This list is almost similar to the last one, but the eighteen themes listed here are completely free yet they provide a level of quality comparable to premium themes. The following link will take you to the desired web site:

`http://hackwordpress.com/best-magazine-style-wordpress-themes/`

Best WP theme

This is a young web site which already features a list of more than 50 very nice free themes. All of the themes have an online demonstration. The following link will take you to the desired web site:

`http://www.bestwptheme.com/`

WPVote WordPress themes

WPVote is a social bookmarking web site where the users discuss WordPress. It features a nice **WordPress Themes** section, where users can freely submit and vote for WordPress themes. I have seen some stunning themes available in the following web site:

```
http://www.wpvote.com/index.php?category=WordpressThemes
```

ThemeLab free themes

This blog features numerous themes for you to download. Most of these themes are simple, clean, and stylish. All of them are free to download and use. Definitely a place to consider while you're looking for a WordPress theme! The following link will take you to the desired web site:

```
http://www.themelab.com/free-wordpress-themes/
```

Important notes about themes

Now that we have learned about the various WordPress themes and the web sites from where you can download them, let's earn some extra knowledge about them. There are a few important points to be considered while dealing with the WordPress themes.

Important factors to consider

Apart from the way a theme looks, there are some important issues to be considered before settling for a theme:

- ▶ **Is it compatible with a range of browsers?** Look for evidence to prove that the theme has been tested in many different browsers, otherwise test it yourself. Many of the free WordPress themes aren't fully compatible with Internet Explorer 6, which may be totally obsolete, but still used by a wide range of people.

- ▶ **Is it accessible?** How will the theme look with a 1024x768 pixel resolution? Does it have a lot of heavy JavaScript coding or very large images? The required loading time is an important factor to be considered, as many Internet users will not wait for your site to load. If your blog's too slow, then visitors will leave.

- ▶ **Will it work with my plugins and widgets?** Most of the recent themes are now fully widget-ready, but there are still a number of them that aren't. For those that are not widget ready, I'll explain how to make a theme widget-ready later in this book.

- ▶ **Do the themes use a specific JavaScript framework?** For example, some themes use the Mootools framework, while some plugins use jQuery, or vice-versa. This can lead to problem and incompatibility.

- ▸ **Does it require you to customize it or create custom graphics?** Even if most themes are ready to use, you may want to modify background images or logos. Are you able to do this?

- ▸ **Is the theme ready to use?** While most classic themes work out of the box, some magazine themes require extra configuration from the user in order to be fully functional. Most themes feature a custom admin panel page, but some others (such as Mimbo 2) require you to directly modify the theme files.

Magazine versus blog themes

Since approximately one and half years ago, magazine themes have become overly popular in the WordPress community. Indeed, these new layouts are a real innovation and it gives the bloggers an opportunity to own a real online magazine instead of a blog.

Nowadays, many bloggers seems to have come back to a simpler layout. For example, two of my three blogs have a normal layout and the last one has a magazine layout, but I'm already thinking about coming back to a more classic theme.

Questions you must ask yourself before choosing a magazine theme

The following are a few questions that you must ask yourself before choosing a magazine theme:

- ▸ **Do you write enough posts per day?** Most magazine themes feature posts by categories on the homepage. If you only write one post per day, then some categories will be updated only once a week, which doesn't look very professional.

- ▸ **Do you blog alone, or with other bloggers?** A magazine style layout is a brilliant idea if you run a multi-author blog. Therefore, I personally think that a classic layout is better for someone who blogs alone.

- ▸ **Why a magazine theme?** Do you need a magazine theme because you actually need the kind of layout it provides, or just because it is popular? Don't follow the hype, be yourself and choose what you really need.

3
Get the most out of your WordPress Theme

Themes are a very important part of any WordPress blog they control the manner in which your content is being displayed and the design of your blog.

As we have seen in Chapter 2, a lot of free and premium themes are available for WordPress. But even if there is a really huge choice of themes, no one wants to use a theme the way it is—without customizing it even a bit.

A lot of customization actions can be performed on an existing theme, such as, changing colors, font families, font size, integrating plugins, logo, and favorite icons.

You don't need to be a code developer, or a designer, to personalize the theme you chose to use. In this chapter, we shall learn many tricks to customize an existing theme and enhance the theme that you've created.

After reading this chapter, you'll be able to pick up any existing WordPress theme, and modify it to make it 100% yours.

In this chapter, you will learn:

- Modifying your theme colors
- Modifying your theme fonts
- Creating and integrating a favicon
- Integrating your own logo
- Adding social bookmarking buttons to your theme
- Integrating Feedburner feeds on your theme
- Integrating Twitter on your theme using the Twitter Tools plugin

- ▶ Displaying your Twitter entries on your blog, using a page template
- ▶ Customizing WordPress admin login page
- ▶ Using conditional tags to display content on specific pages
- ▶ Using page templates in your theme
- ▶ Creating an archive page
- ▶ Creating a custom 404 error page
- ▶ Using a static page as a homepage
- ▶ Creating a Featured Posts block on your homepage
- ▶ Making your new posts stands out with a custom style

Modifying your theme colors

Have you ever come across a WordPress theme available online and thought, 'Wow, this is a great theme but it would look even better if it had a green layout!'? This happens to me really often, and I'm pretty sure it's happened to you as well.

Luckily, changing the theme color scheme isn't as difficult as it seems to be.

Getting ready

Of course, you'll need at least one readily available WordPress theme. You'll also need a text editor. In this example, we shall use the **Vi** text editor—which is my favorite text editor; however, even other decent text editors can do the job (TextEdit on Mac, gEdit on Ubuntu, or Notepad on Windows).

If you don't have a favorite text editor, you can use Vi text editor—which is available by default on Mac and Unix systems and freely downloadable from the link: `http://www.vim.org/download.php#pc`

On Mac and GNU/Linux systems, just open a terminal and type `vi` in order to open the Vi text editor. Type `vi myfile.php in order` to open a file in Vi.

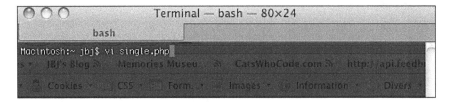

How to do it...

1. The first thing we need to know is the hexadecimal color codes for each of the theme colors. Most WordPress themes use a color scheme of three to five different colors.

2. In order to know which colors are used on the theme, we'll have to open the theme CSS file, named `style.css`.

3. The CSS property used to define a background color is background color (or simply, background). For the foreground color, the property's name is color, and for the border colors, it is border color (or simply, border). For example, here's the color scheme which I use on the OpenBook theme:

    ❏   Background color: `#151515`

    ❏   Content background color: `#fff`

    ❏   Header blocks: `#222`

    ❏   Green (used for links): `#49AB0D`

    ❏   Blue (Titles, hover links): `#109dd0`

4. Once you have known about the colors used on the theme, you'd want to modify the theme. Open the `style.css` file in Vi:

    ```
    vi style.css
    ```

5. Vi has a very useful command to replace all the occurrences of one sting with another. This way, you'll have to run the command only once for changing each color. If you choose to use some other text editor, then look for the search and replace command, which achieves the same result.

6. For example, suppose we are using the OpenBook theme, and you want to replace the dark grey background with a white background. Run the following command in Vi:

    ```
    :%s/151515/ffffff/g
    ```

7. Save your modification with the help of the save command:

    ```
    :w
    ```

8. Repeat the search and replace command as necessary.

How it works...

The command used above is a powerful find and replace feature of Open Source text Editor Vi.

In case you want to learn more about the Vi's features, visit the following link: `http://www.catswhocode.com/blog/100-vim-commands-every-programmer-should-know`

There's more...

Following are a few important points, for your information:

▸ All themes use a `style.css` file, but some themes also use extra stylesheet (for example, using a specific stylesheet for Internet Explorer is very common). Thus, make sure to replace colors in all stylesheets that are part of the theme.

▸ This trick can only replace CSS-based colors. To modify image colors, you'll need to use a design program such as Adobe Photoshop or The Gimp.

▸ If you changed your theme colors and some parts still display the old colors, make sure that the CSS colors are written in hexadecimal codes (for example: `#151515`). Some theme designers use color names instead of hexadecimal codes (for example: they may use background color: white instead of background color: `#ffffff`).

▸ Some color codes can be written by using shorthand, for example, `#006699` can be written as `#069`—therefore, make sure that you've checked for that too.

Modifying your theme fonts

Now that you have learned how to search and replace hexadecimal color codes, let's customize your theme a bit more.

In this recipe, we're going to see how we can easily modify the fonts used in a WordPress theme and also discuss about the good practices for typography on a WordPress blog.

Getting ready

For this recipe, you'll need exactly the same things that were needed in the *Modifying your theme colors* recipe—a theme to customize, and a text editor.

A common beginner mistake is to try and use non web-safe fonts on a web site or blog. For example, there are web sites using the Myriad Pro or Segoe UI fonts. These fonts look beautiful, but what if only 10 or less percent of your readers can render it?

The following web-safe fonts can be used on any web sites:

▸ Times New Roman

▸ Arial

▸ Verdana

▸ Courier

▸ Comic

Installed on more than 80% of computers, these two fonts can be used as well:

- ▸ Trebuchet MS
- ▸ Century Gothic

How to do it...

Most WordPress themes use a maximum of three different fonts. However, it is common to only use one or two different fonts. There's not a big choice, in terms of fonts, due to the fact that a user must have the font installed on his computer to have it render correctly on a web site.

1. In order to modify the fonts of a theme, the first step is to find out which are the fonts used. To do so, open the `style.css` file, in Vi and use the `search` command to find the font and font-family CSS properties:
   ```
   /font
   ```

2. This command will find all the occurrences of font in the stylesheet. To go to the next occurrence, simply type `n`.

3. The font-family CSS property looks as follows:
   ```
   font-family: "Trebuchet MS", arial, serif;
   ```

4. This CSS property allows you to specify one or more fonts to be used. In our example, if in case Trebuchet MS isn't available on the client computer, Arial will be used.

5. The font CSS property is a shorthand which allows you to specify all the font related parameters on a single line:
   ```
   font: italic small-caps bold 12px arial;
   ```

6. To modify the size of a font, you'll look for the `font-size` CSS property.

There's more...

Tips and things to know about fonts

It can be very tempting to **play** with the fonts and CSS fonts related properties. However, there are a few things to be kept in mind:

- ▸ The standard font size of a text is between 11 and 14 pixels; 12px is the most common choice of font size. For titles, (`h1`, `h2`, `h3`, and so on) a font size between 14 and 26 pixels is good.

- ▸ While using a font with a two word name (for example, `Trebuchet MS`), always put it between quotes; that is, `font-family: "Trebuchet MS";)`

- ▸ While defining font families always list at least two fonts, and offer a generic family name as the last alternative. The client's browser will use the first font that it recognizes.

Creating and integrating a favicon

A favicon is a small icon (16 x16 pixel) associated with a web site. The favicon is displayed by modern web browsers in the address bar, tabs, and bookmarks.

Nowadays, almost all the web sites and blogs have their own favicon. The following screenshot shows a favicon displayed in Mozilla Firefox:

Getting ready

You'll need a 16 x 16 pixels image to serve as a favicon. Due to the very small display size of the favicon, the image should be very simple.

 I always tend to use a background color that fits my web site color scheme, and a simplified logo.

Basically, you can use `.jpg`, `.png`, `.gif`, or even `.mng` and `.apng` files to display a favicon. Unfortunately, the Internet Explorer (6 and 7) recognizes only the Windows `.ico` file format named `favicon.ico`.

Therefore, if you want to have an IE-compatible favicon, you'll have to convert your image file from `png`, `gif`, or `jpg` to Windows `.ico`.

Many imaging software applications can convert an image into a Windows icon file. Personally, I use an online service called ConvertIcon (available at the link `http://converticon.com/`) in order to convert my `png` image into Windows `.ico` file. The ConvertIcon application will also resize your image if needed. Therefore, there's no need to worry about your image width and height.

How to do it...

1. Once you have your favicon ready, upload it on your server under the directory of your choice. Personally, I prefer putting it in `wp-content/themes/mytheme/`. However, the choice is yours.

2. Open the `header.php` file from your theme. We now have to place a line of code to specify the location of our favicon. This line can be placed anywhere within the `<head>` and `</head>` tags.

3. Here's the code that we shall use in order to define an Internet Explorer compliant favicon:

```
<link rel="shortcut icon" type="image/x-icon" href="/path/to/
your/favicon.ico" />
```

The preceding line of code is the standard code to integrate a favicon on a web site. Using the `.ico` format, you can make sure that your favicon will be displayed by Internet Explorer, which doesn't happen when using the `.png` version.

4. If you uploaded your favicon into your `wp-content/themes/yourtheme` directory, we can use the `bloginfo()` function in order to automatically retrieve the template path as follows:

```
<link rel="shortcut icon" type="image/x-icon"
    href="<?php bloginfo('template_url'); ?>/favicon.ico" />
```

5. If you chose to use a file format, such as `.gif`, `.png`, or `.jpg`, you can add your favicon with the following code; however, Internet Explorer will not recognize it:

```
<link rel="icon" type="image/png"
    href="favicon.png" />
```

6. Once you have saved your `header.php` file, your favicon will be displayed.

How it works...

The following line of code is the standard code used to integrate a favicon on a web site:

```
<link rel="shortcut icon" type="image/x-icon"
    href="/path/to/your/favicon.ico" />
```

Integrating your own logo

By default, most WordPress themes display a header text—usually the name of the blog and blog description. This is a nice option for personal blogs. However, I personally believe that displaying your own personal logo will make your blog look even more professional.

In this recipe, we shall learn how we can add a logo instead of the default blog name and slogan on a WordPress theme. The following screenshot shows the logo integration on a default WordPress theme:

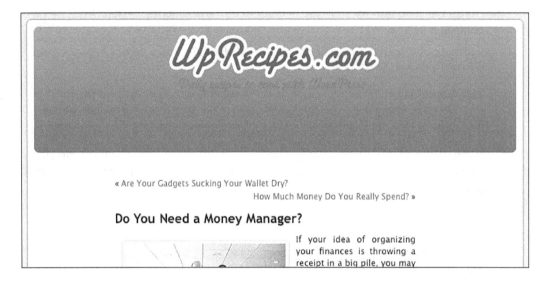

Getting ready

For this recipe, you'll need your own logo and a WordPress theme on which you'd like to integrate your logo. I shall be using the WordPress default theme for this recipe.

However, there are a few things to be kept in mind before getting on with this recipe:

- ▸ Some recent themes don't display blog name and slogan anymore—instead, they display a default logo which can be changed by editing the code or even by defining a new logo in a custom WordPress control panel (which shall be covered in Chapter 3).
- ▸ Due to the fact that each theme is coded differently, the result of this recipe may vary from one theme to another.

How to do it...

1. Open the `header.php` file and locate the part of code where the blog name and description are displayed. In the WordPress default theme, it looks like this:

```
<div id="header">
<div id="headerimg">
<h1><a href="<?php echo get_option('home'); ?>/"><?php
        bloginfo('name'); ?></a></h1>
<div class="description"><?php bloginfo('description'); ?></div>
</div>
</div>
```

2. We can just put an `html` image tag between the `<h1>` and `</h1>` tags, but there's a much better, SEO friendly, way to display our logo—by using CSS.

3. Upload your logo into your `wp-content/themes/default` folder. Once you're done, open the `style.css` file from the WordPress default theme. Go to line number 95. You'll see the CSS properties for the `#headerimg .description` element:

```
#headerimg .description {
font-size: 1.2em;
text-align: center;
}
```

4. Now, replace the preceding piece of code by the following piece of code:

```
#headerimg h1
{
 background: transparent url(images/logo.png) no-repeat 50%
 30px;
 text-indent:-9999px;
}
#headerimg .description
{
    text-indent:-9999px;
}
```

5. Don't forget to change the image name and path if your logo isn't named `logo.png` or is not located at `wp-content/themes/default/images`.

How it works...

As you have seen, we haven't edited a single line of HTML to achieve our logo integration. We didn't have to, and it's better this way. Having `h1`, an html element, as the header text is good for your semantic and SEO. Due to the `text-indent` CSS property, we're able to hide the text by indenting it—this is the reason why we added this property to both `#headerimg h1` and `#headerimg .description`.

We do not want our logo to be hidden, this is why we used the CSS background property to display it.

There's more...

Our logo looks good, but its usability can be improved even more by adding a link to the logo on the blog homepage.

Adding a link to the homepage

To add a link to the homepage, open the `header.php` and replace the following line of code on line 33:

```
<div id="headerimg">
```

With the following line of code:

```
<div id="headerimg" onclick="document.location.href=
'<?php echo get_option(\'home\'); ?>';">
```

Adding social bookmarking buttons to your theme

Social bookmarking web sites are well known among bloggers. Digg, Del.icio.us, StumbleUpon, Reddit, and many more such web sites can drive a huge amount of traffic to your blog.

I have noticed that if you directly add social bookmarking buttons to your theme and give your readers the opportunity to do it in your blog, they'll vote for you more often. In this recipe, we shall learn how to create our own personal social bookmarking buttons.

Getting ready

In this example, I shall be using a background image although, it isn't necessary for achieving this recipe. However, if you don't have a background image and wish to have one you can freely use the basic background that I have created, by visiting the following link: `http://wphacks.com/wp-content/uploads/2008/08/cwc-vote.jpg`

How to do it...

1. First, if you choose to use a background image, upload it into the `wp-content/themes/yourtheme` directory.

2. The social bookmarking button can be added at the end of single posts or on the homepage, after each post excerpt. Personally, I choose to add it on single posts, but the choice is completely yours.

3. We'll have to create a list of HTML elements containing all the links that we want to use, to the social bookmarking sites. In this example, I shall be using Del.icio.us, Digg, Stumble Upon, Reddit, and Dzone. However, you can add more social bookmarking sites or replace the one's which I have chosen with the ones of your choice.

4. Open the `single.php` file from your theme and add the following piece of code where you want the widget to appear:

```
<div id="cwc-vote">
<ul>
<li><a href="http://del.icio.us/post?url=
<?php echo the_permalink(); ?>">Del.icio.us</a></li>
<li><a href="http://digg.com/submit?url=
<?php echo the_permalink(); ?>">Digg</a></li>
<li><a href="http://www.stumbleupon.com/submit?url=
<?php echo the_permalink(); ?>">StumbleUpon</a></li>
<li><a href="http://reddit.com/submit?url=
<?php echo the_permalink(); ?>">Reddit</a></li>
<li><a href="http://www.dzone.com/links/add.html?url=
<?php echo the_permalink(); ?>">Dzone</a></li>
</ul>
</div>
```

How it works...

As you have seen, most—if not all—social bookmarking sites have a URL where you can pass a GET request containing the URL of the web site you'd like to add or vote for. We're using the WordPress `the_permalink()` function to retrieve the URL of any post.

For the markup, using an HTML list is considered a better solution in terms of semantic HTML.

You can easily add others social bookmarking sites; I can't guarantee that it will work for all sites, but basically, the link must look like this:

```
<a href="http://www.yoursite.com/links/submit?url=<?php echo
the_permalink(); ?>">
```

There's more...

Now, we have a fully functional social bookmarking widget. The reason why we have created one manually, instead of using the buttons provided by such sites, is that we can use CSS to integrate it to our theme and make these links looks like a part of the blog.

Using CSS to style the social bookmarking widget

Open your `style.css` file and add the following code:

```
#cwc-vote
{
    /* Don't forget to change the image path */
    background: #fff url(images/cwc-vote.png) no-repeat top left;
    width:600px;
```

```
        height:45px;
        padding-top:35px;
}
#cwc-vote ul
{
        list-style-type:none;
        margin-left:-20px;
}
#cwc-vote ul li
{
        display:inline;
        margin-right:-10px;
}
#cwc-vote ul li a
{
        color:#fff;
        font-size:13px;
}
```

This example CSS will be a good start to personalize the widget. Though, you may have some extra styling to do in order to make it fit your theme color scheme.

Adding Del.icio.us live count

Right now, we have a good looking and functional widget, but we can still improve upon it. I shall teach you how to add a Del.icio.us live count—it will count the number of people who save your post on Deli.cio.us, and print it next to the Deli.cio.us link.

If you want to add the Deli.cio.us live count to your social bookmarking widget, we'll have to edit the list a bit. Simply replace the following line of code:

```
<li><a href="http://del.icio.us/post?url=
<?php echo the_permalink(); ?>">Del.icio.us</a></li>
```

By the following line of code:

```
<li><a href="http://del.icio.us/post?url=<?php echo
the_permalink(); ?>">Del.icio.us (<span id='<?php echo
md5("http://".$_SERVER["HTTP_HOST"].$_SERVER["REQUEST_URI"]);?>'>0
</span>)</a></li>
```

In the preceding piece of code, we have added a zero (the default Del.icio.us count) within a span HTML element. This is the basis of our Del.icio.us live counter. Of course, we have to use a bit of JavaScript to make it work.

Enter the following code in the `single.php` file, below the widget HTML code:

```
<script type='text/javascript'>
function displayURL(data)
{
    var urlinfo = data[0];
    if (!urlinfo.total_posts) return;
    document.getElementById("<?php echo md5("http://".$_SERVER["HTTP_
HOST"].$_SERVER["REQUEST_URI"]);?>").innerHTML = urlinfo.total_posts;
}
</script>

<script src='http://badges.del.icio.us/feeds/json/url/data?url=<?php
the_permalink() ?>&callback=displayURL'></script>
```

We're done! Your widget is now able to count the number of people who have saved your post to Del.icio.us and display the count.

Code explanation

This code uses Del.icio.us **JSON** (**JavaScript Object Notation**) feeds—a lightweight data-interchange format easily used in browser-based mashups, blog badges, and more—to get information about the URL which we have passed as a parameter.

As a callback, we're calling the JavaScript function, `displayURL(data)`. This function retrieves the ID of the span element created in the widget html list and replaces the default value (zero) with the number returned by Del.icio.us JSON feed.

Integrating Feedburner feeds on your theme

Feedburner is a service that allows you to keep a count of the people who have subscribed for your RSS feed. Once you have created a Feedburner feed, you have to integrate it to your theme. In this recipe, we shall learn three different *How to do it...* sections to integrate the Feedburner feeds with your theme.

How to do it...

There are three methods of integrating the Feedburner with a theme. These methods have been explained in the following sections:

Let's start with the manual way by carrying out the following steps:

1. In order to integrate your Feedburner feeds, you can simply edit your theme files and replace the following line of code, `<?php bloginfo('rss2_url'); ?>` with your Feedburner URL.

2. Usually, the RSS feeds are called in the `header.php` file. Many themes also feature RSS links in the `footer.php` and `sidebar.php` files.

3. If you're using a Mac or a Linux machine, you can find any RSS link featured on a theme by executing the following command in the theme directory:

```
find . -type f -print | xargs grep rss2_url
```

Thanks to open source, a WordPress plugin exists to help you with your Feedburner RSS feeds.

1. This plugin that will help you with your Feedburner RSS is called FeedSmith and can be downloaded from the following link: `http://blogs.feedburner.com/feedburner/archives/2007/10/the_feedsmith_plugin_newly_for.php`

2. Install and activate it, just like any other plugin.

How about a bit of WordPress hacking? It is easy to use the `.htaccess` file to automatically redirect any RSS feed top your Feedburner feed.

1. The `.htaccess` file is located at the root of your WordPress installation. This is a configuration file for the Apache web server.

2. While editing `.htaccess`, make sure to create a backup. If you make a mistake or typo in this file, your blog will stop functioning. However, if you create a backup, you can restore the backup file, in order to eliminate that problem.

3. Edit the `.htaccess` file and add the following code (make sure you have replaced my Feedburner feed URL by yours!):

```
<IfModule mod_rewrite.c>
 RewriteEngine on
 RewriteCond %{HTTP_USER_AGENT} !FeedBurner    [NC]
 RewriteCond %{HTTP_USER_AGENT} !FeedValidator [NC]
 RewriteRule ^feed/?([_0-9a-z-]+)?/?$ http://feeds.feedburner.com/
     wprecipes [R=302,NC,L]
</IfModule>
```

How it works...

Let's have a look at the function of the preceding code:

- First, we make sure that the `mod_rewrite.c` module is installed on the server. There's more than 90% of chance that it is installed, however, while developing you must keep in mind every rare possibility.

- We need to make sure that the client user agent isn't the Feedburner itself, or the feed validator. We definitely don't want to redirect bots to our Feedburner feed URL, otherwise they'll be able to grab our new blog content!

- Finally, we shall use a rewrite rule that requests the server redirect any kind of feed URL to our feedburner URL.

Method	Pros	Cons
1	▸ No plugin, just the addition of a small file.	▸ If you switch to another theme, you'll have to replace feeds links again. ▸ If someone subscribed to your old feed, he'll never be redirected to Feedburner.
2	▸ Simple as a plugin! Upload it, activate it, give it your Feedburner feed, and it will do the job for you. ▸ FeedSmith can redirect your old feed subscribers to your Feedburner feed. This way, even the early subscriber will appear on your Feedburner count.	▸ Some people believe that having many plugins activated will slow down their blog. If you don't like using many plugins at the same time you can replace this one by the `.htacess` code.
3	▸ No need to install a plugin. ▸ No upgrade problems if you update your WordPress version or switch theme.	▸ This method might be too hard to implement if you are a beginner or a non-programmer. However, I have clearly explained the method.

Integrating Twitter on your theme using the Twitter Tools plugin

Twitter is a free micro blogging service that allows you to post short messages (less than 140 characters) by answering the simple question—**What are you doing?**.

Getting ready

I must admit that I was very skeptical at first about the use of Twitter for a blog. However, I decided to give it a try and found it really helpful. It is a great way to get in touch with other bloggers, interact with your readers, and promote your blog posts. By the way, my twitter URL is `http://twitter.com/catswhocode`, so don't hesitate to get in touch with me!

However, similar to your RSS feed, in order to invite visitors to your twitter account you have to promote it on your blog—this way your readers will know that you're using Twitter. In my opinion, the best way to tell your readers about your twitter account is to display your tweets on your blog. In this recipe, we'll see how to do it—with and without a plugin.

My favorite Twitter plugin for WordPress is, by far, **Twitter Tools**—created by Alex King who has released numerous popular WordPress plugins, such as **Simple tagging** or **Share This**.

The Twitter Tools plugin is great because it offers so many possibilities; for example, if your theme uses widgets, you can simply drag the Twitter Tools widget to your sidebar and you're done! Twitter Tools also gives you the choice between displaying only your latest Twitter entry or latest page.

Category for tweet posts:	Uncategorized
Tag(s) for your tweet posts:	
	Separate multiple tags with commas. Example: tweets, twitter
Author for tweet posts:	admin
Exclude @reply tweets in your sidebar, digests and created blog posts?	Yes
Tweets to show in sidebar:	1
	Numbers only please.
Create tweets from your sidebar?	No
JS Library to use?	jQuery
Give Twitter Tools credit?	No
Update Twitter Tools Options	

How to do it...

1. To install the Twitter Tools plugin, visit the following link and download it: `http://wordpress.org/extend/plugins/twitter-tools/`. Then, upload the `twitter-tools.php` file into your `wp-content/plugins` directory.

2. Once you have activated the plugin, a new tab—where you can set up your Twitter Tools options—will appear under **Options** in your WordPress **Dashboard**.

3. With the Twitter Tools plugin, displaying your Twitter entries is made very easy. If your theme is widget-ready, go to **Design | Widgets** on your WordPress **Dashboard** and drag the Twitter Tools widget to your sidebar. Once you have saved the modification, your twitter entries will appear on your sidebar.

4. If your theme isn't widget-ready, you have to edit the `sidebar.php` file and add the following function:

5. Display your last tweets: `<?php aktt_sidebar_tweets(); ?>`

6. Display only your latest tweet: `<?php aktt_latest_tweet(); ?>`

How it works...

In order to display your latest Twitter entries, the Twitter Tools plugin uses PHP to parse your Twitter RSS feeds. RSS feeds parsing will be discussed in detail in the following recipe.

Displaying your Twitter entries on your blog using a page template

It is possible to create a **Twitter** page on your blog with the help of the Twitter Tools plugin. How about playing a bit with the code in order to achieve the same result without using any plugin?

Getting ready

To achieve this recipe, you'll need to use a page template. Page templates will be discussed later in this chapter. Therefore, I won't get into details; just the basics—a page template is a PHP file with a custom layout that you can use on your WordPress blog.

How to do it...

1. Let's start by creating a very basic page template. Create a new file on your computer and name it, for example, `twitter.php` and insert the following code in it:

```php
<?php
/*
Template Name: Twitter Page
*/
?>

<?php get_header(); ?>

<div id="content">
<?php //Content goes here ?>

</div>
<?php get_sidebar(); ?>
<?php get_footer(); ?>
```

2. The most important thing to remember while attempting to create a WordPress page template is the template name—your page name comment is always located at the beginning of the file. This PHP comment allows WordPress to know that this file is a page template, and then you'll be able to use it.

3. As you can see, there's nothing hard with page template coding. We just need to import blog header, footer, and sidebar.

4. Now that we have our basic page template layout, we can start to integrate the Twitter entries. Each Twitter account has RSS feeds.

5. The first thing to do is to get the feed URL. To do so, just visit your own Twitter page and get the feed. It might look similar to the following link: `http://twitter.com/statuses/user_timeline/15985955.rss`

6. To integrate this feed into our page template, we shall use the `rss.php` file from WordPress core. This file will allow us to use the `wp_rss()` function, which is a built-in RSS reader. The function can read any RSS feed and display it on your WordPress blog.

7. Let's go back to our page template code, and add the following code instead of the `<?php //Content goes here ?>` comment:

```php
<?php include_once(ABSPATH . WPINC . '/rss.php');
wp_rss('http://twitter.com/statuses/user_timeline/15985955.rss',
        10); ?>
```

8. In the preceding code, we first include the requested `rss.php` file and then we call the `wp_rss()` function, which will read our Twitter feed and display it on our page template.

9. The `wp_rss()` function takes two arguments—the first argument is the RSS feed URL and the second is the number of entries you'd like to display. In the following example, I set 10 as the parameter but it's up to you to choose the number of entries you wish to display. Our final Twitter Page code now looks like this:

```php
<?php
/*
Template Name: Twitter Page
*/
?>

<?php get_header(); ?>

<div id="content">

<?php include_once(ABSPATH . WPINC . '/rss.php');
wp_rss('http://twitter.com/statuses/user_timeline/15985955.rss',
       10); ?>

</div>
<?php get_sidebar(); ?>
<?php get_footer(); ?>
```

10. Save the file under the name `twitter.php`.

11. Now that we have our Twitter Page ready, I'm pretty sure that you can't wait to use it. Great! Upload the file to your `wp-content/themes/yourtheme` directory and login to your WordPress **Dashboard**.

12. Create a new page and name it **Twitter entries,** for example. You don't have to write any content because it isn't needed and our page template doesn't have a function such as `the_content()`. Therefore, it simply can't display any content. The purpose of this page is to display your twitter entries.

13. To use the page template, scroll down until you see the **Page Template** drop-down box. In the drop-down menu options, select **Twitter Page** (the name of the template) and publish the page.

14. You can now go visit your blog. The Twitter entries will be displayed on the page we just created.

CatsWhoCode.com

BloggingCodingAndEvenMore

- 8 Javascript solutions to common CSS problems
  CSS are definitely a great technique for web designers and web developpers. Though, cross-browser problems and lack of CSS3 support in modern browsers are a real problem for your creativity. Today, I have compiled a list of 8 common CSS problems that you can easily resolve with help from Javascript.

- 10 awesome .htaccess hacks for WordPress
  .htaccess, the file which control the Apache webserver, is very useful and allows you to do a lot of things. In this article, let's see how .htaccess can help you with your WordPress blog, for both security, functionnality and usability.

How it works...

To achieve this recipe, we had to make use of a Page Template. Page Template will be discussed later on this chapter so you'll hopefully find an answer to all questions you are currently asking yourself.

The second part of the code is used for parsing the RSS feeds using the PHP language. To learn more about the RSS feeds parsing, you can visit the following link and read the entry on my blog: `http://www.wprecipes.com/how-to-display-your-latest-twitter-entry-on-your-wp-blog`.

Customizing WordPress admin login page

If you're creating a WordPress web site for a client, you'll probably like to make his or her login page a bit more personal than the default. In this recipe, we'll see how to make a custom admin login page for your clients, or even for yourself.

While writing this recipe, I was tempted to provide you two ways to customize your admin login page: with the help of a plugin, and by using a hack. But in the hack method, you are required to edit the WordPress core files, this really isn't a good idea. For example, suppose you hack the WordPress core successfully, but when you update your WordPress installation your hacks will be replaced by the new WordPress files. You'll have to hack again the new version, and so on.

This is the reason why, in this recipe, we shall discuss only about the plugin solution, which I think is really the best for the current scenario. The following screenshot shows a custom admin branding displayed on www.womantribune.com.

How to do it...

Creating a custom login panel is easy using the WordPress custom admin branding plugin and your creativity. Just carry out the following steps to get started.

Carry out the following steps in order to get the plugin:

1. The plugin we shall be using to rebrand or admin login page is called WordPress custom admin branding and can be downloaded for free at the following link: http://pressingpixels.com/wordpress-custom-admin-branding/

2. Once you have saved it in your hard drive, unzip it, and upload the custom_branding file into your wp-content/plugins directory. Login to your WordPress dashboard and activate the plugin.

3. Once activated, you'll be able to notice some changes. For example, in your WordPress dashboard your blog name has been replaced by Pressing Pixel (the plugin author's blog) logo. You should also log out to see your new login form—it also will have the Pressing Pixel logo. Don't worry, we shall learn how to replace this logo with yours!

Carry out the following steps in order to create your own images:

1. Now that we have a functional plugin, it's time to create and use our very own images. Luckily, the plugin author provided some PSD files that we can edit in a program such as Adobe Photoshop or The Gimp.

2. Under the `custom_branding` directory, you'll find a `psd_image_template` directory which contains 3 PSD image templates—`custom_footer.psd`, `custom_header.psd`, and `custom_login.psd`. The plugin author has also provided useful information, such as the part of the login form that may be hidden by the forms elements.

3. Once you have edited the PSD files, export it as `custom_login.jpg`, `custom_header.png`, and `custom_footer.png`. Upload it to your `wp-content/plugins/custom_branding/images` directory and replace the existing images.

How it works...

Using WordPress hooks, the Custom Admin Branding plugin redefine the CSS as well as the images used in WordPress login screen, which are replaced by your custom images.

Using conditional tags to display content on specific pages

Sometimes, you may want to display some content only on specific pages or sections. For example, you may wish to display a welcome message on your blog homepage or show specific information on the **Categories** page. In this recipe, Let's learn how to do it with the help of WordPress conditional tags.

Getting ready

To achieve this recipe, you'll need a WordPress theme that you can edit.

How to do it...

1. WordPress conditional tags are Boolean variables so you have to use them as a condition on a php `if` statement as shown in the following example:

```php
<?php if(is_page())
{
    echo "Page title:";
    the_title;
} ?>
```

2. The preceding `if` statement will return `false` if the current page template isn't a WordPress page template so nothing would happen. Otherwise, the `if` statement will return `true` and will print the page title on screen.

3. Conditional tags can be used in any theme files.

WordPress features a large amount of conditional tags for all needs. They all work as described above. Following are the conditional tags:

- ▶ `is_home()`: It returns true if the current page is the blog homepage
- ▶ `is_front_page()` : It returns true if the current page is the blog front page
- ▶ `is_single()` : It returns true if the current page is a single post template
- ▶ `is_page()`: It returns true if the current page is a page template
- ▶ `is_page_template("about.php")`: It returns true if a page template is currently being used
- ▶ `is_category()`: It returns true if the current page is a category template
- ▶ `in_category('4')`: It returns true if the current posts belongs to the specified category
- ▶ `is_tag()`: It returns true if the current page is a tag template
- ▶ `has_tag("wordpress")`: It returns true if the post have the tag specified in parameter
- ▶ `is_author()`: It returns true if the current page is an author archive
- ▶ `is_date()`: It returns true if the post or page is a date-based archive
- ▶ `is_year()`: It returns true if it's a yearly archive
- ▶ `is_month()`: It returns true if it's a monthly archive
- ▶ `is_day()`: It returns true if it's a daily archive
- ▶ `is_time()`: It returns true if an hourly, minutely, or secondly archive is being displayed
- ▶ `is_archive()`: It returns true if the current page display any type of archives (time, author, tag, and so on)
- ▶ `is_search()`: It returns true if the current page displays search results
- ▶ `is_paged()`: It returns true if the current page is paged
- ▶ `is_404()`: It returns true if the current page is a 404
- ▶ `is_sticky()`: It returns true if the **Stick this post to the front page** check box has been checked for the current post
- ▶ `has_tag("WordPress")`: It return true if the current posted has been tagged with **WordPress**

- ▶ `is_admin()`: It returns true if the dashboard or an admin page is currently displayed

- ▶ `comments_open()`: It returns true if commenting is allowed on the post

- ▶ `pings_open()`: It returns true if pinging is allowed on the post

- ▶ `is_preview()`: It returns true if the post or page is displayed in preview mode

> The `is_home()` function has been deprecated and replaced by the `is_front_page()` function. To ensure backward compatibility with older WordPress versions, you should use the following piece of code:
>
> ```php
> <?php if (is_front_page() || is_home())
> {
>     //Do something
> } ?>
> ```

How it works...

Unless specified, the above tags doesn't take any parameter. They have to be used in a PHP conditional statement.

```php
<?php if (is_404()) "
{
    //Do something only if the post or page is a 404 error.
} ?>
```

On the other hand, some conditional tags request a parameter to work. For example, to use the `is_year()` tag, you have to provide a year in parameter.

```php
<?php if (is_year("2007"))
{
    //Do something only if the post or page was published
        during the year 2007.
} ?>
```

There's more...

Conditional tags, as we have seen, are very useful. But there's more—some conditional tags accept optional arguments that allow you to create a more specific condition. For example, you should create a code snippet that will only be executed if the current page is a WordPress template.

Some conditional tags can accept up to 4 different types of parameters:

- ID: The ID parameter can be used in `is_category, is_page(), is_tag(),`
  `is_single(), is_author(),` and `is_sticky()`.

```php
<?php if (is_category(5))
{
}?>
```

As a result, the preceding code returns true if the category ID is 5.

- Name: The name parameter can be used in is_category, is_page(), is_single() and
  is_author().

```php
<?php if (is_category("Blogging Tips"))
{
}?>
```

As a result, the preceding code returns true if the category name is
`"Blogging Tips"`

- Slug: The slug parameter can be used in `is_category, is_page(), is_tag(),`
  `is_single(),` and `is_author()`.

```php
<?php if (is_category("blogging-tips"))
{
}?>
```

As a result, the preceding code returns true if the category slug is `"blogging-tips"`.

- Array: The array parameter can be used in is_category, is_page(), is_tag(), has_tag(),
  is_single() and is_author().

```php
<?php if(is_category(array(5,'blogging-tips','Blogging Tips')))
{
} ?>
```

As a result, the preceding code returns true if the category of posts being displayed
either has the ID as 5, slug as `"blogging-tips"`, or name as `"Blogging Tips"`.

Using page templates in your theme

Even though most of the WordPress themes use a unique page template, our favorite blogging
engine allows us to create as many different page templates as we want.

Why always use the same page layout in your blog? Using different page templates will make
your blog look a lot more professional.

In this recipe, you'll learn to create and use page templates.

Getting ready

To achieve this recipe, you only need a WordPress theme and a text editor. In the following example, we use the WordPress default theme. If you're using another theme, you'll have to adjust the code a bit to make it fit your theme HTML markup.

How to do it...

Let us start with creating a test page template and learn how to create more page templates in the following recipes.

1. On your theme directory, create a new file and name it `testpage.php`.

2. Open the `testpage.php` file in your favorite text editor and insert the following code in it:

```php
<?php
/*
Template Name: Test Page
*/
?>
<?php get_header(); ?>
<div id="content" class="narrowcolumn">
<h1>My first page template, called <?php the_title(); ?>!</h1>
</div>
<?php get_sidebar(); ?>
<?php get_footer(); ?>
```

3. Login to your WordPress **Dashboard** and go to **Write | Page** and give your page a title. You don't have to write any text in the body since it won't be displayed by the page template.

4. Scroll down until you see a **Page template** link. Clicking on the link will open a drop-down menu from where you can select the page template to use. Select the new template, **Test Page**.

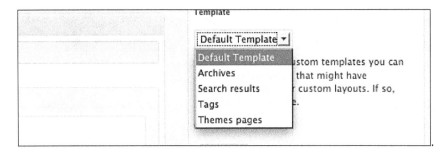

5. Publish the page.

6. Visit your page. You will see a basic page with only a title displaying **My first page template**, called XXX (the name you have given to the page).

Now, you know how easy it is to create and use page templates in your WordPress theme. This example isn't useful at all, therefore, let us see some really interesting uses of page template in the following recipe.

How it works...

The WordPress page template allows you to define special template layouts that can be assigned to pages.

Creating an archive page

More and more blogs feature an archive page where they display all of their posts. There are two good reasons to do it—the first is SEO and second is your visitors. With an archive page, any search engine crawler is able to easily index all your posts. When I find a blog of my choice, I'm used to browsing through their archive page to get a quick view of what might interest me.

In this recipe, you shall learn how to create an useful archive page for your WordPress theme, by using the page template technique.

Getting ready

As I just said, we shall be using a page template to create an archive page, for which you have to understand the page template concept—explained in the previous recipe.

I'm using the WordPress default theme in the following example, so you might have to adapt the HTML markup a bit to make it fit your own theme.

How to do it...

1. Create a file named `archive-custom.php` on your WordPress theme directory.

2. Enter the following code in that file:

```php
<?php
/*
Template Name: Custom Archives
*/
?>
<?php get_header(); ?>
        <div id="content" class="narrowcolumn">
```

```php
<?php
while(have_posts()) : the_post(); ?>
<h2><?php the_title(); ?></h2>
<ul id="archive-list">
<?php
$myposts = get_posts('numberposts=-1&offset=0');
foreach($myposts as $post) :
?>
<li><?php the_time('m/d/y') ?>: <a href="<?php the_permalink();
     ?>"><?php the_title(); ?></a></li>
<?php endforeach; ?>
</ul>
<?php endwhile; ?>
</div>
<?php get_sidebar(); ?>
<?php get_footer(); ?>
```

3. Save the file and upload it to the `wp-content/themes/yourtheme` directory of your WordPress install.

4. Log in to your WordPress **Dashboard**, create a new page, and select **Custom Archives** as a page template. Give it a title of your choice, for example **Archives**.

5. Publish the page. Your theme now features an archive page; cool for both, search engines and visitors!

How it works...

Basically, an archive page is just a page which loops through all posts you wrote, and only display the post title and its date.

In the example, we have used the `get_posts()` function instead of the classic WordPress loop. The reason behind this is that the WordPress loop's purpose is to display posts on your blog homepage depending on certain parameters, such as posts per page or pagination information. However, on our archive page we only need to display all post titles on a single page.

You must have noticed that the `get_posts()` function have two parameters:

1. The first one is `numberposts`, which is used to specify the number of posts you want to retrieve. I have set it up at -1, which means that I want to get all the available posts.

2. The second parameter used is `offset`; which allow you to specify the number of posts that you don't want to be displayed. If you specify `offset=5`, the first post you'll get will be the sixth. The `offset=0` in the example doesn't change anything at all. For example, you should enhance the archive page we just created by creating a first loop which will only get you the most recent posts and style it differently.

There's more...

For those who prefer to use a plugin instead of creating their own archive page, I have used the Smart Archives plugin some time ago and enjoyed it. You can get it for free at the following link, `http://justinblanton.com/projects/smartarchives/`.

Creating a custom 404 error page

Who hasn't seen a 404 error page in his life? I'm sure there rarely is anyone. And you'll probably agree with me that 404 errors are boring—especially when you're looking for something that appears to have been moved.

This is why it is very important to have a custom and useful 404 page. In this recipe, I'll show you how to do it for your WordPress blog.

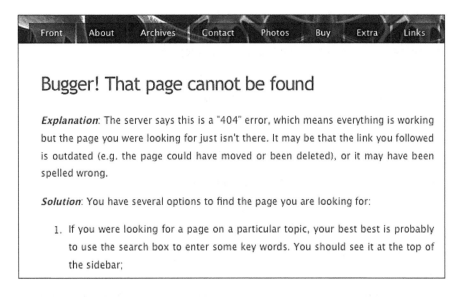

Getting ready

To achieve this recipe, you need a `404.php` file. Most WordPress themes actually feature this kind of page. If, for some reason, your theme doesn't feature such a page, simply create a php file named `404.php` and upload it to your `wp-content/themes/yourtheme` directory. You don't have to add a Page template directive—WordPress automatically recognizes a file named `404.php` as a page designed to be displayed if a 404 error occurs.

In this example, we are using the `404.php` file from the default WordPress theme. If you open the file, you'll find the following code:

```
<?php get_header(); ?>
    <div id="content" class="narrowcolumn">
    <h2 class="center">Error 404 - Not Found</h2>
    </div>
<?php get_sidebar(); ?>
<?php get_footer(); ?>
```

As you can see, this page does nothing except inform the user that nothing was found at the particular URL. Let's enhance it to help the visitor looking for some content, by displaying archives, categories, and a link to the blog homepage.

How to do it...

1. Open the `404.php` file in your favorite editor.

2. Below the `<h2 class="center">Error 404 - Not Found</h2>` line, add the following code to create a link to the blog homepage:

   ```
   <a href="<?php bloginfo("url");?>">Homepage</a>
   ```

3. Add the following code to display your categories:

   ```
   <h2>Categories</h2>
   <ul>
   <?php wp_list_categories("title_li="); ?>
   </ul>
   ```

4. Add the following code to display your monthly archives:

   ```
   <?php wp_get_archives('type=monthly&limit=12'); ?>
   ```

5. Save the file, and you're done!

How it works...

WordPress features an interesting template hierarchy mechanism. When a 404 error appears, WordPress automatically looks for a file named `404.php`. If such a file exists, it is displayed. Otherwise, the `404.php` file is displayed page .

In the `404.php` file we have displayed our blog's monthly archives and categories to make sure that the reader will find the content that he's looking for.

There's more...

In this recipe, we have seen how to create a useful 404 page. However, did you know that some bloggers also enjoy creating funny 404 pages? For example, the 404 error page of my blog **Cats Who Code**, features a picture of a cat trying to repair a PC with the caption, "There's a problem, but someone is fixing it".

For a list of funny an unusual 404 pages, you should take a look at the following link:
`http://blogof.francescomugnai.com/2008/08/the-100-most-funny-and-unusual-404-error-pages/`

Using a static page as a homepage

Almost 90% of blogs use the list of most recent posts as a homepage. However, if you prefer to use a static page as a homepage, the choice is yours. This technique allows you to use WordPress and create different kinds of web sites—not only blogs.

Getting ready

Nothing special is needed here. The possibility of using a static page as a homepage is built-in in the WordPress—however, a lot of bloggers aren't aware of it.

In this recipe, we will learn how to set up a static page as a homepage for your blog, though, we won't create the entire page for you. Now that you have learned how to create and use page templates, setting up a homepage shouldn't be a problem.

How to do it...

1. Log in to your WordPress **Dashboard** and create a page named **Homepage** and publish it.

2. On your WordPress **Dashboard**, go to **Settings | Reading**. You'll see a title saying **Front page displays**.

3. Select the **A static page** radio button and choose your new front page from the drop-down list. If you please, you can also choose a new template for the posts to be displayed.

How it works...

WordPress allows you to choose between the post lists (most used in blogs) and a static page of your choice as homepage.

This second option gives you quite a few of possibilities, in particular if you'd like to create a non-blog site using WordPress.

There's more...

If you have chosen to use a static page as homepage, how about executing some PHP in it? If this idea seems appealing to you, you should definitely check out the Exec-PHP plugin. You can download it for free at the following link: `http://wordpress.org/extend/plugins/exec-php/`.

To install Exec-PHP, simply use the standard *How to do it...* described in Chapter 1. Suppose you want to execute some PHP within a post or a page, you can do it by simply turning the WordPress editor to source mode and starting with coding your PHP.

Creating a Featured Posts block on your homepage

Would you like to make some of your posts stands out of the crowd? If yes, a good solution is to create a **Featured Posts** block on your blog homepage.

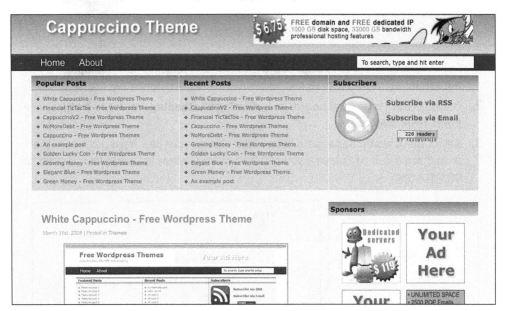

Getting ready

As you can see in the preceding screenshot, before the normal post listing, the blogger set up a **Featured Posts** block where he or she display the most popular posts.

To achieve this recipe, you only need a text editor and a WordPress theme.

How to do it...

1. Log in to your WordPress **Dashboard**, go to **Manage | Categories**, and create a new category named **Featured**.

2. Once you have created your **Featured** category, simply put your mouse cursor on the **edit** link related to this category and look at your browser's status bar—you'll be able to see the `action=edit` and category ID (`cat_ID=1`, in our case), as shown in the following screenshot:

3. Open the `index.php` file from your theme directory.

4. At the location where you want your **Featured Posts** to appear, insert the following code:

```php
<?php if (!$paged) { ?>
<div id="featured">
<?php
    query_posts('showposts=5&cat=5); ?>
    <h2>Featured posts</h2>
<?php while (have_posts()) : the_post(); ?>
    <div class="featuredElement">
      <h3><a href="<?php the_permalink() ?>">
          <?php the_title(); ?></a></h3>
      <?php the_excerpt(); ?>
    </div><!--/featuredElement-->
<?php endwhile; ?>
</div><!--/featured-->
```

5. Don't forget to modify the category parameter on line 4 of the preceding code according to your `"featured"` category ID.

6. Save the file, upload it on the `wp_content/themes/yourtheme` directory of your server, and go back to your WordPress dashboard.

To create featured posts, simply add it to the `"featured"` category. The 5 most recent posts will be shown on your blog homepage.

How it works...

The earlier stated code starts by looking for the $paged variable. If the page isn't paginated, which means the reader is looking at the blog homepage only, the code executes the query_posts() function with the showposts parameter—to display only 5 posts and the cat parameter. This allows us to only get posts from a certain category, that is, the featured category we had created before.

There's more...

Another interesting use of the **Featured Posts** block in your blog homepage is to create a widget-ready zone. Widgets will be discussed in the later chapters of this book.

Making your new posts stands out with a custom style

Creating a **Featured Posts** block, as we have seen earlier, allows you to specify some posts to be displayed on your blog as the featured posts. However, you may prefer to automatically make your latest posts stand out. In this recipe, we shall learn to modify the classic WordPress loop to give another style to your latest posts.

Getting ready

Similar to the previous recipe, you only need a text editor, a WordPress theme, and—of course—this book to achieve the hack. This recipe is based on the WordPress default theme, but can be adapted on any other theme as well.

How to do it...

1. Open the `index.php` file from your theme and look for the WordPress loop. In the WordPress default theme, the WordPress loop is located on line 5 and looks similar to the following code:

```php
<?php while (have_posts()) : the_post(); ?>
<div class="post" id="post-<?php the_ID(); ?>">
    <h2><a href="<?php the_permalink() ?>" rel="bookmark"
    title="Permanent Link to <?php the_title_attribute(); ?>">
    <?php the_title(); ?></a></h2>
    <small><?php the_time('F jS, Y') ?><!-- by
    <?php the_author() ?> --></small>
    <div class="entry">
        <?php the_content('Read the rest of this entry &raquo;');
            ?>
    </div>
    <p class="postmetadata"><?php the_tags('Tags: ', ', ', ',
            '<br />');
    ?> Posted in <?php the_category(', ') ?> |
    <?php edit_post_link('Edit', '', ' | '); ?>
    <?php comments_popup_link('No Comments &#187;',
    '1 Comment &#187;', '% Comments &#187;'); ?></p>
</div>
<?php endwhile; ?>
```

2. Replace that loop with the following code and save the file. You can edit the number of posts that will be marked as `"featured"` on line 4. As the earlier code displays only one featured post, let us use the following code.

```php
<?php $count = 0; ?>
<?php while (have_posts()) : the_post(); ?>
<?php $count++; ?>
<?php if ($count < 2) : ?>
<div class="featured post" id="post-<?php the_ID(); ?>">
    <h2><a href="<?php the_permalink() ?>">New Post:
    <?php the_title(); ?></a></h2>
        <small>Posted in <?php the_category(', ') ?> on
        <?php the_time('F jS, Y') ?>.</small>
        <div class="entry">
```

```
        <?php the_content('Read the rest of this entry &raquo;');
            ?>
    </div>
</div>

<?php else : ?>
<!-- "Normal" posts -->
<div class="post" id="post-<?php the_ID(); ?>">
    <h2><a href="<?php the_permalink() ?>">
    <?php the_title(); ?></a></h2>
      <small><?php the_time('F jS, Y') ?></small>
      <div class="entry">
        <?php the_content('Read the rest of this entry &raquo;');
            ?>
      </div>

      <p class="postmetadata"><?php the_tags('Tags: ', ', ', ' '
      <br />'); ?> Posted in <?php the_category(', ') ?> |
      <?php edit_post_link('Edit', '', ' | '); ?>
      <?php comments_popup_link('No Comments &#187;', '1
      Comment &#187;', '% Comments &#187;'); ?></p>
    </div>
<?php endif; ?>
<?php endwhile; ?>
```

3. Now, edit the `style.css` file from your theme. The preceding code creates and adds a "featured" class to your latest posts—with the help of the "featured" class you can modify the post displays. Add the following code to the `style.css` file and style it your way:

```
post.featured
{
    background:#f9f9f9;
    font-weight:bold;
}
```

How it works...

At the beginning of the code, and before the loop, I have created a PHP variable named `$count` and initialized at the value 0. This variable is a counter—on each iteration through the loop, the code changes its value to its current value + 1.

On line 4 of the earlier code, I test whether the `$count` value is smaller than 2. If yes, a post with the "featured" style is displayed, otherwise the posts are displayed in normal style.

There's more...

The PHP counters are very useful and can be used to achieve various tasks. For example, the following code, similar to our previous code will display some AdSense ads after the first post:

```php
<?php $count = 0; ?>
<?php while (have_posts()) : the_post(); ?>
<?php $count++; ?>
<div class="post" id="post-<?php the_ID(); ?>">
    <h2><a href="<?php the_permalink() ?>">
    <?php the_title(); ?></a></h2>
    <small><?php the_time('F jS, Y') ?></small>
    <div class="entry">
      <?php the_content('Read the rest of this entry &raquo;'); ?>
    </div>

    <p class="postmetadata"><?php the_tags('Tags: ', ', ', '<br />');
    ?> Posted in <?php the_category(', ') ?> |
    <?php edit_post_link('Edit', '', ' | '); ?>
    <?php comments_popup_link('No Comments &#187;',
    '1 Comment &#187;', '% Comments &#187;'); ?></p>
<?php if ($count < 2) : ?>
    <!-- INSERT ADSENSE CODE HERE -->
<?php endif; ?>
</div>
<?php endwhile; ?>
```

That's it! Your latest posts are now displayed with a custom style.

In this chapter, you have learned how to modify and enhance a WordPress theme to definitely make your blog different.

4
Doing anything with Plugins and Widgets

Even if WordPress itself is very powerful and complete, some third party plugins and widgets can enhance its functionality or provide new features, without forcing you to edit a single line of code.

In this recipe, I'm going to show you both basic tasks, installing plugins and widgets, and more complex things such as creating different widget-ready zones on your WordPress theme.

In this chapter, you will learn:

- Installing plugins
- Getting rid of comment spams with Akismet
- Backing up your database with WP database backup
- Optimizing your blog performances with WP Super Cache
- Adding redirects for changed Permalinks
- Getting more comments with the Subscribe to Comments plugin
- Accessing real time statistics with WordPress.com Stats
- Monetizing your blog with ISIS Ads Management
- Extending WordPress search with Search Unleashed
- Installing widgets
- Making your sidebar widget-ready
- Creating two (or more) different widget-ready zones
- Modifying core widgets
- Creating your own widget

Installing plugins

Honestly, I don't know any blogger who doesn't use at least one or two plugin(s) on his or her WordPress blog. In order to make an efficient use of plugins, the first thing to know is how to install one.

Getting ready

Installing a WordPress plugin is easy. In fact, 95% of plugins use the same installation procedure. To install a plugin, you need a working WordPress blog, of course, and a plugin of your choice.

How to do it...

1. Download the plugin archive.

2. Extract the plugin archive on your hard drive.

3. Read the `Readme` or `Install` file from the plugin directory to make sure no additional steps are required.

4. Upload the plugin directory into the `wp-content/plugins` directory of your WordPress install by using an FTP program such as Cyberduck on the Mac or Filezilla on Windows and GNU/Linux.

5. Log in to your WordPress **Dashboard** and go to **Plugins**.

6. Scroll down the plugin list until you see the name of the plugin you'd like to install, and click on the **Activate** button next to the plugin's name. That's all!

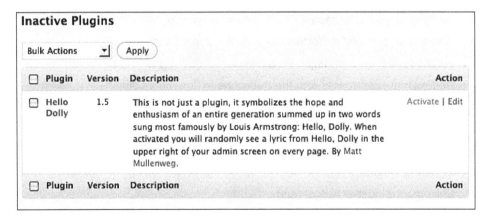

How it works...

When a plugin is installed, its name is registered in the WordPress database, which means that the plugin is active and WordPress will let it execute the tasks it was developed for.

Plugins use hooks (we will discuss it later) and the Plugin API, which provide useful PHP functions to modify WordPress default functions.

Getting rid of comment spams with Akismet

Akismet plugin comes by default with any new WordPress version. As you probably already know, WordPress blogs are heavily spammed. I really think that you should use Akismet instead of boring and non-accessible captchas to prevent blog spam.

Getting ready

As I said, Akismet comes bundled with every WordPress release and so you don't have to download it. The first step is to activate it. Login to your WordPress dashboard and click on **Plugins**. Scroll down until you see **Akismet** in the plugin list and click on the **Activate** button to activate it.

How to do it...

Take note that Akismet is now activated, but it isn't running yet. You have to provide an API key. The API key is free, but you have to create an account at wordpress.com in order to get one.

1. Go to `www.wordpress.com` and create an account.

2. Login to your wordpress.com dashboard and select **Edit Profile** on the drop-down list that you get when you hover the mouse on **My Account**.

3. Your API key is listed here, just below the **Profile** and above the **Personal Options** titles.

4. Report the API key to Akismet. The plugin is now activated and will automatically filter spam comments.

How it works...

When a new comment or trackback is submitted to your blog, Akismet web service runs tests on the comment and returns thumbs up or thumbs down. Akismet works with a shared blacklist of well-known spammers. If a spam comment isn't filtered by the plugin, clicking on the **Spam** button will notify Akismet that you think this comment was a spam.

Backing up your database with WP Database Backup

In case you don't know already, your blog content, comments, and parameters are stored in a MySQL database. So this database is the heart of your blog, and you'll lose all your precious content if any kind of problem occurs on it.

Getting ready

To install this must-have functionality on your WordPress blog, go to http://wordpress.org/extend/plugins/wp-db-backup/ and click on the **Download** button. Once downloaded, follow the *Installing plugins* procedure on page 1.

How to do it...

1. Once WP Database Backup is installed, you'll find a **Backup** tab under **Manage** in your WordPress **Dashboard**. WP Database backup lists all of the tables from your database, including the ones created by plugins.

2. Scroll down until you see the **Backup Options**. Under the **Backup Options**, select the **Download to your computer** option and click on the **Backup now!** button. You'll see a progress bar showing how your backup creation is proceeding. Don't refresh the page or click the **Back** button, as this will cause your backup to fail. Some seconds later, depending on the size of the database, your browser will ask you if you want to download the backup. Click on the **Yes** button and save the backup to your computer.

```
┌─ Backup Options ──────────────────────────────────────────────────┐
│  What to do with the backup file:                                  │
│                                                                    │
│  ○ Save to server ( /home/users/r/roiheenok/www/roiheenok.com/wp-content/backup-fad32/ ) │
│  ◉ Download to your computer                                       │
│  ○ Email backup to:  [ you@yahoo.fr          ]                     │
│  ( Backup now! )                                                   │
└────────────────────────────────────────────────────────────────────┘
```

How it works...

The popular PhpMyAdmin web application allows you to create manual backups of any web site (including, of course, WordPress blogs) but the WordPress Database Backup goes further, letting you create manual database backup without leaving your WordPress dashboard.

Using the **cron** functions of WordPress, WordPress Database Backup is also able to schedule automatic backups for you, which isn't possible with PhpMyAdmin.

There's more...

While creating backups on demand is a cool option, it is even more secure to schedule automatic backups. WP Database Backup can easily do this.

Scheduling automatic backups

Let's learn how how to schedule automatic backups.

How to do it...

To schedule a backup, go to the **Backup** tab under **Manage** on your WordPress **Dashboard** and scroll down until you see the **Scheduled Backup** option. The plugin allows you to schedule a database dump hourly once, daily once, daily twice, or weekly once. Select the frequency that fits your needs (**Once Daily** is my personal choice) and enter your email address. As per your selection of the frequency, you'll receive a database backup by email.

How it works...

WP Database Backup is a PHP script that executes lots of SQL commands using PHP functions to create a database backup.

There's more...

If you're looking for an even more powerful plugin, you should definitely try the WP-DBManager (`http://lesterchan.net/wordpress/readme/wp-dbmanager.html`).

This plugin allows you to create backups of your WordPress database just as WP Database Backup does, but you can also repair and optimize your database, and even, run SQL commands in your WordPress dashboard!

Optimizing your blog performances with WP Super Cache

Would you like to be (or already are) featured on some high-traffic web sites, such as Digg, delicious.com, or StumbleUpon? If the answer is yes, you have to make sure that your blog can survive a 5000/10000 new visitor's rush.

For example, I often click on featured links on Digg. Almost once daily, I'm redirected to a blog that takes forever to load or, even worse, doesn't respond at all. This wouldn't happen in the blog if WP Super Cache is used.

Getting ready

WP Super Cache can be downloaded for free on `http://ocaoimh.ie/wp-super-cache/`. As usual, follow the procedure about installing a plugin on page 1 to install your copy of WP Database Backup.

Once done, you'll find a **WP Super Cache** under the **Settings** tab of your WordPress dashboard.

How to do it...

As the WP Super Cache plugin is a complex piece of code which allows you to do lots of different operations, let's have a step by step look at how to achieve specific tasks:

1. **Turning the cache on/off**: After installing the plugin, you should know that the WP Super Cache is off, which means it is running but inactive. To turn it on and optimize your blog performances, go to **Settings | WP Super Cache** and look for the **WP Super Cache Status** label. Check **ON** and click on the **Update Status** button. Your blog is now protected against huge traffic effects!

2. **Emptying the cache**: When you're modifying of one of your theme files, you need to empty the cache before being able to see it. The principle of caching is to create static pages from dynamic pages, in order to reduce server load and database requests. This explains why you'll not be able to see a recent modification on a theme file until you have cleared the cache. To do so, just login to your WordPress dashboard, then go to **Settings | WP Super Cache** and scroll down until you see the **Delete Cache** button. Click on it and all of the cached pages will be erased. They'll be re-created when someone visits the page for the first time.

How it works...

WP Super Cache's purpose is static caching. The plugin generates HTML files that are served directly by Apache without processing comparatively heavy PHP scripts, resulting in a significant increase in speed for serving of your WordPress blog.

There's more...

While WP Super Cache is very useful, there maybe cases when sometimes you don't want a specific URL to be cached. As a concrete example, I had recently set-up a forum on my blog `www.wprecipes.com`. When I tested it, I realized that if someone leaves a message on the board, no-one was able to read it. Of course, the page is cached, as any other page from my blog, so the forum was a static page! Luckily, this super plugin allows you to prevent URLs from being cached.

Prevent URLs from being cached

To specify an URL which must not be cached, go to the WP Super Cache options panel and scroll down until you see **Accepted filenames, rejected URIs**. By default, **wp-.*.php** and **index.php** are prevented from caching. This makes sure than your index page will not be cached (otherwise you will not be able to see new posts!) as well as any admin page.

Just add your URL below the existing ones. Remember to only put one URL per line.

It is also possible to use wildcards; for example, by specifying that we don't want `wp-.*.php` to be cached, we prevent any file name that starts with `wp-` and ending with `.php` from being cached.

Accepted Filenames & Rejected URIs

Add here strings (not a filename) that forces a page not to be cached. For example, if your URLs include year and you dont want to cache last year posts, it's enough to specify the year, i.e. '/2004/'. WP-Cache will search if that string is part of the URI and if so, it will not cache that page.

```
wp-.*.php
index.php
```

(Save Strings »)

Adding redirects for changed Permalinks

As WordPress uses URL rewriting in Permalinks, you probably know that any change in a permalink will break your **SEO (Search Engine Optimization)** and all of the links will point to the incremented post. Sometimes, you have no other choice than to modify a permalink. Even worse, WordPress itself may have modified your permalink (for example, including the category name in your permalink structure, and add a post to another category after publishing it).

This recipe will show you how to fix this situation, using the Redirection plugin.

Getting ready

Before using it, you need to download, install, and activate the Redirection plugin from `http://urbangiraffe.com/plugins/redirection/`. See the standard plugin installation procedure at the beginning of this chapter.

How to do it...

Let's create a simple redirection as an example. Your post permalink was previously

`http://myblog.com/categorie-one/mypost` and it is now `http://myblog.com/categorie-two/mypost`.

We need to redirect the first URL to the second. This way, if anyone types the old URL in the address bar, or clicks on a link to it, they will automatically be redirected to the new URL, and you'll not lose any traffic.

1. Go to your WordPress **Dashboard | Manage | Redirection**.
2. Define `http://myblog.com/categorie-one/mypost` as the source URL, and `http://myblog.com/categorie-two/mypost` as the target URL.
3. Click on **Add Redirection** and you're done. Your redirected URL will now appear on the Redirection plugin as shown below:

Redirections

	Search:		Per page: 25 ▾	go
Type	URL / Position ▽	Count	Last Access	
301	/blog/featured/6-html-and-javascript-codes-to-cras...	510	March 18, 2009	⊖
301	/blog/featured/mootools-basics-5-useful-tips-524	15	January 15, 2009	⊖
301	/blog/wordpress-ebook.html	1	August 31, 2008	⊖
301	/blog/revolution-theme.html	1	August 31, 2008	⊖
301	/blog/blog-mastermind.html	1	August 31, 2008	⊖
301	/blog/killerdomains.html	777	March 21, 2009	⊖

How it works...

We have redirected the first URL to the second, this way if anyone types the first URL in the address bar, or clicks on a link to it, he or she will automatically redirect to the new URL and you will not lose any traffic.

There's more...

As a must-have plugin, the Redirection plugin can help you achieve lots of different tasks such as creating a redirection to a post which had its URL changed. But as my blogs are monetized, I also use the Redirection plugin to cloak affiliate links.

Using redirects for affiliate marketing and cloaking

Another very interesting point of Redirection is for people doing affiliate marketing on their blog. You can use Redirection to cloak your URLs. This way you can transform an ugly URL such as `https://www.e-junkie.com/ecom/gb.php?ii=153348&c=cart&aff=26621&ev=f19cc82078&ejc=2` to a new and clean URL, for example, `http://www.catswhocode.com/blog/mothertheme.html`.

Getting more comments with the Subscribe to Comments plugin

Comments are very important in blogging, because they encourage discussion. When leaving a comment on a blog post, for example if you are asking a question or requesting some support, it's very boring to come back to the page twice a day and see that no-one has answered you.

With Suscribe to Comments, you'll provide a way for your visitors to receive an email each time someone commented on the post in question. I was skeptical about this plugin at first, but after I tested it, I can say that it increased the average number of comments on my posts, and it helped creating many interesting discussions.

How to do it...

1. The Subscribe to Comments plugin can be downloaded from `http://txfx.net/code/wordpress/subscribe-to-comments`.

2. Next, simply follow the plugin installation procedure as described on page 1.

3. Subscribe to Comments does not require any configuration. Once activated, it is already working. To make sure everything's fine, you can visit any of your blog posts and scroll down until the comment form. You should see a checkbox labeled **Subscribe to Comments**.

How it works...

When someone leaves a comment on your blog, he or she can check the **Subscribe to comments** checkbox. If he or she checks it, the person will receive any other comment posted on the same article through his or her email. This is particularly useful when debating with other readers, or when you have asked a question to the blogger.

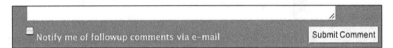

There's more...

If you want, you can check out the subscriber list, see how many people subscribed to your blog posts, and manage subscriptions. To do all of this, login to your WordPress dashboard and go to **Manage | Subscriptions**.

From here, you can perform the following tasks:

▸ Search if a particular email address is subscribing to one or more of your posts

▸ Get email addresses of your subscribers

▸ Get a list of most subscribed posts

▸ Remove subscribers

▸ Change email address

Accessing real time statistics with WordPress.com Stats

Like Akismet, this is a plugin brought to you by Automattic, the company founded by Matt Mullenweg who is the creator of WordPress. The purpose of this plugin is to provide you real time statistics about your blog traffic, your most popular posts, and your referrers. While it is not as powerful as a dedicated solution such as Google Analytics, WordPress.com Stats is a nice solution to watch how your traffic is going real time.

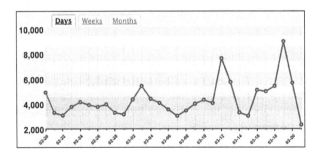

Getting ready

The WordPress.com Stats plugin can be downloaded here:
`http://wordpress.org/extend/plugins/stats/`.

How to do it...

To install it, follow the instructions about installing plugins on page 1.

This plugin requires the use of an API key.

1. Go to `www.wordpress.com` and create an account.
2. Login to your wordpress.com dashboard and select **Edit Profile** on the drop-down list.
3. Your API key is listed here, just below the **Profile** and above the **Personal Options** title.
4. Report the API key to WordPress.com Stats. The plugin is now activated and is already getting information about your visitors.

Right after you have provided your API key to the plugin, your visitors are tracked. Visiting your stats is easy:

1. Login to your WordPress dashboard.
2. Click on the **Blog Stats** link, located below the **Dashboard** tab. Your stats are displayed as soon as you click it.

How it works...

As you can see, the WordPress.com Stats plugin provides a lot of useful information. Some of them are what we can call **Search engine jargon**. Here's a simple way to understand them.

- **Referrers**: The sites linking to your blog, and the number of visits they provided to you
- **Top Posts & Pages**: Your most popular posts and pages.
- **Search engines terms**: The terms searched by visitors that lead them to your blog.
- **Clicks**: The most clicked links on your blog.

There are loads of WordPress plugins dedicated to provide statistics to the blogger. However, WordPress.com Stats is the most efficient one available. Why? Simply because the tracking and recording process runs on Automattic's servers and not your server.

Monetizing your blog with ISIS Ads Management

I would like to quote Michaël Pierard here:

> Most bloggers monetize their blog, do you? If the answer is yes, you probably grew frustrated having one or more 125*125 pixel advertisements. Most people use a text widget with some handmade HTML/CSS to accomplish this. While this is a good way to do it, you're wasting a lot of your precious time.

ISIS Ads Management provides a super clean interface to manage and display 125*125 pixel ads.

Getting ready

Get your copy of the plugin at `http://www.catswhocode.com/blog/featured/isis-ads-management-new-wordpress-widget-to-displaymanage-125125-ads`.

Once you have downloaded the plugin, follow the instructions to install a plugin on page 1.

When ISIS Ads Management will be successfully installed, you'll see an **ISIS Ads Management** tab under **Manage** on your WordPress dashboard.

To utilize this recipe, you'll need a set of 125*125 px ads and their relative links.

How to do it...

Let's create a set of four ads that will be displayed on your blog sidebar.

1. Go to **Manage | ISI Ads Management**. You'll see the ads manager, where you can create and manage ads.
2. Let's give a title to our ads block—**Sponsors** sounds good.
3. It's time to create an ad; populate the **125*125 Ads Link URL** field with the URL of your sponsor, and the **125*125 Ads Image URL** with the image URL.
4. Click on the **Add** button. Your ad is displayed below the form.
5. Repeat the procedure to create as many ads as you need.
6. Drag and drop ads to change their order of appearance, if needed.
7. Click on the **Save** button. Your ad block is now saved!
8. Go to **Appearance | Widgets** and add the **Show Ads** widget to the widgetized zone of your choice.
9. Click on **Save Changes** and you're done!

How it works...

ISIS Ads Management combines the power of a custom admin panel page (we have seen this in Chapter 3) and widgets. The custom admin page allows you to create and manage your ads, while the widget can display it on any widgetized area of your theme.

Extending WordPress search with Search Unleashed

I have heard a lot of WordPress users complaining about the lack of possibilities in the WordPress built-in search. If you ever wished to provide your readers a full text search, wildcards, and even text highlighting across posts, this plugin is for you.

Getting ready

You can grab the Search Unleashed plugin at `http://urbangiraffe.com/plugins/search-unleashed/`. Next, simply install it according to the standard plugin installation procedure described earlier.

Once the plugin is installed successfully, you'll be able to customize its option on a **Search Unleashed** page located under **Manage**.

How to do it...

There's a bit of configuration needed for the plugin to work properly:

1. Login to your WordPress dashboard and go to **Manage | Search Unleashed**.
2. Click on the **Modules** link.
3. Select the data that you want to be indexed by the plugin, as shown in the following screenshot.
4. Click on the **Options** link.
5. Configure the options to fit your needs (Page title, search mode, css color for search results, and so on).

6. Click on the **Save** button and you're done!

How it works...

The default WordPress searching functionality performs searches only over post data. Search Unleashed maintains its own search index which allows searching in comments, tags, categories, and so on, and gets more relevant results.

Search results for 'plugin'

1. **Localization Thanks**

   4

   Mar 9, 2009

   ... by as many different people as possible. Last year I wrote some articles (Translating WordPress Plugins and Localizing WordPress Plugins) detailing how to localize a plugin and theme from both a developers and translators point of view. Since then my plugins have been receiving a steady stream of translations and I'd like to take this opportunity to thank everyone who's not only helped produce translation but also pointed out areas of my code that were not yet localized.

   Thanks go ...

   Comment by shamiao: ... of Redirection plugin. :):P Redirection w/ Chinese ...

   Read more here...

Installing widgets

Now that we have studied how to install WordPress plugins and what plugins can do for you, let's have a look at widgets. A widget does the same thing as a plugin—It adds more functionality to your blog.

When you install a plugin, it automatically adds a new functionality to your WordPress blog. Sometimes, you have to edit one of your files and paste a line of code to make the plugin functional.

On the other hand, widgets have to be dragged to a widget-ready zone, which is a part of your blog that is set up to display widgets. Most recent themes feature at least one widget-ready zone, often located in the sidebar.

The main difference between plugins and widgets is that a widget can be placed on any widget-ready zone on your blog and can be ordered directly from your WordPress dashboard.

Getting ready

Before installing any widget, you must first verify that your theme is widget ready. As I said in the previous section, most recent themes feature a widget-ready zone in the sidebar. You can do the following to verify if a theme is widget-ready:

1. Open the `sidebar.php` file from the theme that you want to verify the widget capacity for.

2. Look for the following code (or similar):

```php
<?php /* Widgetized sidebar, if you have the plugin installed. */
if ( !function_exists('dynamic_sidebar') ||
    !dynamic_sidebar(1) ) : ?>
<?php endif; ?>
```

If you found the code, your theme is widget-ready. If not, don't worry. We'll see how to make any theme widget ready in a few pages.

As we just saw, you need a widget ready theme to be able to use widgets. The WordPress default theme is widget ready, so you can use that one for testing in case the theme you're using can't handle widgets yet. Of course, you will also need a widget of your choice.

How to do it...

Follow these simple steps to add a built-in widget to any of your theme widget-ready zones:

1. Login to your WordPress dashboard and go to **Appearance | Widgets**.

2. On the right-side of the page, you can choose a widget-ready zone. Most themes have only one zone. Click on the **Show** button to display the widgets from that zone.

3. Once you selected the zone that you'd like to use, look on the left of the page where available widgets are displayed. Pick up the one you just installed, and drag it to your widget zone on the right of the page.

4. Click on the **Edit** link on the widget and edit its parameters as desired.

5. Click on the **Save Changes** button below the widget list and you're done!

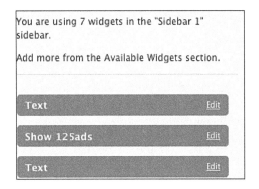

How it works...

WordPress widgets are like plugins, but designed to provide a simple way to arrange the various elements of your sidebar content (known as widgets) without having to change any code.

In this example, I have started by checking if the `dynamic_sidebar()` function exists. If the answer is yes, it means that the WordPress version used by your blog can handle widgets. This same function is called with the widget zone ID as a parameter, (in this example, 1 is the widget zone ID) and widgets belonging to this zone are displayed on screen.

There's more...

Of course, WordPress widgets can be downloaded from the Internet and installed on your own blog. The procedure is almost the same for built-in widgets, except that you have to download the widget, unzip the widget, upload the file, and activate the widget first before you can add it to a zone.

Installing downloaded widgets

The following steps can be used to install widgets downloaded from the Internet:

1. Download the widget you'd like to use on your computer.

2. Extract the zipped archive.

3. Upload the directory to the `wp-content/plugins` directory of your WordPress install.

4. Login to your WordPress dashboard and go to **Plugins**.

5. Scroll down until you see the name of the widget that you have just uploaded.

6. Click on the **Activate** link, just as you do when installing a plugin. The widget is now activated, but it is still not visible on your blog.

7. Go to **Appearance | Widgets**. On the right of the page, you can choose a widget ready zone. Most themes only have one zone. Click on the **Show** button to display the widgets from that zone.

8. Once you have selected the zone you'd like to use, look on the left of the page—available widgets are displayed. Pick up the one that you have just installed, and drag it to your widget zone, on the right of the page.

9. Click on the **Edit** link of the widget and edit its parameters as desired.

10. Click on the **Save Changes** button below the widget list and you're done!

Making your sidebar widget-ready

In the previous recipe, I showed you how to install a widget. Unfortunately, many themes still can't handle widgets by default. In this recipe, I'll show you how to make your sidebar ready for widgets.

Getting ready

First, be sure that your theme sidebar isn't widget-ready. To do so, refer to the previous recipe. If you are sure that it is not widget-ready, proceed with the following steps.

How to do it...

1. Open the `sidebar.php` file from your theme and add the following code:

```
<ul>
<?php /* Widgetized sidebar, if you have the plugin installed. */
    if ( !function_exists('dynamic_sidebar') ||
        !dynamic_sidebar() ) : ?>
<?php endif; ?>
</ul>
```

2.. Save the file and open `functions.php`. If this file doesn't exist, create one. Then, paste the following code in it:

```
if ( function_exists('register_sidebar')) register_sidebar(array(
    'before_widget' => '<li id="%1$s" class="widget %2$s">',
    'after_widget' => '</li>',
    'before_title' => '<h2 class="widgettitle">',
    'after_title' => '</h2>',
));
```

3. Save the `functions.php` file.

4. Login to your WordPress dashboard and go to **Design | Widgets**. You'll see a widget zone (as discussed in the previous recipe) called **Sidebar 1**. That's all! You can now add widgets to your widgetized sidebar.

How it works...

In the `sidebar.php` file, we tested if our sidebar can handle a widget. That way, we avoided any errors if the theme used isn't widget-ready.

Before executing the `register_sidebar()` function I have tested that this function exists. Widgets were introduced with version 2.0, so if someone uses an older version, the `register_sidebar()` function will not be recognized.

The `register_sidebar()` function takes an array as argument. In the previous example, this array contains the following parameters:

▶ `before_widget`: Custom HTML tag to put before any widget. In the example, it is a `<li>` element with custom ID and class.

▶ `after_widget`: Same as `before_widget`, except that the code will be printed after each widget.

▶ `before_title`: HTML tag to put before the title of the widget zone.

▶ `after_title`: Same as `before_title` except that it will be printed after the widget zone title.

Creating two (or more) different widget-ready zones

Widgets are indeed very useful, and can help you to easily achieve a lot of tasks on your WordPress blog. Now, you know how to create a widgetized sidebar for any theme, but what about more than just a widget-ready sidebar?

In this recipe, you'll learn how to create as many widgetized zones as you want.

Getting ready

In this recipe, I assume that you have read and understood the basics about creating a widget ready zone, as described in the previous recipe. To complete the following recipe, all that you need is a theme of your choice.

How to do it...

1. Let's start by creating a widget-ready zone in the theme sidebar. Open the `sidebar.php` file from the theme that you have picked-up. If the theme already has a widgetized sidebar, replace the existing code by the following one, or add it if the sidebar isn't widgetized at all.

```
<ul id="sidelist">
<?php /* Widgetized sidebar */
if ( !function_exists('dynamic_sidebar') ||
    !dynamic_sidebar(1) ) : ?>
<?php endif; ?>
</ul><!--/sidelist-->
```

2. Save the file and open `footer.php` for editing. Enter or add the following code in it:

```
<ul id="footerlist">
<?php /* Widgetized footer*/
if ( !function_exists('dynamic_sidebar') ||
    !dynamic_sidebar(2) ) : ?>
<?php endif; ?>
</ul><!--/footerlist-->
```

3. After you have saved the file, open the `functions.php` file from your theme and add the following code:

```
if ( function_exists('register_sidebars') )
register_sidebars(2,array(
    'before_widget' => '<li id="%1$s" class="widget %2$s">',
    'after_widget' => '</li>',
```

```
'before_title' => '<h2 class="widgettitle">',
'after_title' => '</h2>',
));
```

4. Once you have saved the `functions.php` file, you can login to your WordPress dashboard and visit **Design | Widgets**. In the drop-down list, you now have two different widget ready zones, called **Sidebar 1** and **Sidebar 2** respectively.

How it works...

Although, there's a big difference, the previous code looks a lot like the one that we studied in the previous recipe. When we were adding a single widget-ready zone, we used the `dynamic_sidebar()` function without any arguments. To add more than a single zone, we have to give an ID to each widgetized zone that we'd like to add. This is why I used `dynamic_sidebar(1)` in the sidebar template, and `dynamic_sidebar(2)` in the `footer.php` file.

Then, in the `functions.php` file, the main difference is that I used the `register_sidebars()` function instead of `register_sidebar()`, which can only handle a single widget-ready zone.

The parameters used in the `register_sidebars()` function are the same that we used in the previous recipe.

There's more...

In the previous example, we have added two different widget-ready zones to our theme. Of course, we can create as many as we want. The thing to keep in mind is that any zone must have a unique numerical ID. Note that Widget zones may also be given text names. For example, let's say we'd like to add a third zone. We can add the following code in such a case:

```
<ul id="3rdzone">
<?php      /* Widgetized footer*/
    if ( !function_exists('dynamic_sidebar') ||
        !dynamic_sidebar(3) ) : ?>
    <?php endif; ?>
</ul><!--/3rdzone-->
```

In the `functions.php` file from your theme, you have to specify how many zones are used. In case you added a third widget-ready zone, you'll have to do the following:

```
if ( function_exists('register_sidebars') )
    register_sidebars(3,array(
        'before_widget' => '<li id="%1$s" class="widget %2$s">',
        'after_widget' => '</li>',
        'before_title' => '<h2 class="widgettitle">',
        'after_title' => '</h2>',
    ));
```

Modifying core widgets

In the previous recipes, I showed you how easy it is to add widgets and widget-ready zones to your theme. As you may know, every new WordPress version comes with some built-in widgets such as page list, categories list, search form, and so on. These widgets are useful for most of our requirements, but sometimes you may need something more specific. For example, you might want to exclude some pages to appear from the list.

In this recipe, I'll show you how you can modify WordPress core widgets without editing any core files.

Getting ready

To execute this recipe, you just need a widget-ready theme and a `functions.php` file. Most recent themes feature this file, however, if it doesn't exist, just create it.

I have read lots of WordPress related tutorials all over the Web, where people have posted about editing WordPress core files. In my opinion, this is a really, really bad idea. The reason is simple—on an average a new WordPress version is released every two months. If you have modified any core file, you'll have to redo the modification every time you upgrade your blog, which would be a big waste of time.

How to do it...

Let's say that you'd like to use the WordPress **Pages** widget, but you'd like to exclude pages with IDs 3, 5, and 9.

1. Open your `functions.php` file and paste the following code in it:

```
function widget_new_pages(){
    wp_list_pages('exclude=3,5,9&title_li=');
}
if ( function_exists('register_sidebar_widget') ){
    register_sidebar_widget('pages', 'widget_new_pages');
}
```

2. Save the file and login to your WordPress dashboard.

3. Go to **Design | Widgets** and add a **Pages** widget.

4. Visit your blog and you will see that pages with IDs 3, 5, and 9 aren't listed within the **Pages** widget!

How it works...

First, I created a simple PHP function called `widget_new_pages()`. This function uses the `wp_list_pages()` WordPress function with the exclude parameter to specify which pages I don't want to be listed on the **Pages** widget.

Next, after I tested that the `register_sidebar_widget()` function exists, I used it to tell WordPress to execute the `widget_new_pages()` function when a **Pages** widget will be added.

Creating your own widget

Even though there are a lot of quality WordPress widgets available, sometimes you will find that no single one fits your exact requirements. In such a case, you'll have to create your very own widget. It may sound difficult at first, but if you have any programming experience it is very easy.

Getting ready

To create your very own widget, you need nothing but a text editor. Start by creating a directory on your hard drive that will contain the widget file(s). In this example, I have called this directory `test`.

How to do it...

1. In the `test` directory, create a file named `test.php`.

2. Edit the `test.php` file and paste the following code, which tells WordPress that this file is a widget:

```php
<?php
/*
Plugin Name: Test
Plugin URI: http://www.yourblog.com
Description: Testing custom widgets
Author: You!
Version: 1
Author URI: http://www.yourblog.com
*/
```

3. Now, we have to create the function that will be displayed when your widget will be added to a widget-ready zone. Append the following code to the `test.php` file:

```
function test()
{
    echo "<p>My first widget works!</p>";
}
```

4. One more function to be added—this one gets display parameters from the user's `functions.php` file and uses it to make the widget perfectly integrated with the user's theme.

```
function widget_test($args) {
extract($args);
echo $before_widget;
echo $before_title;?>Test&lt?php echo $after_title;
sampleHelloWorld();
echo $after_widget;
}
```

5. We're almost done. We now have to create an initialization function, and hook the widget:

```
function test_init()
{
    register_sidebar_widget(__('Test'), 'widget_test);
}
add_action("plugins_loaded", "test_init");
?>
```

6. Once you have saved the file, install the widget as described earlier, and add it to the widget-ready zone of your choice.

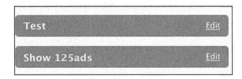

Visit your blog and you can see your first custom widget!

How it works...

Now that we have created a working widget, let's take a function-by-function look at its code.

First, you have to tell WordPress that this file is a widget or a plugin by adding the PHP comments at the beginning of the file. The information will be used by your WordPress dashboard when you activate the widget. If WordPress can't find these comments, the file won't be recognized as a widget.

The `test()` function is our widget function that will be executed when the widget has been activated and inserted into a widget ready zone. In this example, its purpose is really basic because it only writes some random text on screen. You can easily replace it with the any function that you want it to perform, for example, `widget_new_pages()` from the previous recipe.

Try to recollect when I showed you how to make your theme widget-ready. I had shown you how to use the `register_sidebars()` function and to specify its arguments such as `before_widget`, `after_widget`, and so on:

```
register_sidebars(3,array(
        'before_widget' => '<li id="%1$s" class="widget %2$s">',
        'after_widget' => '</li>',
        'before_title' => '<h2 class="widgettitle">',
        'after_title' => '</h2>',
    ));
```

The `widget_test($args)` function from our widget gets the arguments specified by the user with the `register_sidebars()` function, and uses them. With this function, we make sure that our widget will be totally integrated in the user's theme.

The last function used in the widget file is `register_sidebar_widget()`. This function will add your widget to the admin interface, and the user will be able to drag and drop it into one of his widget-ready zones.

Lastly, I have used the `add_action("plugins_loaded", "test_init")` function to hook the widget, which means that when WordPress will execute the `plugins_loaded()` function, it will then execute our `test_init()` function, and add the widget to the theme and admin interface.

There's more...

Now that you have seen how to create a simple WordPress widget in detail, here is the complete code used so you can re-read it, or use it as a base for the widget you'll create soon!

Complete widget code

```
<?php
/*
Plugin Name: Test
Plugin URI: http://www.yourblog.com
Description: Testing custom widgets
```

```
Author: You!
Version: 1
Author URI: http://www.yourblog.com
*/
function test()
{
  echo "<p>My first widget works!</p>";
}
function widget_test($args) {
  extract($args);
  echo $before_widget;
  echo $before_title;?>Test&lt?php echo $after_title;
  sampleHelloWorld();
  echo $after_widget;
}
function test_init()
{
  register_sidebar_widget(__('Test'), 'widget_test);
}
add_action("plugins_loaded", "test_init");
?>
```

In this chapter, you learned two very important aspects of WordPress blogs—plugins, and widgets. At this point of the book, you should now be able to install and create your own plugins and widgets, as well as add widget-ready zones to any WordPress theme.

5
Displaying Posts

Did you ever want to have total control over how your posts are being displayed? Indeed, the way you display your posts is important. It changes the feel and look of your blog. I am sure you always wanted to know how some blogs display only posts from one category, embed thumbnails within their excerpts, or display posts like a newspaper.

In this chapter, I'll show you the various ways to display your posts and we'll also study the extremely useful `query_posts()` function—which is used to control the WordPress loop.

In this chapter, you will learn:

- ► Getting posts within the WordPress loop
- ► Retrieving posts from a particular category only
- ► Getting an exact number of posts
- ► Retrieving posts by date
- ► Getting posts published today
- ► Getting posts published exactly a year ago
- ► Using two different loops without duplicate posts
- ► Accessing post data outside of the WordPress loop
- ► Accessing permalinks outside the loop
- ► Displaying any RSS feed on your blog
- ► Displaying thumbnails on your blog homepage
- ► Alternating background color on post list
- ► Displaying posts in two columns
- ► Saving time by using WordPress shortcodes
- ► Creating a nice download message box using a shortcode

Getting posts within the WordPress loop

What is the WordPress loop? The loop is a group of PHP instructions that allows you to retrieve your posts from the database. In this recipe, you'll learn how to use the WordPress loop efficiently.

Getting ready

The WordPress loop is basically a simple PHP loop that fetches posts from the database and displays it on the page. It can be placed anywhere on your theme files. All available themes use it to retrieve the posts, for example on `index.php`, `single.php`, or `page.php`.

How to do it...

Paste the following code where you'd like to display the list of posts. Most of the time, the loop is used on the `index.php`, `category.php`, `search.php` files, but you can use it wherever you want, for example, on a page using a custom page template.

```
if ( have_posts() ) :
    while ( have_posts() ) : the_post(); ?>
       <?php the_title();?>
       <?php the_content();?>
       <?php endwhile;
endif; ?>
```

How it works...

This basic piece of code first checks if posts exist. If the answer is yes, every post title and their contents are displayed on the page by using the `the_title()` and `the_content()` WordPress functions. If the GET parameter exists, only the post with the ID will be displayed. Otherwise, it will display a group of posts, according to the number of posts to show per page specified in your admin dashboard.

Retrieving posts from a particular category only

Are you using a sideblog, or any kind of special category on your theme? If so, you may want to be able to get posts from this category only. Let's see how to do it.

Latest Tutorials and Resources

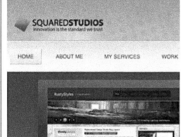

Design Studio Layout #2

May 19th in **Photoshop** by Matthew Heidenreich

In this tutorial you will learn how to make a clean layout for your design company. If you have any questions about this tutorial be sure to ask in the comments. Also, remember with all the tutorials, the psd is available for download.

8 Comments   Continue Reading

How to Create a "Worn Paper" Web Layout

May 15th in **Photoshop** by Matthew Heidenreich

In this tutorial, you'll learn how to create a textured "worn paper" web design theme using some basic Photoshop techniques. The design incorporates some free stock images to let you create a beautiful layout in a jiffy.

4 Comments   Continue Reading

Clean Photo Gallery Website Layout

Apr 28th in **Photoshop** by Matthew Heidenreich

In this tutorial you will learn how to make a clean photo gallery

Getting ready

To complete this recipe, you need a WordPress loop, and the super useful `query_posts()` function along with the `cat` parameter.

How to do it...

Paste the following code anywhere in your theme, where you'd like to display posts from a single category only. As I said previously, most of the time you'll use the loop on the `index.php` file but there are no restrictions—the loop can be used everywhere.

```php
<?php
query_posts("cat=5");
if (have_posts()):
    while (have_posts()) : the_post(); ?>
      <h3><a href="<?php the_permalink() ?>" rel=
          "bookmark" ><?php the_title();?></a></h3>
      the_excerpt();
    endwhile;
endif;
?>
```

How it works...

The `query_posts()` function, used with the `cat` parameter, allows you to specify one or more categories that you want to get the posts from.

For example:

`query_posts("cat=5");`: Get posts from the category with id 5 only

`query_posts("cat=5,6,9");`: Get posts from the category with ids 5,6, and 9

`query_posts("cat=-3");`: Get posts from all categories, excepted 3

Getting an exact number of posts

If you're using a sideblog or a featured posts block, you may want to be able to display only a desired number of latest posts. In this recipe, we're going to see how to control the number of posts to display within the loop.

Getting ready

To complete this recipe you again need a WordPress loop and the `query_posts()` function.

How to do it...

Simply paste the following code anywhere in your theme files, where you'd like your posts to be displayed:

```php
<?php
query_posts("showposts=5");
if (have_posts()):
    while (have_posts()) : the_post();
        the_title();
        the_excerpt();
    endwhile;
endif;
?>
```

How it works...

Just like in the previous example, we're using the powerful `query_posts()` function. This time, we use the `showposts` parameter that allows you to specify how many posts must be displayed.

Retrieving posts by date

Another very handy use of the `query_posts()` function is to get posts according to specific date and time parameters. Let's see how to use `query_posts()` to get posts from a specific date.

Getting ready

Retrieving posts by date can be a bit more complex than, for example, getting an exact number of posts, because you sometimes need to use multiple parameters, or combine some custom PHP code along with the `query_posts()` function.

However, this first example is rather simple. We'll see more complex uses of `query_posts()` date and time parameters in the next recipes.

How to do it...

The following code displays all posts which have been published in October. Simply paste this code anywhere in your theme files:

```php
<?php
query_posts("monthnum=10");
if (have_posts()):
    while (have_posts()) : the_post();
        the_title();
        the_excerpt();
    endwhile;
endif;
?>
```

How it works...

The `monthnum` parameter allows you to specify a month number, and retrieve only the posts published in the given period. You can also get posts by day, year, hour, and even minutes and seconds.

Here are the date and time parameters which can be used within the `query_posts()` function:

- `hour`: Number from 0 to 24, displays posts made during this time
- `minute`: Number from 0 to 59
- `second`: Number from 0 to 59
- `day`: Number from 0 to 31, shows all posts made, for example on the 15th
- `monthnum`: Number from 1 to 12
- `year`: Year, show all posts made in for example, 2007

Getting posts published today

If you publish more than one post per day on your blog, it would be a good idea to display other posts that you have written on the current day to encourage your visitors to read them as well.

Getting ready

Mixed with some easy PHP, `query_posts()` date and time parameters can be very useful. For example, the following code gets today's date with PHP, and then display all posts published within the day.

How to do it...

Simply paste this code anywhere on your template where you'd like your posts to be displayed. A good idea should be to display it on `single.php`, just after the main post and before the comments.

```php
<?php
$current_day = date('j');
$current_month = date('m');
$year = date('Y');
query_posts('day='.$current_day.'&month='.$current_month.
            '&year='.$year);
if (have_posts()) :
```

```
    while (have_posts()) : the_post(); ?>
      // WordPress loop
    endwhile;
endif;
?>
```

How it works...

In the preceding code, I started with creating two PHP variables named $current_day and $year; initialized with the PHP date() function. Then, I used the query_posts() function along with two parameters—day and year.

Getting posts published exactly a year ago

Here's a nice idea to give a second life to your old posts—automatically displaying the posts you published exactly one year ago. In this recipe, you'll learn how to do just that by using some simple PHP, the WordPress loop, and the super-useful query_posts() function.

Published one year ago...

8 Javascript solutions to common CSS problems

>More posts

Getting ready

In the previous recipe, I showed you how to get posts for the day. Now, let's use the same code and modify it a bit to get all posts published exactly one year ago.

How to do it...

This code can be used anywhere in your theme files. However, I recommend using it in single.php, between display of the post and the comments template.

```php
<?php
$current_day = date('j');
$current_month = date('m');
$last_year = date('Y') -1;
query_posts('day='.$current_day.'&month='.$current_month.
```

```
            '&year='.$last_year);
if (have_posts()) :
    while (have_posts()) : the_post(); ?>
        // WordPress loop
    endwhile;
endif;
?>
```

How it works...

This useful code works exactly as the previous example does. First, we have to use the PHP `date()` function to get the current day and month number, and then we subtract 1 from the current year. Once done, we simply use `query_posts()` and the WordPress loop to display our posts.

Using two different loops without duplicate posts

If you have created a **Featured posts** section on your blog homepage, you probably have the problem of showing duplicate posts when running two distinct loops. In this recipe, you'll learn how to use two (or more) distinct loops while being sure not to get any duplicated posts.

Featured Post	Get Your Own Copy of the 31 Days to Build a Better Blog WorkBook
90 Comments	Join over 14,000 other bloggers and Give your Blog a Kick Start with this 31 Day Challenge.
	Regular readers of ProBlogger are familiar with the 31 Days to Build a Better Blog project that we ran here recently.
	The concept was simple: bloggers set aside 31 days to be intentional about improving their blogs.
	Each day for 31 days readers were presented with a daily task and ...

Recently at the Blog

13 Things I've Learned about Successful Blogging [My 5000th Post on ProBlogger]

10 JUN 2009 / 37 Comments

This is my 5000th post here on ProBlogger.net. To commemorate the moment I thought I'd share some of the lessons that I've learned in building my blogs.

I was recently asked as the last ...

Click Here to Continue Reading

13 Lessons (& Tips) Learned Launching an eBook

09 JUN 2009 / 55 Comments

It's been 10 days since I excitedly launched the 31 Days to Build a Better Blog workbook. When it launched I wasn't quite sure what to expect but I was sure ...

Click Here to Continue Reading

Weekly Video Post

5 Tips to Help You Get a Blogging Job

05 JUN 2009 / 47 Comments

More and more people are looking to add a second income stream to their lives by landing a blogging job. In this video I share 5 tips for increasing the chances of finding a blogging job.

This video was sponsored by eHow.com - a place for writers to make money, promote their blog, and share their knowledge.

See the full sized video at YouTube.

If you're looking for a blog job don't forget to check out the ProBlogger Job Boards mentioned in the video.

Share This

Best of Problogger

All Time	This Month	For Beginners	Darren's Favs

How to Write Your "About Me" Page

by Darren Rowse / 120 comments

How to do it...

1. Let's start with the first loop. Nothing difficult in this case, we're just going to get the latest eight posts by using the `showposts` parameter. Open the `index.php` and paste the following code to output your **Featured posts**:

```php
<?php
query_posts('showposts=8');
$saved_ids = array();
while (have_posts()) : the_post();
    $saved_ids[] = get_the_ID();
    the_title();
    the_content();
endwhile;
?>
```

2. Once complete, it's time to apply the second loop and get all posts, except the ones that we have already output in the first loop:

```php
<?php
query_posts(array('showposts' => 1, 'cat' => 3,
    'post__not_in' => $saved_ids));
while (have_posts()) : the_post();
    the_title();
    the_content();
endwhile;
?>
```

3. Save your `index.php` file, and admire the results!

How it works...

In the first loop, I have created an array variable called `$saved_ids`. Each time a post is retrieved from the database, its ID is added to the `$saved_ids` array.

Then, in the second loop, I have used the `query_posts()` function with the `post__not_in` parameter that allows you to specify a list of posts IDs in a PHP array variable that you don't want to retrieve.

As the `$saved_ids` array contains the IDs of posts that we previously displayed on the **Featured posts** first loop, they're not displayed again in the second loop.

Here's the complete code that you can use for your theme:

```php
<?php
/* FEATURED POSTS */
query_posts('showposts=8');
$saved_ids = array();
while (have_posts()) : the_post();
    $saved_ids[] = get_the_ID();
    the_title();
    the_content();
endwhile;
?>
<?php
/* "CLASSIC" LOOP */
query_posts(array('showposts' => 1, 'cat' => 3,
    'post__not_in' => $saved_ids));
while (have_posts()) : the_post();
    the_title();
    the_content();
endwhile;
?>
```

Accessing post data outside of the WordPress loop

Sometimes, you may want to access post data outside of the WordPress loop. Unfortunately, WordPress functions such as `the_title()` or `the_content()` can't be used outside the loop. In this recipe, I'll show you how to access post data anywhere on your theme, without using the loop.

Getting ready

Before I show you the code, you have to know that each time you'll use the following function, it will execute a SQL query on your WordPress database. This isn't a problem itself, but you shouldn't use the following function usually, in order to avoid extra loading time.

How to do it...

1. As we have seen, WordPress has a very useful function to get post data outside the loop called `get_post()`. Carry out the following steps to create a PHP variable that will contain all of the available data from the post:

```php
$data = get_post(10);
```

2. You now have a `$data` object which contains all post data available. To display the data, add the following code:

```
echo $data->post_title; //Print post title
echo $data->post_date; //Print post date
```

How it works...

The `get_post()` function that we just used takes a single argument—the ID of the post you'd like to get the data from. Once called, the function use the `$wpdb` object to execute an SQL query which will get all available information about the selected post from WordPress database.

Then, to display post data, you have to specify the name of the data that you'd like to show.

Following is the available data from the database:

- `post_author`: ID of the post author
- `post_date`: Publication date; according to your date settings
- `post_date_gmt`: Publication date; according to GMT time
- `post_content`: Post content
- `post_title`: Post title.
- `post_category`: ID of the post category
- `post_excerpt`: Post excerpt
- `post_status`: Post status (Publish, draft, and so on)
- `comment_status`: If comments are open
- `ping_status`: If pingbacks are allowed
- `post_password`: Post password, if any
- `post_name`: Post permalink %postname%
- `to_ping`: Sites to ping
- `pinged`: Sites pinged
- `post_modified`: Last modified date; according to your time settings
- `post_modified_gmt`: Last modified date; according to GMT time
- `post_content_filtered`: Post content, filtered
- `post_parent`: ID of the post parent, if any
- `guid`: Standard URL (http://blog.com/?p=10)
- `menu_order`: Order in the menu
- `post_type`: Post or page
- `post_mime_type`: Mime time of the post
- `comment_count`: Number of comments or trackbacks of the posts

The previous data should be used in the following way:

```
echo $data->post_title;
echo $data->post_date_gmt;
echo $data->post_content;
echo $data->post_category;
echo $data->post_excerpt;
echo $data->post_status;
echo $data->comment_status;
echo $data->ping_status;
echo $data->post_password;
echo $data->post_name;
echo $data->to_ping;
echo $data->pinged;
echo $data->post_modified;
echo $data->post_modified_gmt;
echo $data->post_content_filtered;
echo $data->post_parent;
echo $data->guid;
echo $data->menu_order;
echo $data->post_type;
echo $data->post_mime_type;
echo $data->comment_count;
```

Accessing permalinks outside the loop

While the previous recipe may be very useful to get access to post data outside the loop, there's still something very important that the get_post() function can't do—retrieving a permalink. Sure, it can retrieve the guid (the classic URL which looks like http://www.yourblog.com/?p=15) but it cannot retrieve the permalink. In this recipe, I'm going to show you how it is possible.

Getting ready

As for the get_post() function, we're going to use the get_permalink() function that will execute one more SQL query on your WordPress database. Therefore, use it—only when you have no other choice—to reduce page loading time.

How to do it...

To get the permalink of a specific post, simply paste the following code anywhere on your template:

```
<a href="<?php echo get_permalink(10); ?>" >Link to the post</a>
```

How it works...

Just like `get_post()`, the `get_permalink()` function takes a single argument—the ID of the post you'd like to retrieve the permalink of.

There's more...

The following is one of the few additional things you may want to try.

Using the $post global variable

When you're on a post or page, and within the loop, a `$post` global variable is initialized. This variable contains all of the data you can get with the `get_post()` function that we have seen earlier. The `get_permalink()` function can be used along with the `$post` global variable:

```
<a href="<?php echo get_permalink($post->ID); ?>" >Link
    to the post</a>
```

Sure, the `$post` global variable can be used without the `get_permalink()` function, as shown in the following example:

```
The post "<?php echo $post->post_title; ?>" has been written
    on <?php echo $post->post_date; ?>.
<a href="<?php echo $post->guid; ?>" >Read the post</a>
```

As you can see, the `$post` variable works exactly the same as the `get_post()` function using the returned value from the function. So, in order to minimize database requests, you should always try to use the `$post` variable when possible. As I previously said, the `$post` variable is initializated with the loop. Once you're outside of the loop the data can't be accessed again.

Displaying any RSS feed on your blog

Let's use my personal example—I have two blogs, `catswhocode.com` and `wprecipes.com`. In order to get one blog to promote the other, and vice-versa, why not put a list of posts from one blog in a separate page or in the sidebar of the other.

Let's see how we can display any RSS feed on a WordPress blog, without even using a plugin.

DesignM.ag - All Inclusive-Feed

Pipes Output

- How to Make Unique Front Page Teasers for Wordpress Posts
  Want some distinction between your blog's front and post pages? Wish your post displayed differently when viewed in a list? With Wordpress, it's easier than you think. Visit Source. Looking to Hire a Designer or Developer? Post a free job listing to the DesignM.ag job board for freelance, part-time or full-time positions. Your listing will be [...]

- World's Best Programmer is... [w/ Communication]
  One of those conditions prevalent within the environment of the World's Best Programmer is Communication. Our journey in discovering (and coming announcement of who is) the World's Best Programmer starts with understanding the ideal environment within which s/he will/can thrive. This series explores what it takes to craft that ideal programmer [...]

Getting ready

Do you know that WordPress has a function, called `wp_rss()`, that is simply a built-in RSS reader? It is used on the WordPress dashboard, to display news from the WP team.

How to do it...

1. Edit your sidebar, or create a page template (refer to Chapter 3 for using and creating page templates).

2. Paste the following code where you'd like to display the feed item. It can be a page template, your sidebar (`sidebar.php`), or your blog footer (`footer.php`):

```php
<?php
include_once(ABSPATH.WPINC.'/rss.php');
wp_rss('http://feeds.feedburner.com/wprecipes', 3);
?>
```

3. Save the file and visit the page that you just edited. It displays feeds!

How it works...

To display feeds on a blog, we have to use the `wp_rss()` function. As this function is located in the `rss.php` file, we first have to include it on our page by using the `include_once()` PHP function.

Once `rss.php` is included, we can use `wp_rss()`. This function takes two arguments—the first is the feed URL, and the second is the number of items you'd like to display. In this example, the code will display the three latest posts from `WpRecipes.com` using the feed located at `http://feeds.feedburner.com/wprecipes`.

There's more...

Have you ever see your blog content published exactly as you did on your own blog elsewhere, with a consequent amount of ads? Many blogs or **splogs (spam blogs)** to be exacted can be found over the internet. They're automated blogs which steal valuable content from real blogs using this technique. Of course, I expect you not to use this recipe to steal content from other bloggers!

Displaying thumbnails on your blog homepage

You must have heard many times that 'A picture is worth a thousand words'. In the case of blogging, this is particularly true. Many blogs use thumbnails, displayed next to post excerpts on their homepage, to visually enhance their blog and give it a more professional look.

In this recipe, I'll show you how you can easily add thumbnails to your homepage, independent of the theme you're using.

10 awesome .htaccess hacks for WordPress
61 comments

.htaccess, the file which control the Apache webserver, is very useful and allows you to do a lot of things. In this article, let's see how .htaccess can help you with your WordPress blog, for both security,functionnality and usability.

10 free professional websites templates PSD files
39 comments

Studying and working on PSD files is a very good way to learn using Photoshop for Web Design. In this article, I have compiled 10 gorgeous, professional and 100% free website templates that you can use and customize to fit your needs.

Getting ready

This recipe can be achieved on any WordPress theme. So, you don't need anything else except your favorite WordPress theme and a text editor. To add thumbnails to your blog homepage, we'll use custom fields. Custom fields are one of the most powerful WordPress possibilities. It allows you to define a key and give it a value. In your template, you simply have to get the key to display the custom value. Custom fields are individually defined on each post or page.

How to do it...

1. Let's start by writing a post. Log in to your WordPress **Dashboard**, then go to **New Post** or pick up an existing post and edit it.

2. On the writing panel, upload an image and copy its URL. A good size is 120*120 pixels.

3. Scroll down the page until you see **Custom fields**. Click on the tab to open it. Fill the **key** field with the image and the **value** field with the URL that you previously copied. Once done, publish the post.

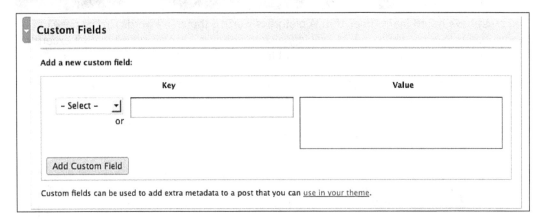

4. If you visit your blog now, you won't see any changes. The custom field is defined and it has a value, but for now our theme can't handle it. Open your `index.php` file for editing and find the WordPress loop. Then, add the following code:

```php
<?php
$value = get_post_meta(the_ID(), 'Image', true);
if (isset($value)) : ?>
    <a href="<?php the_permalink() ?>"><img src=
        "<?php echo $value; ?>" alt="<?php the_title();
        ?>" /></a>
<?php endif; ?>
```

5. Once you've saved `index.php`, visit your blog to see the thumbnails displayed!

How it works...

To be fully functional, a custom field has to be entered on any post where you'd like to use it, and your theme must have the preceding code to handle it. Some recent WordPress themes can natively handle custom fields, but a majority of themes still can't.

To get the value of the custom field, I have used the `get_post_custom_value()` function, which takes the key name of your custom field as an argument. Then, I have checked to see if a value exists. This prevents us from trying to display an image that doesn't exist. If the custom field has a value, we can display it.

There's more...

For now, our theme can display thumbnails defined via a custom field. But what if someday you forget to define the field while writing a post? Your layout will be broken, or at least will look slightly bad. The solution to this is explained in the following section.

Defining a default image

The solution to the problem mentioned in the previous section is to define a default image which will be displayed if the custom field isn't displayed.

1. Create a default image, named `default.png`, and upload it at the following directory: `wp-content/themes/yourtheme/images/`.

2. Paste the following code in your `index.php` file, within the WordPress loop:

```php
<?php
$value = get_post_meta(the_ID(), 'Image', true);
if (isset($value)) :
    $img = $value;
else:
    $img = TEMPLATEPATH."/images/default_thumb.jpg";
    <a href="<?php the_permalink() ?>"><img src="<?php
        echo $img; ?>" alt="<?php the_title(); ?>" /></a>
<?php endif; ?>
```

Alternating background color on post list

In order to visually enhance your blog, you should definitely consider using alternate background colors on your blog homepage where your posts are listed.

Getting ready

There's nothing difficult with this recipe. All you have to do is to edit the WordPress loop located in your `index.php` file.

How to do it...

1. Open `index.php` for edition, and find the loop.

2. Replace your current loop with the following one:

```
<?php $odd_or_even = 'odd'; ?>
<?php if ( have_posts() ) : while( have_posts() ): the_post(); ?>
<div class="post <?php echo $odd_or_even; ?>">
<?php $odd_or_even = ('odd'==$odd_or_even) ? 'even' : 'odd'; ?>
<?php the_title(); ?>
<?php the_content; ?>
</div>
<?php endwhile;
endif;
?>
```

3. Save `index.php` and open `style.css` for editing.

4. Add the following CSS classes to `style.css`:

```
.post.odd{
    background: blue;
}
.post.even{
    background: red;
}
```

5. Save `style.css` and visit your blog. Post background colors are now alternated between blue and red. Indeed, theses colors are ugly—replace these with the colors of your choice.

How it works...

The principle used here is fairly simple. We alternate two CSS classes. To achieve this, I have used a PHP ternary operator, which is a short way to write:

```
<?php
if ('odd' == $odd_or_even){
    $odd_or_even = 'even';
}else{
    $odd_or_even = 'odd';
}
?>
```

Displaying posts in two columns

Recently when the **Magazine** layouts were introduced in WordPress themes, displaying posts by columns became quite popular. In this recipe, you'll learn how to easily display your posts in two columns.

Userfly: Usability Testing Made Easy

By: Matthew Kammerer | 19 Comments

Userfly is described as usability testing made easy. Since my review of Feedback Army I have been overwhelmed with different websites offering usability services in a quick and easy package. However, Userfly seems to stand out from the crowd! I have put it to the test and brought you my findings.

Read This Post »

Feedback Army Contest Winners

Usability Review: www.SignOnSanDiego.com

☆ ☆ ☆ ☆ ☆

April 20th. 2009 | 3 Comments

Sign On San Diego (http://www.signonsandiego.com) is a newspaper by the Union-Tribune that covers news from San Diego to national news. It communicates it's purpose clearly, though there are several things that would make the browsing experience more pleasurable.

Read This Review »

Getting ready

The following code is simply a WordPress loop containing several PHP instructions to order posts in two distinct columns. It can be used for any WordPress theme.

How to do it...

1. Open `index.php` and find your current loop. Replace the loop by the following code:

```php
<?php $hol = 1; ?>
<?php if (have_posts()) : while (have_posts()) : the_post(); ?>
<?php if ($hol == 1) echo "<div class=\"row\">"; ?>
<div class="post hol<?php echo $hol;?>" id="post-<?php
    the_ID(); ?>">
<h2><a href="<?php the_permalink() ?>" rel="bookmark"><?php
    the_title(); ?></a></h2>
<p><?php the_excerpt(); ?></p>
<?php if ($hol == 1) echo "</div>";
        (($hol==1) ? $hol=2 : $hol=1); ?>
</div><!--/post-->
<?php endwhile; ?>
<?php endif; ?>
```

2. Save the file and append the following styles to `style.css`:

```
.row {
    clear: both;
}
.hol1 {
    width: 200px;
    float: left; padding: 0 10px;
}
.hol2 {
    width: 200px;
    float: right;
    padding: 0 10px;
}
```

3. Save `style.css` and visit your blog. Posts are now displayed in two columns.

How it works...

Before the loop starts, I have initialized a PHP variable called `$hol`. This variable will contain a value (1 or 2) and will be useful to know if we must start a new row or continue on the existing one.

After the loop displays the post data, I have used the `$hol` variable to check out if I must close the `div` tag. Finally, I used a ternary operator to give `$hol` a value of 1 or 2 depending on its current value.

Saving time by using WordPress shortcodes

When writing posts, don't you feel a bit tired because you had to repeat a lot of information? For example, a styled `<div>` element to display a downloadable file, or some information about the author?

When you know that you'll have to insert the same code snippets on many posts, you should definitely create a shortcode.

Getting ready

Introduced in WordPress 2.5, the shortcode APIs are a simple set of functions for creating macro codes for use in post content. A classic shortcode looks like this:

```
[author_info]
```

Shortcodes can handle attributes. For example:

```
[download file="myfile.zip"]
```

Also, a shortcode can have embedded content:

```
[mycode] Some Content [/mycode]
```

How to do it...

Creating shortcodes is a lot easier than it looks. For your first shortcode, let's create a simple one which will only display a disclaimer.

1. The first thing we have to do is to create a simple PHP function. To do so, open the `functions.php` file from your theme and add the following code:

```
function displayDisclaimer() {
    return 'This product is meant for educational purposes only.
    Use of the programs or procedures in such a manner, it is
    at your own risk.';
}
```

2. What a great disclaimer we have here! Now, we have to turn it into a shortcode:

```
add_shortcode('disclaimer', 'displayDisclaimer');
```

3. You're now able to use the `disclaimer` shortcode.

4. Write a new post, or edit an existing one. Switch the editor to HTML mode, and insert the shortcode you just created:

```
[disclaimer]
```

5. Publish the post and visit your blog. Instead of `[disclaimer]`, the text that you have defined on the `displayDisclaimer()` function is shown.

How it works...

The `add_shortcodes()` takes two arguments—the first is the shortcode name, and the second is the function to call when the shortcode will be used.

In this example, I first wrote a very basic function and then used the `add_shortcode()` function to turn it into a shortcode.

Every time WordPress displays a post, it will look for shortcodes and executes the associated functions.

There's more...

By default, WordPress comes with some useful shortcodes. Here's the list:

- **[audio]**: converts a link to an mp3 file into an audio player
- **[digg]**: embeds a voting button for your link on Digg
- **[flickr]**: embeds a Flickr video
- **[googlemaps]**: embeds Google Maps
- **[googlevideo]**: embeds a Google Video
- **[livevideo]**: embeds a video from LiveVideo
- **[odeo]**: embeds an Odeo audio file
- **[podtech]**: embeds audio or video from the PodTech Network
- **[polldaddy]**: embeds a PollDaddy poll(use without the space)
- **[redlasso]**: embeds a video from Redlasso
- **[rockyou]**: embeds a slideshow from RockYou
- **[slideshare]**: embeds a slideshow from Slideshare.net
- **[sourcecode]**: preserves the formatting of source code
- **[splashcast]**: embeds Splashcast media
- **[vimeo]**: embeds a Vimeo video
- **[youtube]**: embeds a YouTube video

Creating a nice download message box using a shortcode

Many bloggers like to provide free downloads to their readers. If you want to provide free downloads as well you have the choice between adding a simple text link, and inserting a fancy box to embed your download. Of course, the second solution is, at least visually, the best. But the problem is that anytime you'd like to provide a downloadable file to your readers, you'll have to copy and paste the code within your post.

In this recipe, I'm going to show you how you can easily create a nice **Download** message box, and insert it even more easily by using a custom WordPress shortcode.

Since shortcode was introduced in Wordpress 2.5 it's been possible to do many cool things. Everything from simple donate buttons to more advance things. In this article I will show you a simple

Getting ready

To achieve this hack, you all you need is WordPress 2.5 or a later version, and a functions.php file in your theme directory. If you haven't already read the previous recipe, you should definitely read it before this one.

How to do it...

1. First, create a nice image that will be the background of your download box and upload in the wp-content/theme/yourtheme/images directory. This isn't necessary, but don't hesitate to do it if you have any design talent.

2. Open the functions.php file from your theme and paste the following function:

```
function myUrl($atts, $content = null) {
    extract(shortcode_atts(array(
    "href" => 'http://'), $atts));
        return '<div class="download"><ahref="'.$href.'">'.
        $content.'</a></div>;
}

add_shortcode("download", "myUrl");
```

3. Open the style.css file from your theme and add the following code:

```
.download{
width:500px;
height:80px;
background: transparent url (images/yourimage.png)
    norepeat top left;
}
.download a{
font-weight:bold;
font-size:16px;
}
```

4. Once you have saved both the files, write a new post or edit an existing one. Simply type the following shortcode anywhere that you'd like to display your download box: Many bloggers like

```
[download href="http://www.yourblog.com/path/to/
    downloadable/file.zip"]
```

5. Publish the post and visit your blog—the [download] shortcode has been replaced by your fancy "Download" box.

How it works...

To create this "Download" box, I have used a shortcode with a href attribute. Just like in the previous recipe, I started by creating a function named myUrl() to return the necessary code for our box.

First, the myUrl() function looks for passed arguments. If no href attribute was used along with the [download] shortcode, a default link is defined. I have defined http:// as default in this example, but you can define any link you want.

Once done, the function will return the link to the downloadable file and embedded with a div element. Using CSS, I gave a style to this container.

As usual with shortcodes, the last thing we have to do is to create a new shortcode by using the add_shortcode() function.

Now, every time you'll use the [download] shortcode within your posts, it will output your downloadable file embedded within the "Download" box.

6

Managing and Enhancing Multi-Author Blogs

Are you running a multi-author blog, or at least hiring some guest bloggers? Indeed, the more authors you have, the more content you will have, along with a greater number of visits. In the beginning of 2009, many successful blogs such as, Smashing Magazine, Lifehacker, or Mashable, were powered by a team of bloggers.

In this chapter, we are going to learn how to create, enhance, and get the most out of your multi-author WordPress blog.

In this chapter, you will learn:

- ▶ Creating an author page template
- ▶ Displaying a custom login form in your blog's sidebar
- ▶ Adding a control panel to your blog's sidebar
- ▶ Configuring author roles
- ▶ Displaying author-related information on posts
- ▶ Displaying author picture on posts
- ▶ Displaying the author's gravatar picture on posts
- ▶ Adding moderation buttons to the comments
- ▶ Getting notified when a new draft is saved
- ▶ Allowing multiple authors on posts
- ▶ Displaying a list of all of the authors

Creating an author page template

In Chapter 3, I had explained how to create and use page templates. Well, it's now time to make efficient use of page templates. If you have different authors on your blog, then my suggestion to you would be to display the biographical and contact information of each author on his own dedicated page. Luckily, WordPress allow us to do just that.

Getting ready

In this recipe, we're going to create an author page template for the purpose of displaying author related information. Make sure that you have understood the creation and usage of a page template. This has been explained earlier, in Chapter 3.

How to do it...

1. Create a new file named `authors.php` on your WordPress theme directory.

2. Insert the following code into your file named `authors.php`:

```php
<?php
/*
Template Name: Authors Page
*/
?>
<?php get_header(); ?>
    <div id="content" class="narrowcolumn">
    <?php
    if(isset($_GET['author_name'])) :
        $curauth = get_userdatabylogin($author_name);
    else :
        $curauth = get_userdata(intval($author));
    endif;
    ?>

    <h2>About <?php echo $curauth->nickname; ?></h2>
    <div class="excerpt">
        <?php echo $curauth->nickname; ?> personal website:
        <a href="<?php echo $curauth->user_url; ?>">
        <?php echo $curauth->user_url; ?></a>
    </div>

    <?php echo $curauth->user_description; ?>

    <h2>Latest posts by <?php echo $curauth->nickname; ?>:</h2>
```

```
<ul>
    <?php if ( have_posts() ) : while ( have_posts() ) :
      the_post(); ?>
    <li>
        <a href="<?php the_permalink() ?>"><?php the_title();
          ?></a> on <?php the_time('d M Y'); ?>
    </li>
    <?php endwhile; else: ?>
        <p><?php _e('No posts by this author.'); ?></p>
    <?php endif; ?>
</ul>
</div><!--/content-->
<?php get_sidebar(); ?>
<?php get_footer(); ?>
```

3. Save the file and upload it to the `wp-content/themes/yourtheme` folder of your WordPress install.

4. Log in to your WordPress dashboard, create a new page, and select the **Authors Page** as a page template. Give it the title of your choice, such as, **About the Author** and publish the page.

5. Open the `single.php` file from your theme. Depending on the theme that you're using, you may need to add the following code in order to display the author's name and a link to the author's page:

```
Posted by <?php the_author_posts_link(); ?>
```

6. Once you have saved the modifications made in your `single.php` file, visit one of your blog posts and click on the author name. The author page is displayed showing the author name, description, and web site.

How it works...

The first thing that we need to know is the name of the author whose information is to be displayed. To do so, we have to get the `author_name` parameter sent via the GET method. With this value, we can initialize a `$curauth` php object that will allow us to get some personal information about the author, such as his web site, email, biography, and so on, with the help of the classic php syntax, that is, `$curauth->nickname;`.

Once the author data, that is to be displayed, has been retrieved, we shall add a WordPress loop in order to be able to view the recent posts by this author.

The following screenshot shows a well-prepared author page:

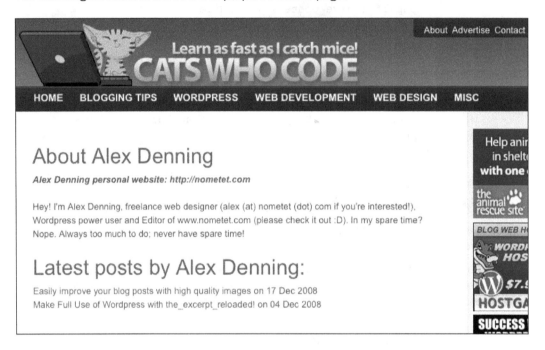

There's more...

In the preceding example we retrieved the author name, description, and web site URL. However, as you may know, users can provide much more information (in **Administration**, **Profile**, **Your Profile** options) such as their email address, AIM and Yahoo! messenger nickname, and login information.

A few more template tags can be used to retrieve another kind of information from the author data. These tags are listed under the *There's more!* section of *Displaying author-related information on posts*, which we will see later in this chapter.

Displaying a custom login form in your blog's sidebar

It doesn't matter whether you're running a multi-author blog, or a blog where readers can register. Having a login form embedded in your sidebar will make your blog look a lot more professional and user friendly.

Here is what you can expect from this recipe. In the following screenshot, a login form has been added to the K2 theme sidebar.

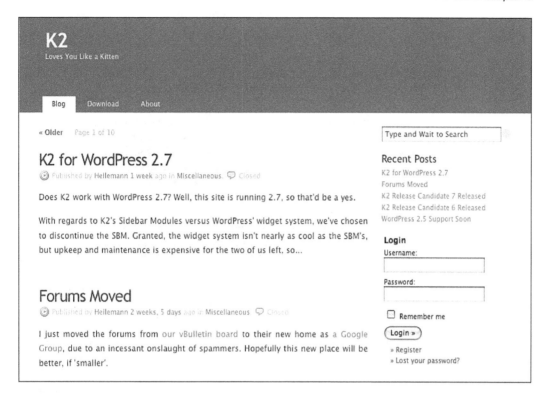

Getting ready

To achieve this recipe, you'll have to edit the `sidebar.php` file from your theme. The following hack works with WordPress 2.0 to 2.8.

How to do it...

1. Open the `sidebar.php` file for editing.

2. Find the opening `<ul>` tag and paste the following code under it:

```
<li>
  <?php global $user_ID, $user_identity, $user_level ?>
  <?php if ( $user_ID ) : ?>
    <h2><?php echo $user_identity ?></h2>
    <ul>
      <li><a href="<?php bloginfo('url') ?>/wp-login.php?action=
                logout&amp;redirect_to=<?php echo urlencode
                ($_SERVER['REQUEST_URI']) ?>">Logout</a></li>
    </ul>
  <?php elseif ( get_option('users_can_register') ) : ?>
```

```
<h2>Identification</h2>
<ul>
  <li>

  <form action="<?php bloginfo('url')
              ?>/wp-login.php" method="post">

  <p>
    <label for="log"><input type="text" name="log"
      id="log" value="<?php echo wp_specialchars (stripslashes
      ($user_login), 1) ?>" size="22" /> User</label><br />
      <label for="pwd"><input type="password"
        name="pwd" id="pwd" size="22" /> Password</label><br />
        <input type="submit" name="submit" value="Login"
          class="button" />
      <label for="rememberme"><input name="rememberme"
        id="rememberme" type="checkbox" checked="checked"
        value="forever" /> Remember me</label><br />
  </p>
    <input type="hidden" name="redirect_to" value="<?php echo
      $_SERVER['REQUEST_URI']; ?>"/>
  </form>

  </li>
  <li><a href="<?php bloginfo('url')
              ?>/wp-register.php">Register</a></li>
  <li><a href="<?php bloginfo('url') ?>/wp-login.php?action=
              lostpassword">Recover password</a></li>
</ul>
<?php endif ?>
</li>
```

3. Save the file. Your users can now login directly from your blog's sidebar.

How it works...

The working of this code is quite simple. First, you initialize the global variables to get the user ID, name, and level. Then, you check the value of the $user_ID variable. If the value is not null, which means that the current user is logged in, you then display a quick **hello user** text and a link to log out.

If the user isn't logged in, you check whether registering is allowed on the blog. If the user is logged in, then you simply display an HTML form that allows the user to log in directly from the blog. A link has also been included for registration if the current user doesn't have an account yet.

This code was inspired from a tutorial available at www.wpdesigner.com.

Adding a control panel to your blog's sidebar

Now that you have learned how to check whether a user is logged in or not, why not learn how to add a small control panel to your blog's sidebar that is only visible to the logged in users.

In this recipe, you'll learn how to achieve this task.

Getting ready

The upcoming piece of code works in exactly the same way as the code from the previous recipe does. It is all about checking if the user is logged in and whether he or she has the right to do a certain kind of thing.

The following screenshot shows a simple, but useful, control panel which is similar to the one we're about to create:

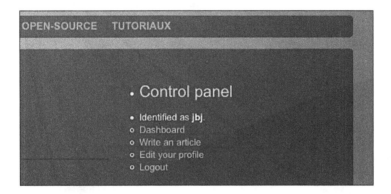

How to do it...

1. Open `sidebar.php` for editing.

2. Find the first opening `<ul>` HTML tag, and paste the following code under the `<ul>` tag:

```
<li>
  <?php global $user_ID, $user_identity, $user_level ?>
  <?php if ( $user_ID ) : ?>
    <h2>Control panel</h2>
    <ul>
      <li>Identified as <strong><?php echo $user_identity ?>
      </strong>.
```

```
    <ul>
        <li><a href="<?php bloginfo('url') ?>/wp-
        admin/">Dashboard</a></li>

            <?php if ( $user_level >= 1 ) : ?>
                <li><a href="<?php bloginfo('url') ?>/wp-admin/
                post-new.php">Write an article</a></li>
            <?php endif; ?>

            <li><a href="<?php bloginfo('url') ?>/wp-admin/
            profile.php">Profile and personal options</a></li>
            <li><a href="<?php bloginfo('url') ?>/wp-login.php?
            action=logout&amp;redirect_to=<?php echo
            urlencode($_SERVER['REQUEST_URI']) ?>">Logout</a></li>
        <?php
        if (is_single()) {?>
            <li><a href="<?php bloginfo('wpurl');?>/wp-admin/
            edit.php?p=<?php the_ID(); ?>">Edit Post</a>
            </li>
        <?php } ?>
        </ul>
    </li>
    </ul>
<?php endif; ?>
</li>
```

3. Once you are done, save the file. The allowed users can now go to their dashboard, edit their profile, or write a new post directly from the blog.

How it works...

As mentioned earlier, this code works in the same way as the code that was used to create a login form in the sidebar.

After you've made sure that the `$user_ID` variable isn't null, you work towards displaying the options available to the user. It is possible to define what a user can perform according to his role (administrator, author, contributor, subscriber, and so on). We're going to have a look at this in the next recipe.

There's more...

Now that you have learned how to add a control panel to the blog's sidebar, let's go ahead and try out something new.

Adding a login form and a control panel

Now that you know how to add a login form and a mini control panel to your blog's sidebar, why not try mixing the two codes? If the user isn't logged in, we'll display the login form. Otherwise, the custom panel will be shown to the user.

The code below works in the same way as the two that we studied previously. Add the following code to the `sidebar.php` file of your theme:

```
<li>
  <?php global $user_ID, $user_identity, $user_level ?>
  <?php if ( $user_ID ) : ?>
    <h2>Control panel</h2>
     <ul>
       <li>Identified as <strong><?php echo $user_identity ?>
       </strong>.
       <ul>
          <li><a href="<?php bloginfo('url') ?>/wp-admin/">
          Dashboard</a></li>
            <?php if ( $user_level >= 1 ) : ?>
               <li><a href="<?php bloginfo('url') ?>/wp-admin/
               post-new.php">Write an article</a></li>
            <?php endif; ?>
            <li><a href="<?php bloginfo('url') ?>/wp-admin/
            profile.php">Profile and personal options</a></li>
            <li><a href="<?php bloginfo('url') ?>/wp-login.php?
            action=logout&amp;redirect_to=<?php echo urlencode
            ($_SERVER['REQUEST_URI']) ?>">Logout</a></li>
          <?php
          if (is_single()) {?>
            <li><a href="<?php bloginfo('wpurl');?>/wp-admin/
            edit.php?p=<?php the_ID(); ?>">Edit Post</a>
            </li>
          <?php } ?>
     </ul>
     </li>
     </ul>
  <?php elseif ( get_option('users_can_register') ) : ?>
    <h2>Identification</h2>
    <ul>
      <li>
      <form action="<?php bloginfo('url') ?>/wp-login.php"
      method="post">
      <p>
        <label for="log"><input type="text" name="log" id="log" value
        ="<?php echo wp_specialchars(stripslashes($user_login), 1)
        ?>" size="22" /> User</label><br />
```

```
            <label for="pwd"><input type="password" name="pwd" id="pwd"
            size="22" /> Password</label><br />
            <input type="submit" name="submit" value="Login"
            class="button" />
            <label for="rememberme"><input name="rememberme" id=
            "rememberme" type="checkbox" checked="checked"
            value="forever" /> Remember me</label><br />
         </p>
            <input type="hidden" name="redirect_to" value="<?php echo
            $_SERVER['REQUEST_URI']; ?>"/>
         </form>
         </li>
         <li><a href="<?php bloginfo('url') ?>/wp-register.php">
         Register</a></li>
         <li><a href="<?php bloginfo('url') ?>/wp-login.php?
         action=lostpassword">Recover password</a></li>
      </ul>
   <?php endif; ?>
   </li>
```

The custom logging form for unregistered users will look similar to the following screenshot:

And the control panel for logged in users will look similar to the following screenshot:

Configuring author roles

Now that you have learned about the different aspects of the user's roles and capabilities, there's probably something that you're finding a little frustrating. By default, you can't configure author roles to fit your blog's needs. For example, a contributor can't upload images. Moreover, by default, you can't change it. Luckily, there's a plugin called **Role Manager** which allows you to configure author roles in the way that you want.

Getting ready

The Role Manager plugin can be found at the following link:

```
http://www.im-web-gefunden.de/wordpress-plugins/role-manager/
```

Download it, unzip it onto your hard drive, and install it as any other WordPress plugin. If you need help to install the plugin, just follow the simple steps described in Chapter 3 of this book.

How to do it...

1. Once the Role Manager plugin is installed, log in to your WordPress dashboard and go to **Users | Roles**.

2. A list of all of the available user roles will be displayed. For each role you can define what the user can do. For example, you can choose to let a contributor upload images.

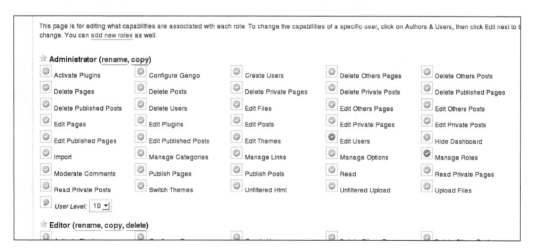

3. What is even better is that you're not limited to the 5 default user roles that are provided by WordPress. The Role Manager plugin allows you to create new roles, as well as the ability to rename, copy, or delete existing ones.

How it works...

The job of the Role Manager plugin is pretty easy. It simply creates custom roles with the options that you have defined and save it on the WordPress database.

There's more...

Now that we have configured the author roles, let's learn how to control the author's actions.

Controlling what authors can do

Even if your blog is powered by multiples authors, it is still your blog. Therefore, you shouldn't allow every author to have the right to edit posts or delete comments.

Since version 2.0, WordPress features user roles. **User roles** are defined as a group of actions that can be accomplished by a specific range of users. For example, the administrator can edit theme files, but the subscribers can't.

User roles and their capabilities

Here are the 5 predefined roles for WordPress users:

1. **Administrator**: The administrator is the blog owner. He has unlimited access to all of the administration features such as writing posts, editing his own posts along with the posts from other authors, installing plugins, selecting a new theme, editing themes, and editing plugin files.

2. **Editor**: The editor can write or publish posts, upload images, edit his own posts, and manage other's posts.

3. **Author**: The author can write, publish, and edit his own his own posts. He's also allowed to upload images for use in his posts.

4. **Contributor**: A contributor can write posts but can't publish them himself. Once he has written a post, the post is pending approval from the administrator. The contributor can't upload images either. This role is very good for guest authors on your own blog.

5. **Subscriber**: A subscriber is a registered user of your blog, but can't write posts.

For an exhaustive description of user roles and capabilities, you should read the related page in WordPress Codex: `http://codex.wordpress.org/Roles_and_Capabilities`.

Controlling what users can see in your theme

In the previous example, we built a sidebar control panel that allows the user to edit the current post. However, the code doesn't let you control which kind of author is allowed to edit the current post. For now, even if only the users with a sufficient role level will be capable of editing the post, every logged in user can see the related link.

The solution to that problem is a built-in WordPress function, called `current_user_can()`. As an argument, this function takes a string describing the action or the required role level to perform a specific task. For example, the following code will provide a link to edit the current post to the administrators only:

```php
<?php
if (current_user_can('level_10')){ ?>
    <a href="<?php bloginfo('wpurl');?>/wp-admin/edit.php?p=
            <?php the_ID(); ?>">Edit Post</a>
<?php } ?>
```

The `current_user_can()` function accepts `user_0` to `user_10` as a parameter. Here is the conversion table between the role levels and the roles:

▶ Suscriber: `level_0`

▶ Contributor: `level_1`

▶ Author: `level_2` to `level_4`

▶ Editor: `level_5` to `level_7`

▶ Administrator: `level_8` to `level_10`

The `current_user_can()` function can also be used with a specific action as a parameter. This is the recommended use, as the level parameter is becoming obsolete.

The following example checks if the current user can edit a post he previously published. If yes, then a link to edit the post will be displayed.

```php
<?php
if (current_user_can('edit_published_posts')){ ?>
    <a href="<?php bloginfo('wpurl');?>/wp-admin/edit.php?p=
            <?php the_ID(); ?>">Edit Post</a>
<?php } ?>
```

Here are all of the arguments that are accepted by the `current_user_can()` function:

- `switch_themes`
- `edit_themes`
- `activate_plugins`
- `edit_plugins`
- `edit_users`
- `edit_files`
- `manage_options`
- `moderate_comments`
- `manage_categories`
- `manage_links`
- `upload_files`
- `import`
- `unfiltered_html`
- `edit_posts`
- `edit_others_posts`
- `edit_published_posts`
- `edit_pages`
- `edit_others_pages`
- `edit_published_pages`
- `edit_published_pages`
- `delete_pages`
- `delete_others_pages`
- `delete_published_pages`
- `delete_posts`
- `delete_others_posts`
- `delete_published_posts`
- `delete_private_posts`
- `edit_private_posts`
- `read_private_posts`
- `delete_private_pages`
- `edit_private_pages`
- `read_private_pages`
- `delete_users`
- `create_users`
- `unfiltered_upload`

- ▸ `edit_dashboard`
- ▸ `update_plugins`
- ▸ `delete_plugins`

Displaying author-related information on posts

In a multi-author blog, it's always good for the reader to know the author of the article that they're currently reading. It's even better if they can grab some extra information about the author, such as his website, a short bio, and so on.

In this recipe, you'll learn how to edit your `single.php` theme file to automatically retrieve the author-related information, and display it at the top of the page.

Getting ready

As we're going to display author information on posts, the first thing to do is to make sure that your contributing authors have entered their biography and other information into the WordPress database.

Any author can enter his information by logging in to the WordPress dashboard, and then going to **Profile**. The blog administrator can edit all of the profiles. The following screenshot shows the WordPress 2.7 profile editor for the authors.

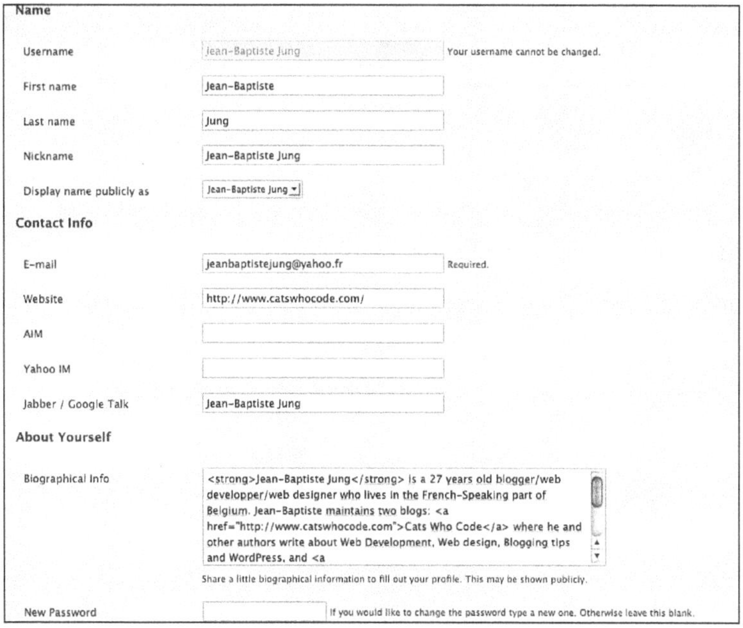

How to do it...

Once you have made sure that your authors have successfully filled their information, you can start coding by carrying out the following steps:

1. Open the file `single.php` for addition.

2. Paste the following code within the loop:

```
<div id="author-info">
<h2>About the author: <?php the_author();?></h2>
<?php the_author_description(); ?>
<?php the_author();?>'s website: <a href="<?php the_author_url();
 ?>"><?php the_author_url(); ?></a><br />

Other posts by <?php the_author_posts_link(); ?>

</div><!--/author-info-->
```

3. Save the file and visit your blog. You will notice that your posts now automatically display the author-related information, as shown in the following screenshot:

About the author: Jean-Baptiste Jung

Jean-Baptiste Jung is a 27 years old blogger/web developper/web designer who lives in the French-Speaking part of Belgium. Jean-Baptiste maintains two blogs: Cats Who Code where he and other authors write about Web Development, Web design, Blogging tips and WordPress, and WpRecipes where Jean shares useful WordPress snippets on a daily basis.

Tags : **WordPress**

How it works...

WordPress provides a dozen of author-related template tags, which are an easy way to retrieve information that is entered by authors in their profile.

Note that all of these tags must be used within the loop for them to work.

There's more...

Here are all the available template tags related to authors:

the_author	Display the author public name
the_author_description	Display author description (Bio)
the_author_login	Display author login
the_author_firstname	Display author's first name
the_author_lastname	Display author's last name
the_author_nickname	Display author's nickname
the_author_ID	Display author's ID
the_author_email	Display author's email address
the_author_url	Display author's website URL
the_author_link	Display a link to the author website—anchor text for the link is the author display name
the_author_aim	Display author's AIM screen name
the_author_yim	Display author's Yahoo! Messenger email
the_author_posts	Display how many post have been written by the author
wp_list_authors	List of all the authors (This will be discussed later in this chapter)

Displaying author picture on posts

Did you like the previous recipe? I hope you did! But personally, I must admit that even though displaying author information looks very cool, something is missing from the previous recipe. Can you guess what is it? It is a picture of the author, of course.

Even if your author-related information is precise and complete, a picture is still essential. This is because it is the easiest, and quickest, way for a reader to recognize an author. But sadly, WordPress can't handle author pictures by default. Let's learn how to create a **hack** that will allow us to display the author's picture in the way that we want to.

Getting ready

As we'll be using author pictures in this recipe, you should start by requesting a picture of all of your authors. Although it isn't necessary, it will be really better if all of the pictures have the same width and height. A square of 80 to 110 pixels is a good standard.

Also, make sure that all of your pictures have the same format, such as .jpg, .png, or .gif.

How to do it...

Now that you have collected pictures of all of your authors, we can start to hack WordPress and insert author pictures in the posts.

1. First, you have to rename your images with the author IDs. You can also use author's last name if you prefer, but in this example I am going to use their IDs.

2. Once you have your renamed authors' pictures, upload them to the `wp-content/themes/yourtheme/images` directory.

3. Open the file `single.php` and add the following code within the loop:

```
<img src="<?php bloginfo('template_url); ?>/images/<?php the_
author_ID(); ?>.jpg"  alt="<?php the_author(); ?>" />
```

4. Save the `single.php` file and you're done. Each post now displays a picture of its author!

How it works...

The working of this code is pretty simple. You simply concatenated the result of the `the_author_ID()` function with the theme URL to build an absolute URL to the image. As the images are named with the author ID (for example, `1.jpg`, `4.jpg`, `17.jpg`, and so on), the `the_author_ID()` function gives us the name of the picture to be displayed. You just have to add the `.jpg` extension.

There's more...

Now that you've learnt how to display the picture of the current author, you should definitely use this recipe to enhance the previous recipe. The following code will retrieve the author information, and display the author picture as we have learnt earlier:

```
<div id="author-info">
  <h2>About the author: <?php the_author();?></h2>
  <img src="<?php bloginfo('template_url); ?>/images/<?php the_author_
                ID(); ?>.jpg"  alt="<?php the_author(); ?>" />
  <?php the_author_description(); ?>
  <?php the_author();?>'s website: <a href="<?php the_author_url();
?>"><?php the_author_url(); ?></a><br />
  Other posts by <?php the_author_posts_link(); ?>
</div><!--/author-info-->
```

The outcome of the preceding piece of code will look similar to the following screenshot:

 About the author: Jean-Baptiste Jung

Jean-Baptiste Jung is a 27 years old blogger/web developper/web designer who lives in the French-Speaking part of Belgium. Jean-Baptiste maintains two blogs: Cats Who Code where he and other authors write about Web Development, Web design, Blogging tips and WordPress, and WpRecipes where Jean shares useful WordPress snippets on a daily basis.

 Tags : **WordPress**

Displaying the author's gravatar picture on posts

Gravatars (which stands for **Globally recognized avatars**) is a popular service, that allows you to associate an avatar image to your email address.

On October 18, 2007, **Automattic** (The company behind WordPress) acquired Gravatar. Since WordPress 2.5 the popular blogging engine is fully gravatar-compatible, which results, in the ability to include gravatars in comments.

In this recipe, I'll show you how to modify the previous code to use the author gravatar instead of a personal picture.

Getting ready

As we're going to use Gravatars, you (and each of your authors) first need a gravatar account. Carry out the following steps to create a gravatar account and associate an image to your email address.

1. Go to the web site `http://en.gravatar.com/site/signup`, and enter your email address into the text field. Gravatar will send you a confirmation via email.

2. Check your emails and open the one received from Gravatar. Click on the link to confirm your email address.

3. Choose a username and a **Password** for your account.

Finish creating your account by choosing your finishing touches!

Choose your Gravatar nickname, using only lowercase letters and numbers. This will be used to identify you later on with features which are coming soon to gravatar. As an added bonus you will be able to log into WordPress.com using this nickname! Finally choose a password, and once we make sure that your nickname is available for use you'll be all set! **Please only use lowercase numbers and letters, no spaces or punctuation**

Email: adecek@gmail.com

Nickname: catswhocode
               Your nickname will be permanent,
               choose wisely.

Password: ••••••••••

Password (again): ••••••••••

               (Signup)

AN **AUT⊚MATTIC** JOINT

4. Once your username and **Password** has been created successfully, you'll see a text that reads **Whoops, looks like you don't have any images yet! Add an image by clicking here**. Click on the given link, and choose to upload a picture from your computer's hard drive, or the Internet.

5. Once you are done choosing and cropping (if necessary) your picture, you have to rate it. Click on **G** unless—except, if your avatar is meant for mature audiences only.

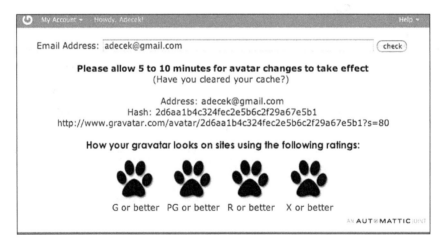

6. Done! You now have your own gravatar.

How to do it...

Open the `single.php` file from the theme you're using and paste the following code:

```
$md5 = md5(get_the_author_email());
$default = urlencode( 'http://www.yoursite.com/wp-content/themes/
yourtheme/images/default_avatar.gif' );

echo "<img src='http://www.gravatar.com/avatar.php?gravatar_id=$md5&am
p;size=60&amp;default=$default' alt='' />";
```

How it works...

The first thing to do is to get an **md5** sum from the author's email address. To do so, I used the php `md5()` function along with the `get_the_author_email()` function. I didn't use `the_author_email()` because this function directly prints the result without allowing you to manipulate it with PHP.

I then encoded the URL of a default picture that is to be shown if the author hasn't signed up to Gravatar yet.

Once done, the gravatar can be displayed. To do so, visit the web site `http://www.gravatar.com/avatar.php` with the following parameters:

- **gravatar_id**: The gravatar id, which is an md5 sum of the user email
- **size**: The gravatar size in pixels
- **default**: The absolute URL to an image which will be used as a default image if the author hasn't signed up to gravatar yet

Adding moderation buttons to the comments

A common problem with comments is spam. Sure, you can moderate comments and use the Akismet plugin. However, sometimes someone leaves a normal comment, you approve it, and then the spammer—who knows that his comments aren't being accepted by the moderator—starts to spam your blog.

Even though you can do nothing against this (except moderating all of the comments), a good idea is to either add spam and delete buttons to all of the comments. This way, if you see a comment saying **spam** while reading your blog, then you can edit it, delete it, or mark it as spam. I got this useful tip from Joost de Valk, who blogs at `www.yoast.com`.

Getting ready

The following screenshot shows normal comments without the edit, delete and spam buttons:

Agolf Cartson

Dec 28 at 10:55

Will this always work no matter what theme you might be using?

Plurkr

Dec 28 at 12:23

@Agolf - I think it will not.

Some theme designers may forget adding this class.

If someone knows this for sure can correct me 😃

There's nothing complicated at all with this recipe. However, you must be sure to know which kind of blog the users are allowed to edit or delete your comments. For a list of actions and user roles, see the section named *Controlling what users can do*, which is later in this chapter.

How to do it...

1. Open the file `functions.php` and paste the following piece of code:

```
function delete_comment_link($id)
{
  if (current_user_can('edit_post'))
{
    echo '| <a href="'.admin_url("comment.php?action=cdc&c=$id").'
                                         ">del</a> ';
    echo '| <a href="'.admin_url("comment.php?action=cdc&dt=spam&c
                                       =$id").'">spam</a>';
  }
}
```

2. Save the `functions.php` file and open the `comments.php` file. Find the comments loop and add the following lines:

```
<?php
edit_comment_link();
delete_comment_link(get_comment_ID());
?>
```

3. Save the file `comments.php` and visit your blog. You now have three links on each of the comments to **edit**, to delete **(del)**, and to mark as **spam** as shown in the following screenshot:

Jean-Baptiste Jung (edit | del | spam)

Dec 08 at 10:37

@Sarbjit Singh: Glad to see you enjoyed this recipe!

Nihar (edit | del | spam)

Dec 25 at 10:00

This will really help. thanks for the tip. I have edit this link i will put call to this function beside this in comments.php.

Thanks

How it works...

In this recipe we started by creating a function. This function first verifies whether the current user has the right to edit posts. If yes, then the admin URLs to mark the comment as spam or delete it are created and displayed.

In the file `comments.php`, we have used the `edit_comment_link()`, which is a built-in WordPress function. Some themes include this by default. We then used the comment ID as a parameter to the `delete_comment_link()` function that you had created earlier.

Getting notified when a new draft is saved

As a blog administrator, you have to know what your authors and contributors are working on. Sure you can ask them, but it can become a boring task quickly if you have many different contributors.

Getting ready

The solution to the stated problem is a plugin called **Draft Notification**. When someone creates a new draft on your blog, you'll automatically receive an email.

How to do it...

1. Of course, the first thing to do is to get the plugin. You can download it from the following URL: `http://www.dagondesign.com/articles/draft-notification-plugin-for-wordpress/`.

2. Once you have downloaded the file, rename the `.txt` extension to `.php` and install it according to the standard installation procedure, as described in Chapter 4.

3. That's all! Now, every time a new draft will be saved you'll receive an email notification. Please note that the creation of this plugin is such that it also sends out an email when an existing draft has been modified and saved again.

4. Since dates aren't saved in the WordPress database for drafts, there does not seem to be an efficient way to check if it is the first time the draft has been saved.

How it works...

Once installed, the Draft Notification plugin starts to look up when a draft is saved. When it does, the plugin automatically sends an email to the blog admin.

Allowing multiple authors on posts

In a multi-author blog, sometimes an author starts a post and another one finishes it. Or, perhaps, two (or more) contributors share their ideas and create a great article together.

Unfortunately, by default, WordPress allows only one author per post. Although this is good for most blogs, it can quickly become very frustrating for contributors on a multi-author blog. Just imagine that two authors have worked together to write a post, but only one can be rewarded. In my opinion, that's not a very comfortable situation for either of them.

Getting ready

Luckily, a very cool WordPress plugin allows your blog to assign more than one author to a post. The plugin is simply named **Co-Authors** and was created by Weston Ruter.

How to do it...

1. The Co-Authors plugin can be downloaded from the web site `http://wordpress.org/extend/plugins/co-authors/`. Once you have it, extract it onto your hard drive and install it by following the standard installation procedure that was described in Chapter 4.

2. Write a post, or edit an existing one. When you scroll down the page, you'll see a box named **Post Author(s)**. This is where you can add as many authors as you want.

3. Now, you have to modify your template files a bit to where you want the co-authors to be listed. The Co-Authors plugin provides the following co-authors tags:

- ❏ `coauthors()`
- ❏ `coauthors_posts_links()`
- ❏ `coauthors_firstnames()`
- ❏ `coauthors_lastnames()`
- ❏ `coauthors_nicknames()`
- ❏ `coauthors_links()`
- ❏ `coauthors_IDs()`

4. They work exactly the same way as the built-in author's tags. For example, let's modify the `single.php` file of our theme and display the co-authors. Add the following code anywhere within the loop:

```
if(function_exists('coauthors'))
{
    coauthors();
}
else
{
    the_author();
}
```

How it works...

When installed, the Co-Authors plugins creates news tags to return multiple authors. If only one author wrote the post, only his name is displayed.

In the preceding piece of code, we check if the `coauthors()` function exists. If yes, then we use it to display co-authors. If the function doesn't exist (which means that the plugin isn't installed) we use the built-in `the_author()` function instead.

Displaying a list of all of the authors

In my opinion, in a multi-author blog it is a good thing to display a list of all of the authors, such as in your **About** page. In this recipe, I'm going to show you how to easily display the list of your authors and control its display.

Getting ready

To achieve this recipe and enhance your **About** page, you should definitely create a page template. This is not mandatory, though. To get information about the page template and learn how to use them on your WordPress blog, please refer to Chapter 3.

How to do it...

Edit the desired file and insert the following line of code to where you want your list of authors to be displayed:

```php
<?php wp_list_authors(); ?>
```

Save the file, publish the page, and visit your blog. You will notice that all of your authors are now listed.

How it works...

To display the list of your blog authors, you only need the `wp_list_authors()` function. This function can be inserted anywhere into your theme files. Once called, `wp_list_authors()` executes a database query to get the list of authors. The function can be controlled with parameters.

There's more...

Now that we have learned how to display the list of authors, let's learn how to the function used to display the list of authors.

Controlling the wp_list_authors() function

The `wp_list_authors()` function can be controlled with a few parameters:

- `Optioncount`: Display the number of published posts by each author (1 = true, 0 = false).

- `exclude_admin`: Exclude the `admin` from the authors list (1 = true, 0 = false).

- `show_fullname`: Display the first and last name of the authors (1 = true, 0 =false).

- `hide_empty`: Do not display authors with 0 posts (1 = true, 0 =false).

- `feed`: The text to be displayed for a link to each author's RSS feed. The default choice is no text and no feed displayed.

- `feed_image`: This is the path or filename for a graphic image. This acts as a link to each author's RSS feed, and overrides the `feed` parameter.

The following line of code will list the author's full names along with the number of posts that they have published:

```php
<?php wp_list_authors('show_fullname=1&optioncount=1'); ?>
```

The following code will not exclude the `admin`, as well as the authors who haven't published any post yet:

```php
<?php wp_list_authors('exclude_admin=0&hide_empty=0'); ?>
```

7
Securing your WordPress Blog

A very important point in managing a blog is **security**. Even though nobody wants to lose all of their data, security is often neglected by many WordPress users. Hacking into blogs is far more prevalent than you may think. A Google search for 'My blog was hacked' gives a count of around two million web pages.

In this chapter, you'll learn how to protect your blog from various sorts of hacking by creating database backups to protect your `wp-admin` directory from brute force attacks.

In this chapter, you will learn:

- ▸ Creating manual backups of your WordPress blog
- ▸ Restoring a MySQL backup
- ▸ Creating backups of your WordPress files
- ▸ Using a shell script to create automatic files and database backups
- ▸ Securing your plugins directory
- ▸ Removing a WordPress version from the theme files
- ▸ Getting rid of the Administrator account
- ▸ Automatically forbid login after some failed login attempt
- ▸ Protecting the wp-admin directory against brute force with the help of AskApache plugin
- ▸ Restricting wp-admin directory to your IP address
- ▸ Testing your blog security
- ▸ Denying comment posting on no referrer requests

Creating manual backups of your WordPress blog

If you must remember only one recipe from the entire book, then it has to be this one. All of your WordPress data (posts, pages, categories, comments, and so on) are saved in a MySQL database. Without the database, the only thing you'll get is an empty theme. Having backups of your WordPress database is not just important, it's mandatory.

Getting ready

In this recipe, we're going to manually create a backup of your MySQL database using phpMyAdmin.

To achieve this recipe, you have to be sure that phpMyAdmin is successfully installed on your web server. Most web hosts have it installed by default. However, you will have to check and see whether it is installed on yours or not.

How to do it...

1. Log in to your phpMyAdmin (the phpMyAdmin URL depends of your server, ask your web host if you don't know its URL yet).

2. If you're using multiple databases, then select the one related to your WordPress blog.

3. Click on the export button on the horizontal menu.

4. From the lefthand side of the page, select the database tables that you'd like to export (except for special circumstances, you should always export the whole database).

5. Scroll down the page until you see the **Execute** button. Just before executing, you can choose to compress the backup, which I would recommend. I always use the Gzip compression on my database backups.

6. Then, click on the **Execute** button. Wait a few seconds and your browser will ask you to download the backup. Keep it in a secure place, like a USB drive.

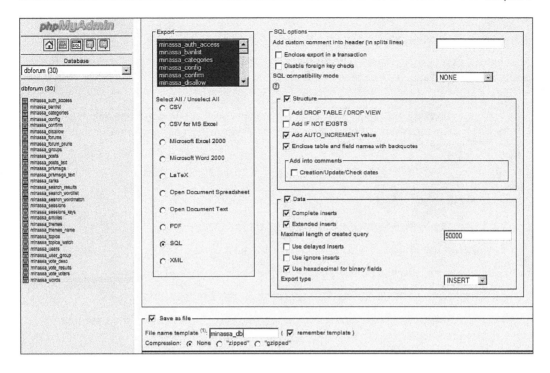

How it works...

The phpMyAdmin application is a very useful web application. It allows you to visually manage, create, export, and delete, the MySQL databases.

The **export** option is one of the numerous things that phpMyAdmin can do for you. Creating manual backups using the command line is easy as well, but novice users may find it a bit more difficult than creating backups visually.

There's more...

If you're interested in having a plugin that can perform backups for you, and can even schedule automatic backups, then you should definitely refer to the Backing up your database with WP Database Backup recipe from Chapter 4.

Restoring a MySQL backup

Now that you know how to create a backup of your blog database, the next very important point is to know how to restore it when needed. Believe it or not, I have read about a lot of users asking for help on the forums, as they had the backup of their database, but were not able to restore it in their database.

Getting ready

To achieve this recipe, you need a backup of your blog database. If you don't have one, then create one by carrying out the steps in the previous recipe.

 Don't try this recipe on a production blog! This is for emergencies only. If you want to test it, then you should install WordPress locally and perform your tests on this local install.

How to do it...

1. Log in to **phpMyAdmin** and select your WordPress database.

2. Click on the **Import** tab from the horizontal menu.

3. Click on the **Browse** button and select the backup on your hard drive.

4. Once done, scroll down the page and click on the **Execute** button.

5. The database backup has been imported into your database and the data has been replaced.

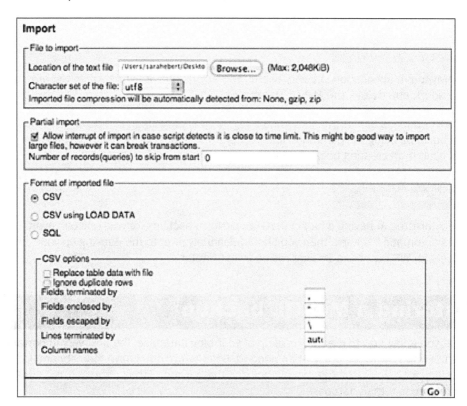

How it works...

When you import a MySQL backup with phpMyAdmin, your database is truncated (which means that the database becomes empty), and the previous data is replaced by the ones contained in the backup. This is why I warned you while introducing this recipe that restoring a backup causes the replacement of your data.

This is the reason why you should create backups frequently. The more frequently you create backups, the less the data you could possibly lose.

Creating backups of your WordPress files

As we have seen earlier, having backups of your WordPress database is really important, but what about the files? Core files aren't really a problem because you can download them when you want from `www.wordpress.org`. However, when you're writing posts, you often upload pictures, and maybe even modify your theme.

This is another reason why it is very important to create backups of your blog files. You have a better chance to avoid data loss if your blog is hacked some day, accidentally.

Getting ready

This recipe is very easy to achieve. You only need an FTP program and some space on your hard drive or USB device. The following screenshot shows the transferring of a file via FTP using the Cyberduck program on Mac OS X.

How to do it...

1. On your computer, create a directory and name it as `backup-myblog-20090106`.

2. Open your favorite FTP program, and connect to your blog's web host.

3. Select all of your files, including the `.htaccess` file, and copy them into the `backup-myblog-20090106` directory on your hard drive.

4. That's all. If for some reason you lose your WordPress files someday, due to an attack or a technical problem, then you'll just have to open the `backup-myblog-20090106` director, and copy anything from it to the root of your blog's web host.

How it works...

There is really nothing hard here. In this recipe, you created a directory on your computer and then copied the files from your server to this directory, using an FTP program. The result is a backup of your files on your computer that can be used to replace your WordPress files, if any kind of problem occurs.

Using a shell script to create automatic files and database backups

If you read the previous two recipes, then you'll know how to backup your MySQL database as well as your WordPress files. Let's go a step further with the backups. In this recipe, I'm going to show you how to use a shell script to create automatic backups of both your database and WordPress files.

Getting ready

To use the following shell script, you must have physical or **SSH** (**Secure Shell**) access to your server. Confirm with your web host if you are not sure whether you have an SSH access.

How to do it...

1. Connect to your server using SSH.

2. Get the script with the help of the following command:

```
wget http://www.tomsquest.com/blog/wp-content/
            uploads/2008/09/wpbackupsh.zip
```

3. Unzip the script files:

```
unzip wpbackupsh.zip
```

4. Make the script executable:

```
chmod 700 wpbackup.sh
```

5. Edit the script and modify the following lines:

- `EMAIL=monemail@mail.com`: Your email address (The script sends an email when the backup is finished)
- `WORDPRESS_PATH="/opt/wordpress"`: WordPress install path
- `BACKUP_PATH="/mnt/backups"`: Path to your backups

6. Save the script and run it:

```
./wpbackup.sh
```

How it works...

The shell script, created by Thomas Queste, does not need to know your WordPress database login and password. It automatically parses the `wp-config.php` file from your WordPress install to get it. Once the script gets the requested information from `wp-config.php`, it backs up your MySQL database and then, your files. The backup is saved on the specified directory.

Securing your plugins directory

The fact that WordPress is open source software has many good points. One is that anyone can create a plugin and make it available to the community. However, this can also become a bad point if the plugin contains security holes.

A hacker often checks out the `wp-content/plugins` directory of the blog they're attempting to hack. Since this directory doesn't contain any `index.html` file, the server creates a listing of files letting the hacker know which plugins you're using. If one of your plugins contains a security hole, the hacker may exploit it to hijack your blog.

Getting ready

Even if there are not a lot of plugins containing security problems, it's always better to be proactive to prevent any kind of damage. In this recipe, you'll learn how to easily protect your `wp-content/plugins` directory.

How to do it...

1. Visit the link `http://www.yourblog.com/wp-content/plugins`. You'll see a listing of the directory's content. Anyone can view it and have a look at the plugins being used by your blog.

2. On your computer's hard drive, create a new blank file and call it `index.html`.

3. With your favorite FTP program, upload the `index.html` file into the `wp-content/plugins` directory.

4. Visit the link `http://www.yourblog.com/wp-content/plugins` again. The page is now blank, which means that no one can see the plugins that you're using.

Index of /wp-content/plugins

```
Name                 Last modified       Size  Description
Parent Directory                          -
akismet/             01-Oct-2008 23:14    -
hello.php            16-Jun-2008 23:30   2.0K
redirection/         02-Oct-2008 06:55    -
stats/               02-Oct-2008 15:19    -
wp-db-backup.php     02-Oct-2008 15:19   42K
```

Apache/2.2.8 (Unix) mod_vdbh/1.0.3 mod_ssl/2.2.8 OpenSSL/0.9.8c PHP/5.2.6 S

How it works...

When an `index.html` file can't be found on a directory, Apache servers, buy default display a listing of available files and subdirectories. As you can see in the preceding screenshot, anyone can see the plugins that you're using.

Creating a blank `index.html` file and uploading it into your blog's `wp-content/plugins` directory eliminates the listing. The only thing that can be seen at the address `http://www.yourblog.com/wp-content/plugins` is a completely blank page.

Removing a WordPress version from the theme files

By default, WordPress adds a meta tag in your blog header containing the WordPress version you're using. This is used by the WordPress team to obtain stats about version usage.

The problem is that some older versions of WordPress contain security holes. Imagine that you're using an older WordPress version and a hacker wants to hack your blog. He looks in your blog source, finds the meta tag, and discovers that you're using a WordPress version that contains a security problem. You've guessed it right! The hacker can now easily destroy your blog.

Getting ready

This meta tag may be useful to the WordPress team, but for you and your blog, it is absolutely unnecessary. You can get rid of it without losing any functionality.

```
<meta http-equiv="Content-Type" content="text/html; charset=UTF-8" />

<meta name="generator" content="WordPress 2.7" /> <!-- leave this for stats please -->


<link rel="stylesheet" href="http://www.undabgesehendavon.com/wp-content/themes/o2/styl
```

How to do it...

1. Open the `functions.php` file from your theme. If that file doesn't exist, then create it.

2. Enter the following code inside the `functions.php` file:
   ```
   add_filter( 'the_generator', create_function('$a,
   "return null;"));
   ```

3. Save the file and you're done. The WordPress version isn't displayed publicly anymore.

How it works...

In the older WordPress versions, the meta tag was included in the `header.php` file so it was very easy to remove. However, in the newer versions, the WordPress version is directly injected into your blog header.

The reason you need to add a filter on `the_generator()` function is to avoid displaying your WordPress version. This is done by creating a basic function which returns null instead of the WordPress version.

Getting rid of the Administrator account

By default, all of the WordPress blogs have an **Administrator** account that is automatically created when you install WordPress. It is understood that this account has administrator rights, which means that someone logged in with the **Administrator** account can create other accounts with administrator rights, change WordPress password, and so on.

Getting ready

Before getting rid of the **Administrator** account, make sure to have a backup of your WordPress database.

How to do it...

As every WordPress blog is supposed to have an **Administrator** account, chances are that when a hacker tries to crack your password, he or she will use the `admin` account as the login.

The solution to this problem is to create another account for yourself and then delete the `admin` account.

1. If you're currently using the name `admin` for posting and managing your WordPress blog, then you have to create another administrator account. To do so, log in to your WordPress dashboard and go to **Users** page. Click on the **Add new** button and enter the details for your new account. Select the role to be **Administrator**.

2. Once you have created your new account, log out and log in again. This time use your new account. Go to **Users | Authors and users**, find the **Administrator** account, and delete it.

How it works...

We have simply used the `admin` account to create another account here and gave it the **Administrator** rights.

Once done, we logged out of the `admin` account and logged in again, this time in our newly created account with the administrator rights. Then, we finally deleted the `admin` account.

Forbiding login automatically after some failed login attempt

By deleting the `admin` account, as described in the previous recipe, you reduced a major threat of being hacked. However, hackers are (usually) smart and could also try other logins, such as your author name. For example, my name is Jean-Baptiste Jung and a hacker will also probably try it as a login on a brute force attempt.

Getting ready

The solution to this problem is the **Login LockDown** plugin. The purpose of this plugin is to record the IP address and the timestamp of every failed WordPress login attempt. If more than a certain number of attempts are detected within a short period of time from the same IP range, then the plugin automatically disables the login function.

How to do it...

To install the Login LockDown plugin on your WordPress blog, carry out the following steps:

1. Visit the link `http://www.bad-neighborhood.com/login-lockdown.html`, and download the plugin.

2. Install the plugin on your blog by using the standard plugin installation procedure, as described in Chapter 4.

3. To access the **Login LockDown** options, go to **Settings | Login LockDown**. You can specify the maximum number of failed login attempts, the logout length, and so on here.

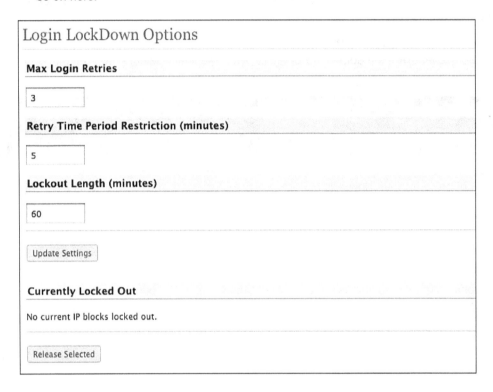

How it works...

The Login LockDown plugin records the IP address and timestamp of every failed login attempt. If more than a certain number of attempts are detected within a short period of time from the same IP range, then the login function is disabled for all of the requests from that range. This helps in preventing brute force password discovery.

Currently, the plugin defaults to a 1 hour lock out of an IP block, after 3 failed login attempts within 5 minutes.

Protecting the wp-admin directory brute force with the help of AskApache

According to Wikipedia, a brute force attack is a method of defeating a cryptographic scheme, by systematically trying a large number of possibilities. Due to the success of WordPress, hackers have tools to try and discover your administrator password.

Getting ready

A great way to get protected from brute force attacks is to use HTTP authentication. When someone tries to access the `wp-login.php` file, a pop up window, created by the server, will be launched asking for a password. With no password, the person attempting to view the `wp-login.php` file will never be able to see it.

In my opinion, HTTP authentication is the best method of protection against brute force attacks (Internet bots wont be able to fill the fields of the server-generated pop up window), even though you'll then have to log in twice (one for the HTTP authentication and once for WordPress).

An HTTP authentication can be set manually. However, it is much easier to use the **Ask Apache Password Protect** plugin.

How to do it...

1. Visit the following link and download the plugin: `http://wordpress.org/extend/plugins/askapache-password-protect`.

2. To install the plugin, follow the general plugin installation procedure described in Chapter 4.

3. Once the plugin is activated, log in to your WordPress dashboard and go to **Settings | AA PassPro**. The plugin starts by verifying your server configuration. Scroll down and click on the **Continue to AskApache Password Protection Setup** button.

4. You have to define your password settings (as shown in the upcoming screenshot). Pick a **Username**, a **Password**, and a message to be displayed on the pop up. The **Username** and **Password** have nothing to do with WordPress so they don't need to match your WordPress login ID and password.

Setup Password Protection

Create User

Admin Email Username and Password sent here in case you forget it.	
Username	
Password (twice)	•••••••••• ••••••••••

Authentication Scheme

Choose Scheme

⊙ **Digest** — Much better than Basic, MD5 crypto hashing with nonce's to prevent cryptanalysis.
○ **Basic** — Cleartext authentication using a user-ID and a password for each authname.

This is the mechanism by which your credentials are authenticated (Digest is strongly preferred)

Authentication Settings

Password File Location

Use a location inaccessible from a web-browser if possible. Do not put it in the directory that it protects.

Realm Name

    Protected By AskApache

The authname or "Realm" serves two major functions. Part of the password dialog box. Second, it is used by the client to determine what password to send for a given authenticated area.

Protection Space Domains

One or more URIs in the same protection space (i.e. use the same authname and username password info). The URIs may be either absolute or relative URIs. Omitting causes client to send Authorization header for every request.

Encryption Preferences

Password File Algorithm

○ **CRYPT** — Unix only. Uses the traditional Unix crypt(3) function with a randomly-generated 32-bit salt (only 12 bits used) and the first 8 characters of the password.
○ **MD5** — Apache-specific algorithm using an iterated (1,000 times) MD5 Digest of various combinations of a random 32-bit salt and the password.
○ **SHA1** — Base64-encoded SHA-1 Digest of the password.

Note I do not store or save your password anywhere, so you will need to type it in each time you update this page.. for now.

(Save Settings »)

5. Once done, click on the **Submit Settings** button. On the next screen, you can manage **Security Modules**. A **Security Module** is basically a piece of code dedicated to perform a particular action (for example, auto-denying comments from no referrer's requests) inserted in your `.htaccess` file.

6. The **AskApache** plugin lets you activate or deactivate the module, just like plugins. Therefore, don't hesitate to try as many modules as you wish.

In my opinion, the following modules should always be enabled:

- Password Protect wp-login.php
- Password Protect wp-admin
- BAD Content Type
- Stop Hotlinking

7. If you have activated both the password protect wp-login.php file and the password protect wp-admin file, then the HTTP **Authentication request** pop up window will appear instantly, asking you for the login and the password that you just defined:

8. Enter your information, and don't forget to set your browser to remember it, otherwise you'll have to retype it each time you'll try to access the wp-admin directory and the wp-login.php file.

How it works...

Once activated and configured, the AskApache plugin generates a server-side password verification using the WordPress .htaccess file. The most interesting part of this is, as you can see in the preceding screenshot, the password is requested by a pop up window, which means that no Internet bots can even try to fill and submit it.

Restricting wp-admin directory to your IP address

A very radical, but effective, solution to protect your `wp-admin` directory from brute force attacks, as well as any kind of intrusion, is to restrict access to this directory to a single IP address, yours.

Getting ready

Before applying this recipe, you need to make sure that you're using a static IP address. To do so, ask your **Internet Service Provider** (**ISP**). This recipe can't be achieved if you're using dynamic IP addresses.

How to do it...

1. The first thing to do is to find out your IP address. There's many way to obtain it, but the simplest is to go to `http://whatsmyip.org/`. Once you visit the site, your IP address will appear, as shown in the following screenshot:

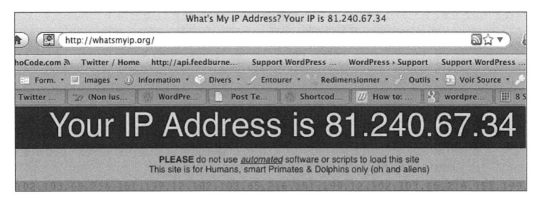

2. Then, create a file named `.htaccess` on your computer and enter the following lines in it. Do not edit the `.htaccess` file located at the root of your WordPress install.

```
AuthUserFile /dev/null
AuthGroupFile /dev/null
AuthName "Example Access Control"
AuthType Basic
<LIMIT GET>
order deny,allow
deny from all
allow from xx.xx.xx.xx
</LIMIT>
```

3. On the last line of the preceding code, you can specify the IP address that shall be allowed access to the `wp-admin` directory.

4. Save the `.htaccess` file on the `wp-admin` directory of your WordPress blog. Now, if your IP address isn't listed in the `.htaccess` file, you'll see a **403 Forbidden** error.

How it works...

In this recipe, we have used the authentication functionalities of the Apache web server to restrict access to the `wp-admin` directory to a specific IP address. Any other requests, coming from unspecified IP addresses, will be rejected.

There's more...

Right now, I have shown you how to restrict the `wp-admin` directory to a single IP address. However, in the case of a multiauthor blog, you may want to be able to authorize more than just one IP address.

Allowing access to more than one IP

Simply use the following syntax (one IP address per line) to authorize more than a single IP address:

```
AuthUserFile /dev/null
AuthGroupFile /dev/null
AuthName "Example Access Control"
AuthType Basic
<LIMIT GET>
    order deny,allow
    deny from all
    allow from xx.xx.xx.xx
    allow from xx.xx.xxx.xx
    allow from xx.xx.xxx.xx
    allow from xx.xx.xx.xx
</LIMIT>
```

It's possible to specify more than a single IP address. Just put them on a new line, with the `allow from` text before specifying the IP.

Testing your blog security

A difficult aspect of blog security is to know what a potential security risk is. Luckily, there are tools to help you in the quest for a secure blog. In this recipe, I'm going to show you how to use the **WP Security Scan** plugin to scan your blog, get a listing of security problems, and fix them.

Getting ready

In order to scan your WordPress blog for security problems, you have to install the WP Security Scan plugin. This plugin can be downloaded by visiting the following link:

`http://wordpress.org/extend/plugins/wp-security-scan/`

I recommend creating a backup of both your database and files, as described earlier in this chapter. Install WP Security Scan by following the general plugin installation procedure described in Chapter 4.

How to do it...

Once installed, the plugin will scan the following:

- passwords
- file permissions

And perform the following actions:

- database security
- version hiding
- WordPress admin protection and security
- removes WP Generator META tag from the core code

On your WordPress dashboard, you'll find a new top-level tab titled **Security Scan**. This tab contains a submenu composing of the following five items:

1. **Security**: The first menu item is **Security**. As you can see in the upcoming screenshot, the **Security** option gives you a lot of useful information about your blog and server configuration, such as your **Server**, **Operating System**, **MYSQL Version**, **PHP Safe Modes**, and so on.

It also provides a particularly interesting tool, which is the database prefix switcher. If your tables' prefixes are the default `wp_`, then you'll see a red line towards the left of the page asking you if you'd like to change your database prefix. Having `wp_` as a prefix is a potential security risk, because many people use it. Therefore, this will be the first thing a hacker will try in order to hijack your blog.

The **Security** tab will also let you know about the WordPress version, and hide it from the source code.

Lastly, WP Security Scan will check for an `.htaccess` file in your `wp-admin` directory. It will also verify whether an **Administrator** account is available or not.

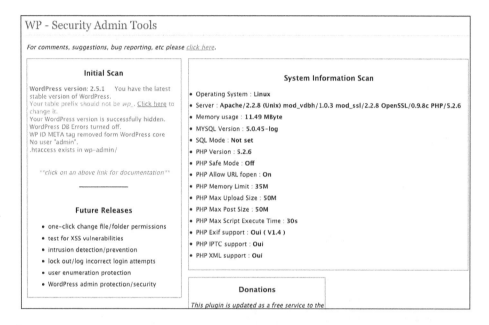

2. **Scanner**: The second tab is called **Scanner**. Basically, it automatically scans your blog file permissions to ensure that they do have the needed `chmods`. In case one of your directories doesn't have the needed chmod, then it appears in red. Just use your favorite FTP program to correct it.

WP - Security Scan

Name	File/Dir	Needed Chmod	Current Chmod
root directory	../	0755	755.
wp-includes/	../wp-includes	0755	755.
.htaccess	../.htaccess	0644	644.
wp-admin/index.php	index.php	0644	644.
wp-admin/js/	js/	0755	755.
wp-content/themes/	../wp-content/themes	0755	755.
wp-content/plugins/	../wp-content/plugins	0755	755.
wp-admin/	../wp-admin	0755	755.
wp-content/	../wp-content	0755	755.

3. **Password Strength Tool**: It is obvious that a strong password is necessary to protect your blog. Just enter the password that you'd like to use and the **WP-Password Tools** will tell you if it's **Weak**, **Average,** or **Strong**. It is recommended to use a password that is suggested to be **Strong** by the **Password Strength Tool**.

WP - Password Tools

Password Strength Tool

Type password: ●●●●●●●●●●●●

Minimum 6 Characters

Password Strength:

————————————— ▬▬▬ Strong

Strong Password Generator
Strong Password: !h!9ZMTIdx9IK@

4. **Database**: As we have seen earlier, having the default `wp_` table prefix is a potential security risk. Sure, you can rename your tables using phpMyAdmin, but the WP Security Scan can do that job for you as well. To do so, you first need to make sure to backup your database. Then, simply enter the prefix that you want to use in the text field input and click on the **Start Renaming** button as shown in the following screenshot. After a short bit of time, your tables will be renamed with the selected prefix.

WP - Database Security

Make a backup of your database before using this tool:

Change your database table prefix to mitigate zero-day SQL Injection attacks.

Before running this script:

- wp-config must be set to writable before running this script.
- the database user you're using with WordPress must have ALTER rights

Change the current: wp_   prefix to something different if it's the default wp_

Allowed Chars are all latin Alphanumeric Chars as well as the Chars – and _. (Start Renaming)

5. **Support**: As you can expect, the **Support** tab contains links to the plugin documentation and change log. In the future, more features need to be added.

How it works...

The WP Security Scan plugin is a very complete plugin as its role is to scan your WordPress installation in order to find potential security vulnerabilities.

The WP Security Scan plugin performs operations on:

- ▶ Passwords
- ▶ File permissions
- ▶ Database
- ▶ WordPress admin protection/security

Moreover, the plugin can hide your WordPress version by removing the WP Generator META tag from the core code.

There's more...

In the future, WP Security Scan developers plan to release the following functions:

- ▶ one-click change file or folder permissions
- ▶ test for XSS vulnerabilities
- ▶ intrusion detection and prevention
- ▶ lock out and log incorrect login attempts
- ▶ user enumeration protection
- ▶ `.htaccess` verification
- ▶ doc links

Denying comment posting on no referrer requests

Comment spam isn't a security risk, but a boring reality for every blogger. Sure, the **Akismet** plugin is very good at avoiding spam, but what about preventing spam instead of simply putting it in a specific queue?

Getting ready

In this recipe, I'm going to show you how to block comment postings to no referrer requests. This hack consists of looking up the referrer (the page from where the comment posting request comes) and blocking it, if the request doesn't come from your blog.

Most spammers don't even go to your blog to post their spam comments, they use a dedicated script or software to do it. As the request comes from a specific script instead of your blog, the following codes will block the spam comments.

How to do it...

There are two different ways to achieve exactly the same goal, which is blocking spam comment posting. The first method uses an `.htaccess` file and rewrites rules, and the second uses PHP. They're both great in my opinion, so you can pick the one you prefer.

You can adopt the `.htaccess` method by carrying out the following steps:

1. Create a backup of your `.htaccess` WordPress file, which is located in the root of your WordPress install.

2. Open it and insert the following code:

```
RewriteEngine On
RewriteCond %{REQUEST_METHOD} POST
RewriteCond %{REQUEST_URI} .wp-comments-post\.php*
RewriteCond %{HTTP_REFERER} !.*yourblog.com.* [OR]
RewriteCond %{HTTP_USER_AGENT} ^$
RewriteRule (.*) ^http://%{REMOTE_ADDR}/$ [R=301,L]
```

3. . Replace `yourblog.com`, on line 4, with your blog's URL.

4. Save the file and you're done.

You can adopt the PHP method by carrying out the following steps:

1. Open the `functions.php` file from your blog, and add the following piece of code:

```
function check_referrer()
{
    if (!isset($_SERVER['HTTP_REFERER']) ||
    $_SERVER['HTTP_REFERER'] == "")
    {
        wp_die( __('Please enable referrers in your browser, or,
        if you\'re a spammer, bugger off!') );
    }
}
add_action('check_comment_flood', 'check_referrer');
```

2. Save the `functions.php` file.

How it works...

Even if one code uses an `.htaccess` file and the other uses the PHP programming language, they work in exactly the same way:

1. They check out the referrer's request.

2. If the referrer doesn't exist, then it means that the request doesn't come directly from your blog. The user is then redirected to the home page (`.htaccess` code) or simply sees a blank page (PHP code).

8
SEO Tips and Tricks to Get More Visits

Having a blog is cool, but it doesn't have any value if people don't even know about its existence. Getting online exposure isn't easy and it can often cost a lot of money. Luckily, being featured on search result pages is absolutely free. However, the competition is very tough. Let's do a Google search about a topic. For example, let's use WordPress—there are more than 306,000,000 results! To make your blog stand out, you have to pay a lot of attention to **SEO** (**Search Engine Optimization**).

SEO is an ensemble of techniques dedicated to obtaining a higher rank in search results pages. While SEO for WordPress should be a book of its own, I'll show you some SEO basics, WordPress specific tips and tricks, and a few more techniques in this chapter.

In this chapter, you will learn:

- Optimizing your permalinks for SEO
- Migrating your permalinks safely
- Optimizing your title tag for SEO
- Creating Meta descriptions for your posts
- Avoiding duplicate content with a robot.txt file
- Adding a sitemap to your blog
- Using Google Webmaster Tools
- Pinging third party services
- Enhancing your WordPress blog SEO with the All in One SEO Pack plugin

Optimizing your permalinks for SEO

In my opinion, one of the most important things to ensure a good SEO is to use pretty URLs.

Pretty URLs use a technique called URL rewriting, which basically consists of transforming an URL with GET parameters to a human-readable URL.

Getting ready

For example, here's a dirty URL:

```
http://www.mysite.com/index.php?page=start&access=1&category=25
```

And now the same URL after some rewriting:

```
http://www.mysite.com/wordpress
```

It's a sure thing that the second one is really a lot more pretty and readable. With this rewritten URL, a reader, as well as a search engine crawler, instantly knows that this page talks about WordPress. How can you guess the subject with the non-rewritten URL?

How to do it...

1. By default, WordPress URLs aren't rewritten so as to avoid compatibility problems with non-Apache servers, and look like this:

   ```
   http://www.catswhocode.com/blog/?p=1526
   ```

2. To modify your blog permalink structure, carry out the following steps:
   - Login to your WordPress dashboard.
   - Go to **Settings | Permalinks**.
   - Select the permalink structure you'd like to use, or enter a custom structure.

3. As you can see in the following screenshot, WordPress offers the default structure and three others. You can also define a custom URL structure and enter it in the **Custom Structure** text field.

○ Default	http://www.catswhocode.com/blog/?p=123
○ Day and name	http://www.catswhocode.com/blog/2009/01/16/sample-post/
○ Month and name	http://www.catswhocode.com/blog/2009/01/sample-post/
○ Numeric	http://www.catswhocode.com/blog/archives/123
● Custom Structure	/%postname%

Which permalink structure is the best?

There are many online discussions about which permalink structure is the best. In my opinion, the best structure possible is the following one, using only the post title:

```
http://www.catswhocode.com/blog/blogging-
contest-win-the-blog-and-make-cash-ebook
```

4. To apply this structure, simply enter the following code in the **Custom Structure** text field:

```
/%postname%
```

5. Scroll down until you see the **Save changes** button and click on it. The permalink change is functional.

How it works...

The whole permalinks functionality uses the Apache `mod_rewrite` module that allows you to rewrite URLs.

In my opinion, there are many reasons why this structure is the best:

▶ It contains only the most important thing, that is, the post title. It keeps your URL short and readable.

▶ It doesn't include the category name in the URL, which is a big problem when your want to move a post from one category to another.

▶ It doesn't include any numbers (except if you have numbers in your post). Google reported they don't like numbers in URLs.

On the other hand, you may want to avoid this structure if you are habituated to using duplicated titles. In fact, if you're using the permalink structure that I just described and have a duplicated title, WordPress will automatically add a "-2" or "-3" at the end of the permalink, which isn't pretty at all.

There's more...

Now that I have shown you how to define permalinks in your WordPress blog, let's have a look at the possible structure tags. Then, I'll show you a method to further optimize your permalinks.

Structure tags reference

By default, WordPress allows you to use ten structure tags to personalize your permalink structure:

- **%year%**: The year the post has been published, for example, 2009

- **%monthnum%**: The month the post has been published, for example 01 for January

- **%day%**: The day the post has been published, for example 03 for the third day of the month

- **%hour%**: The hour the post has been published

- **%minute%**: The minute the post has been published

- **%second%**: The second the post havs been published

- **%postname%**: The name of the post

- **%post_id%**: The post ID, for example, 735

- **%category%**: The post category

- **%author%**: The post author

Structure tags can be mixed up together to create a personalized structure. Don't forget to use a separator between structure tags.

Following are the recommended separators:

- the slash (/)

- the underscore (_)

- the hyphen (-)

Further optimizing your permalinks

Now that you have a SEO friendly permalink structure for your blog, it is still possible to optimize it even more.

This trick is about getting rid of words which aren't needed in your URL. For example, if you wrote a post entitled "Creating user-defined RSS feeds in WordPress" then, the permalink created by WordPress should be:

```
creating-user-defined-rss-feeds-in-wordpress
```

In this permalink a few words such as "on" or "your" aren't necessary at all. Some others can be removed as well to keep your URL short and concise.

To do so, click on the **Edit** link under the post title as shown in the following screenshot:

After you click on the **Edit** link, the permalink will become editable. To continue with the previous example, you should replace

```
creating-user-defined-rss-feeds-in-wordpress
```

by:

```
google-search-wordpress
```

Once done, click on the **Save** button and your changes will be recorded.

Migrating your permalinks safely

As we discussed previously, permalinks are a must have for any serious blog because it will definitely increase your blog's SEO. In the previous recipe, I have shown you why some permalink structures are better than some others. Now the problem is what to do if you have chosen another structure prior to reading this book?

Of course, you can do the enormous mistake of modifying your permalinks as is. This is a very common beginner's mistake. While all looks fine, all links from social bookmarking sites, trackbacks as well as search engine results, are now broken and will only lead to your blog's 404 page.

By modifying permalinks this way, you can lose up to **40% of your traffic**!

Getting ready

Luckily, it is possible to change your permalinks the safe way by using an extremely useful plugin created by Dean Lee, called **Dean's Permalinks Migration Plugin**.

How to do it...

1. First, you have to download the plugin. It can be found at the following address `http://www.deanlee.cn/wordpress/permalinks-migration-plugin`.

2. Once you have the plugin, install it by following the standard plugin installation procedure as described in Chapter 4 of this book.

3. After you have successfully installed the Dean's Permalinks Migration Plugin, you'll find a new tab entitled **Permalinks Migration** under **Settings** on your WordPress dashboard.

4. Enter your **Old Permalink Structure** in the text field. Your old permalink structure can be found under **Settings | Permalinks**. After you have entered it in the text field, click on the **Update options** button.

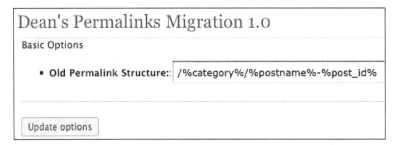

5. Now, you have to define your new permalink structure. Go to **Settings | Permalinks** and type the desired structure in the **Custom Structure** text field. Personally, I recommend using **/%postname%**.

6. That's it, you're done. Your permalinks have been modified but you'll not suffer any loss of traffic due to broken links on other web sites and search engines results pages.

How it works...

To avoid broken links in search engines results pages and other sites, the Dean's Permalinks Migration Plugin creates 301 redirect rules for every post that experimented a permalink change.

For example, if your previous permalink structure was:

```
/%category%/%postname%-%post_id%
```

It is now:

```
/%postname%
```

The Dean's Permalink Migration Plugin automatically creates a rule to redirect any URL having the old structure to the new structure. In fact if a search engine indexed one of your posts with the following URL:

```
http://www.catswhocode.com/blog/wordpress/integrate-google-
     search-on-your-blog-526
```

The visitor will be redirected to the following URL that will match your new permalink structure:

```
http://www.catswhocode.com/blog/integrate-google-search-on-your-blog
```

Optimizing your title tag for SEO

The `<title>` HTML tag, located within the `<head>` and `</head>` tags, is very important in terms of Search Engine Optimization. First of all it is the first thing that people will notice in search engine results, pages as well as for example, linking social bookmarking sites. Secondly, search engines give a lot of importance to the keywords in that tag when ranking pages. You guessed it; if you want your blog to be optimized for search engines, you have to make your `<title>` tag SEO-friendly. It may be hard to believe, but more than 80% of WordPress themes don't have a SEO optimized title tag by default.

Getting ready

Most WordPress themes display the title tag like this:

Blog name >> Category >> Post name

Let's do a Google search and look at the results:

BlogSecurity » Blog Archive » WordPress Security Whitepaper - [Traduire cette page]
BlogSecurity » Blog Archive » WordPress Whitepaper and ModSecurity now available in Espanol on 6 March, 2008 at 8:37 pm # ...
blogsecurity.net/wordpress/wordpress-security-whitepaper/ - 160k -
En cache - Pages similaires

BlogSecurity » Blog Archive » WordPress BlogWatch - [Traduire cette page]
BlogSecurity » Blog Archive » WordPress BlogWatch **BlogSecurity's WordPress** BlogWatch gives you a central location to check out the latest **WordPress ...**
blogsecurity.net/wordpress/blogwatch/blogwatch/ - 61k - En cache - Pages similaires
Autres résultats, domaine blogsecurity.net »

As you can see, these two posts, which are slightly different, are seen by Google as almost similar. Why? Because both of them have **BlogSecurity >> Blog Archive** in their title tag.

Sometimes the result of a non-optimized tag can be even worse: due to the useless blog name and category, the post names don't appear completely:

> **BlogSecurity » Blog Archive » WordPress** Scanner ... - [Traduire cette page]
> Last night I used the **WordPress** Scanner on two of my blogs and I got this message.dangerous-check-[0] PHP configuration file found in.
> wehuberconsultingllc.com/**wordpress**/2008/03/23/**blogsecurity-blog-archive-wordpress-scanner**/ - 43k - En cache - Pages similaires

In this recipe, I'm going to show you how to avoid these problems and create a perfectly SEO optimized title tag.

How to do it...

The solution to this problem is to modify the way your WordPress theme displays the title tag.

1. To do so, open the `header.php` file from your theme. The code used to generate the title tag might look like this:

   ```
   <title><?php bloginfo('name'); ?><?php if ( is_single() ) {
       ?> » Blog Archive <?php } ?><?php wp_title(); ?></title>
   ```

2. Once you have found it, replace it with the following:

   ```
   <title><?php if (is_home () ) { bloginfo('name'); }elseif (
       is_category() ) { single_cat_title(); echo ' - ' ;
   bloginfo('name'); }

   elseif (is_single() ) { single_post_title();}

   elseif (is_page() ) { bloginfo('name'); echo ': ';
       single_post_title();}

   else { wp_title('',true); } ?></title>
   ```

3. Save your `header.php` file. The modification has been made and your titles are now SEO-friendly.

4. You should wait some days until Google updates its index, and then your posts will appear on search engines results pages as shown in the following screenshot:

Top 10 **CSS buttons** tutorial list - [Traduire cette page]
14 Oct 2008 ... Sadly, even theses days many web pages still displays ugly **buttons**. Here's our " Top Ten" **CSS buttons** tutorial list, for giving your **buttons**, ...
www.catswhocode.com/blog/top-10-**css-buttons**-tutorial-list - 69k -
En cache - Pages similaires

How it works...

This code works by using WordPress conditional comments. It will generate title tags according to the following model:

- ▸ **If the visitor is on the blog homepage**: We'll display the blog name
- ▸ **If the visitor is on a category page**: We'll display the category name and the blog name
- ▸ **If the visitor is on an article page**: We'll only display the article title
- ▸ **If the visitor is on a static page**: We'll display the blog name, and the page title

Creating Meta descriptions for your posts

Believe it or not but by default, WordPress doesn't add any Meta descriptions to the posts you write. Sure, in terms of SEO, Meta descriptions aren't as important as they used to be, but good Meta descriptions are always a plus for both your visitors and search engines bots.

CSS Buttons is the Plug and Play Solution for Web Designers and ... - [Tra
CSS Buttons is the Plug and Play solution for web designers and developers looking to use accessible and flexible **buttons** on their web pages.
www.**cssbuttons**.net/ - 11k - En cache - Pages similaires

Getting ready

The HTML Meta tag is used to tell things about the web page to search engines crawlers. The description attribute is used to give a short description of the web page. Actually, it is supported by all major search engines such as Google, Yahoo, and MSN/Live search.

The bigger advantage of this tag is that it gives you control over the description that will be displayed on search engines' results pages, because the Meta description is often—but not always—used by search engines to give the visitor a brief description of the page. Without the Meta description tag, the search engine will usually take the first phrases from the page and use it as a description. You guessed it, using a custom description is better than letting Google create it for you.

In this recipe, you'll learn how to use WordPress post excerpts as Meta description.

How to do it...

1. Open `header.php` for editing.

2. Customize the blog description on line 2 and paste the following code between the `<head>` and `</head>` tags:

```php
<?php if (  (is_home()) || (is_front_page())  ) { ?>
<meta name="description" content="Blog description goes here" />
<?php } elseif (is_single()) { ?>
<meta name="description" content="<?php the_excerpt();?>"/>
<?php } ?>
```

3. Save `header.php`. Meta descriptions are now displayed on the head part of your WordPress posts and pages.

How it works...

Just like the previous recipe, this code is based on WordPress conditional tags. It first checks if the current page is the homepage or the front page. If the answer is yes, it will display your custom description. If the page is a post, the post excerpt that will be used as a Meta description.

There's more...

While the above code is good, it is still possible to make it better and get more control over the descriptions by using a custom field instead of the post excerpt.

A more sophisticated code by using custom fields

Like the previous code, the descriptions of this code have to be customized, and then the code will have to be pasted between the `<head>` and `</head>` tags, in your `header.php` file.

```php
<meta name="description" content="
<?php if ( (is_home()) || (is_front_page()) ) {
    echo ('Your main description goes here');
    } elseif(is_category()) {
        echo category_description();
```

```
    } elseif(is_tag()) {
        echo '-tag archive page for this blog' . single_tag_title();
    } elseif(is_month()) {
        echo 'archive page for this blog' . the_time('F, Y');
    } else {
        echo get_post_meta($post->ID, "Metadescription", true);
}?>">
```

To create a description for your posts, you'll have to create a custom field. Name it as **Metadescription** and enter your description as a value.

Avoiding duplicate content with a robot.txt file

As a WordPress user, you must have probably already experienced sites stealing your content and republishing elsewhere. This is called **duplicate content**. In order to fight this practice, Google uses some filters to detect similar contents. When the crawler detects two (or more) similar pages, only one of them will be shown in search engines results pages. Additionally, some sites providing duplicate content can experience page rank loss.

Unfortunately, it is quite easy to duplicate content from your WordPress blog. For example, feeds have the same content as posts. Same goes for the trackback URLs, and so on.

Getting ready

To avoid any kind of duplicate content, we have to use a file dedicated to that task. This file is a simple text file, named `robots.txt` that is located at the root of your WordPress blog. The file is used to tell the search engines crawlers that they don't have to follow or index some pages or directories.

How to do it...

1. To start, create a new blank file on your computer. Name it `robots.txt`.

2. Copy and paste the following code in the `robots.txt` file:

```
User-agent: *
Disallow: /wp-
Disallow: /search
Disallow: /feed
Disallow: /comments/feed
Disallow: /feed/$
Disallow: /*/feed/$
Disallow: /*/feed/rss/$
Disallow: /*/trackback/$
Disallow: /*/*/feed/$
```

```
Disallow: /*/*/feed/rss/$
Disallow: /*/*/trackback/$
Disallow: /*/*/*/feed/$
Disallow: /*/*/*/feed/rss/$
Disallow: /*/*/*/trackback/$
```

3. Save the file and upload it to your WordPress blog root.

How it works...

This `robots.txt` file prevents duplicate content by telling all search engines crawlers not to index search results, feeds, trackbacks URLs as well as `wp-*` directories.

There's more...

The `robots.txt` file is the most common technique used to avoid duplicate content on web sites. Though, as you can guess, this isn't the only way to protect your WordPress blog from search engine optimization problems caused by duplicate content.

PHP code to avoid duplicate content

In case you don't want to use a `robots.txt` file, you can use a single piece of code in your `header.php` file, to help preventing duplicate content. Please note though, that this method isn't as good as the one that uses the `robots.txt` file.

1. Open the `header.php` file from your theme.

2. Find the `<head>` and `</head>` tags.

3. Paste the following code between these tags:

```php
<?php if (is_home() && !is_paged()) || is_single() || is_page()
    || is_category()){
    echo '<meta name="robots" content="index,follow" />';
    } else {
        echo '<meta name="robots" content="noindex,follow" />';
```

4. And you're done! You have successfully implemented a rudimentary, but working, protection against duplicate content.

Adding a sitemap to your blog

A very important point in Search Engine Optimization is to be sure that search engines crawlers can access all of your blog pages and posts, so they all can be indexed. There are many ways to make sure that all of your pages and posts can be accessed by crawlers, such as creating an archive page template. Therefore, the best way to guarantee that crawlers can see and index all of your site pages is to use a sitemap.

According to `sitemaps.org`,

> *Sitemaps are an easy way for webmasters to inform search engines about pages on their sites that are available for crawling. In its simplest form, a Sitemap is an XML file that lists URLs for a site along with additional metadata about each URL (when it was last updated, how often it usually changes, and how important it is, relative to other URLs in the site) so that search engines can more intelligently crawl the site.*

In other words, using a sitemap doesn't guarantee that absolutely all your pages will be indexed by search engines (from my experience, even if a WordPress blog uses a sitemap there are 99% of chances that all their posts and pages will be indexed), but it gives crawlers some information to do a better job.

Getting ready

In this example, we're not going to manually create a sitemap. A really easier solution is to use the **Google (XML) Sitemaps Generator for WordPress** plugin. Before we move any further, let's have a look at the sitemap protocol first.

A sitemap is, as a RSS feed, a good old XML file, encoded in UTF-8. Here's an example sitemap:

```
<?xml version="1.0" encoding="UTF-8"?>
<urlset xmlns="http://www.sitemaps.org/schemas/sitemap/0.9">
<url>
    <loc>http://www.example.com/</loc>
    <lastmod>2005-01-01</lastmod>
    <changefreq>monthly</changefreq>
    <priority>0.8</priority>
</url>
<url>
    <loc>http://www.example.com/catalog?item=73&amp;desc=
        vacation_new_zealand</loc>
    <lastmod>2004-12-23</lastmod>
    <changefreq>weekly</changefreq>
</url>
<url>
<loc>http://www.example.com/catalog?item=74&amp;desc=
    vacation_newfoundland</loc>
    <lastmod>2004-12-23T18:00:15+00:00</lastmod>
    <priority>0.3</priority>
</url>
<url>
    <loc>http://www.example.com/catalog?item=83&amp;desc=
        vacation_usa</loc>
    <lastmod>2004-11-23</lastmod>
</url>
</urlset>
```

Let's have a look at the different attributes of this standard sitemap:

- ▶ `urlset`: Reference the sitemap protoc (required)
- ▶ `urn`: This is the parent tag for each URL of your site (required)
- ▶ `loc`: The URL of the page; must start with `http://` (required)
- ▶ `lastmod`: The date of last modification on the page; format must be YYYY-MM-DD (optional)
- ▶ `changefreq`: How frequently the content of the page is updated; values can be `always`, `hourly`, `daily`, `weekly`, `monthly`, `yearly`, or `never` (optional)
- ▶ `priority`: The importance of this URL relative to other URLs from your site; values range from 0.0 to 1.0 and the default priority is 0.5 (optional)

We need to follow a few general rules for creating sitemaps:

- ▶ Sitemaps must have an `.xml` extension.
- ▶ Sitemaps must be encoded using UTF-8.
- ▶ All data in a sitemap must be entity-escaped. For example, you can't include the minor than character (<). You have to use the related escaped entity, which is `&lt;`.
- ▶ A sitemap must always begin with the `<urlset>` tag, and close with the corresponding closing `</urlset>` tag.
- ▶ `<url>` and `<loc>` tags are mandatory.

Now that we briefly saw how the sitemap protocol works, let's install the sitemap plugin on your WordPress blog.

How to do it...

1. Get the **Google (XML) Sitemaps Generator for WordPress** plugin at `http://www.arnebrachhold.de/projects/wordpress-plugins/google-xml-sitemaps-generator/`. It is available in many different languages, such as Arabian, Brazilian, Portuguese, Bulgarian, Czech, Danish, English, French, German, Hungarian, Italian, Japanese, Korean, Polish, Portuguese, Russian, Slovenian, Spanish, Swedish, Simplified, Traditional Chinese, and Turkish.

2. Unzip the plugin on your hard drive and install it according to the standard plugin installation procedure as described in Chapter 4. **Do not** activate the plugin for now.

3. Use your favorite FTP program to create two files in your WordPress install root, namely, `sitemap.xml` and `sitemap.xml.gz`. Make these files writable.

4. Login to your WordPress dashboard, go to **Plugins** and activate the Google XML Sitemaps plugin.

5. Once done, you can check the plugin options by using the XML-Sitemap menu that you'll find under the **Settings** tabs.

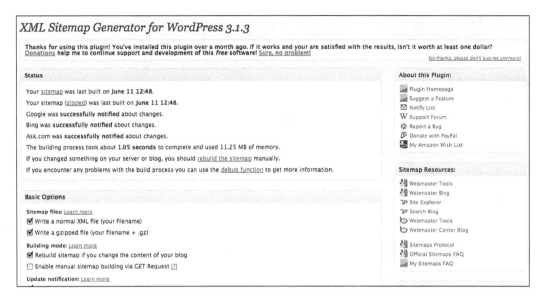

As you can see in the preceding screenshot, the plugin offers loads of options for you to customize.

The first thing to do is to click on the **Click here to generate your first sitemap** button. Once done, the page will tell you when the last sitemap was generated.

Don't forget to re-generate a new sitemap when you change something on your blog, such as switching the theme. Don't worry about blog updates, the plugin will automatically regenerate a sitemap when your blog content changes.

How it works...

After you have installed and activated the "Google (XML) Sitemaps Generator for WordPress" plugin on your blog, you probably noticed that it has a lot of options for you to configure. Let's take a look at theses options and their possible values.

The basic options are:

- **File types**: Specify the type of files to write. You should check both `sitemap.xml` and `sitemap.xml.gz`.
- **Construction mode**: Specify how and when the sitemap is updated. You should check **Generate sitemap when blog content changes**.
- **Notifications**: Specify which search engines have to be informed on your content updates. You should check all the options available. Please note that to enable Yahoo notifications, you'll have to provide a valid Yahoo ID. If you don't already have one, you can get one here: `https://developer.yahoo.com/wsregapp/`.

> ► **Advanced options**: Specify advanced options for sitemap creation. If you don't have any memory or MySQL errors, you should only check the last option to generate the sitemap without extra loading time when saving a post.

Adding more pages:

This allows you to add external pages to your blog sitemap.

Article priority:

You can choose how the priority parameter is defined. The possible options are:

- ► Same priority to all articles
- ► Number of comments
- ► Average comments

In my opinion, the number of comments is the best way to define article priority.

Sitemap path:

Simply defines where your sitemap is. Automatic detection is the option to be chosen.

Sitemap content:

Specify what should be included on your sitemap. Homepage, articles, and static pages have to be selected. Don't select archives, tags, and author pages as this could risk forming duplicate content.

Data to exclude:

Allows you to exclude categories or posts.

Excluded items

Excluded categories:
Note: Using this feature will increase build time and memory usage!

- ☐ News
- ☐ Photoshop
- ☐ Resources
- ☐ Uncategorized

Exclude posts:
Exclude the following posts or pages: List of IDs, separated by comma

Note: Child posts won't be excluded automatically!

Modify frequencies:

This allows you to modify the `<changefreq>` value of each post. Note that search engines consider this only as an indice.

Priorities:

This allows you to manually change the pages priority. You wouldn't have to edit any of these options, except if you deactivate the automatic priorities definitions.

Using Google Webmaster Tools

Now that you have created an XML sitemap, you can take advantage of a Google service called Google Webmaster Tools.

As the name says, Google Webmaster Tools is a set of tools and reports that allows you to see how your blog is ranked by Google and what you can do to enhance it.

How to do it...

Once you're connected to Google Webmaster Tools, the first thing to do is to add a site. To do so, carry out the following steps:

1. Click on the **Add Site** link to add your blog. Your blog will be instantaneously added, but you have to verify it in order to gain access to all features from Google Webmaster Tools.

2. To validate your blog, Google will give you the choice between a few methods. Personally, I prefer the **Upload HTML file** method. If you choose this, you'll be asked to upload a file on your server with a name that looks similar to `google87503ad5f1bcb124.html`.

3. Simply create a blank file on your computer, using a program such as TextEdit (Mac OS), Gedit (GNU/Linux), or Notepad (Windows). Do not add any content to. Save the file with the name that Google gave you, for example, `google87503ad5f1bcb124.html`.

4. Use your favorite FTP program to upload the file to your server. Place it in WordPress root.

5. Once done, go back to Google Webmaster Tools and click on the **Verify** button. That's all! You have successfully verified your blog!

How it works...

In order to use Google Webmaster Tools, you need a Google account. If you're already using one of Google services, such as Adsense or Gmail, then you have a Google account which can be used for Google Webmaster Tools. If you don't, you'll be prompted to create an account while accessing Google Webmaster Tools homepage.

Once you're connected using your Google account, you'll be able to access all tools and reports from this service.

Statistics	Indexing | Top search queries »	
Links	Home page crawl:	✓ Googlebot last successfully accessed your home page on **Apr 5, 2008**.
Sitemaps	Index status:	✓ Pages from your site **are** included in Google's index. See Index stats. ⑦
Tools		✓ Pages in your Sitemap(s) **are** included in Google's index. See Sitemaps overview.

Web crawl errors		
All errors for URLs in Sitemaps	⚠ 278	Details »
HTTP errors	✓ 0	--
Not found	⚠ 437	Details »
URLs not followed	⚠ 88	Details »
URLs restricted by robots.txt	⚠ 301	Details »
URLs timed out	✓ 0	--
Unreachable URLs	✓ 0	--
Total:	1104	

Find more answers in our help center, **including:**

How can I improve my site's ranking?
Why doesn't my site show up for a specific keyword?
Why is my page's location in the search results lower than before?

There's more...

Once your blog is verified, you can access all of the powerful features and reports provided by Google Webmaster Tools.

Overview

As the name says, the overview page displays basic information about your web site: when it was crawled by Google for the last time, how many errors the Googlebot has encountered, and the number of unreachable URLs.

Statistics

The statistics page gives you access to Google reports about your web site—top search queries, searches, what googlebot sees, crawl stats, and subscribers' stats.

Top search queries		
#	Query	Position
1	ipod touch	7
2	pidgin	10
3	telecharger deezer	7
4	extjs	5
5	demo	9
6	texte	18
7	theme	14
8	fichier flv	10
9	telecharger sur deezer	5
10	wget	7
More »		

In my opinion, the most interesting pages of the statistics section are crawl stats, which allow you to see your page rank per page, and subscribers' stats. These subcribers' stats tell you how many people are reading your RSS feeds through Google Reader, iGoogle, or Orkut. You can also see if people are subscribing to the main feed, or category/comment feed. The disadvantage is that people reading your feeds with other readers, such as Netvibes for example, aren't tracked.

Links

Guess what, the **Links** section is all about links. You'll be able to know almost everything about your internal and external link structure. For example, which amongst your blog page has the most links to external sites, and so on.

http://www.lyxia.org/	25 893
http://www.lyxia.org/blog/actualite/deezercom-apparement-ca-downloade-plein-pot-37	1
http://www.lyxia.org/blog/actualite/nouveau-theme-wordpress-cat-print-145	39
http://www.lyxia.org/blog/actualite/ubuntu-un-dock-pour-votre-bureau-42	15
http://www.lyxia.org/blog/author/jbj	1
http://www.lyxia.org/blog/category/featured	1
http://www.lyxia.org/blog/design/10-tutos-pour-creer-de-sublimes-boutons-en-css-311	95
http://www.lyxia.org/blog/design/30-effets-de-texte-avec-photoshop-269	83

Sitemaps

In the previous recipe from this chapter, I have shown you how to create an XML sitemap to help your blog SEO. In this section, I'll show you how Google lets you upload your own sitemap so that the Googlebot can make sure to crawl and index all pages of your blog.

Statistics provided include date of sitemap submission, last download, and how many URLs your sitemap contains.

Tools

Tools is the last section of Google Webmaster Tools and contains many very useful tools. The first is **Remove URL** which allows you to manually remove URLs of your blog from Google index. A tool to analyze your `robots.txt` file and ensure it isn't blocking good content is available. It also allows you to create a `robots.txt` file if you don't already have one.

The last tool provided is called **Enhanced image tool** and it allows you to label your images to make it easier to find when people are searching images on Google images.

Pinging third party services

If you're interested in SEO, then you are interested in getting more visitors. A good way to bring new readers is to ping third party services.

In this example, we're looking forward to third party services which are web sites such as Technorati or Google blog search. They are related blogs and they publish links to popular posts, as well as allow their visitors to search amongst blogs using a powerful search engine.

On the other hand, pinging is the action of notifying a web site that you have updated your content. After you have successfully pinged for example, Technorati, a crawler from that site will visit your blog and index your newest content, making it available to their visitors.

Getting ready

To ping a web site, you have to get the trackback URL. For example, Technorati trackback URL is `http://rpc.technorati.com/rpc/ping`.

Finding trackback or ping URLs isn't always easy as most web sites just display a link on their footer, or even worse, on a specific page. When I'm looking for a particular ping address, I found that the quickest way to get it is to launch a Google search on the web site where I'm looking for the ping URL.

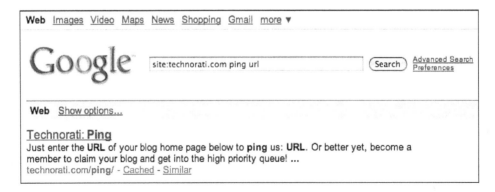

To perform a site specific search on Google, you have to use the following specific syntax:

```
site:technorati.com ping url
```

This way, you'll be able to find the ping URL of the web site as quickly as possible. Also, if the web site doesn't allow pings, you'll know it. In fact, it is quite hard to know if a particular web site allows pings or not.

How to do it...

Once you have the ping URLs of the web sites you'd like to notify about your new content, you have to configure WordPress so that it can automatically ping the selected web site when you write new posts or pages.

To do so, follow this short procedure:

1. Login to your WordPress dashboard and go to **Settings | Writing**.

2. Scroll down to the bottom of the page. You'll see a **Update Services** paragraph, featuring a text area for you to specify the URL that you'd like to ping.

Update Services

When you publish a new post, WordPress automatically notifies the following site update services. For more about this, see Update Services on the Codex. Separate multiple service URLs with line breaks.

```
http://rpc.pingomatic.com/
http://rpc.technorati.com/rpc/ping
http://blogsearch.google.com/ping/RPC2
```

Save Changes

3. Simply specify your ping URLs in the text area as shown in the preceding screenshot. Make sure to write each URL on a new line. Note that by default, WordPress pings Pingomatic.com.

4. Save your URLs by clicking on the **Save Changes** button. Your ping URLs are now recorded and will be notified when you'll add new posts.

How it works...

To notify other web sites about the changes that you made in yours, WordPress uses the **RPC (Remote Procedure Call)** technology that consists of an inter-process communication technology to send a signal to another web site. When a web site (one that accepts pings) receives a ping, it automatically executes a bunch of functions. For example, it can tell a crawler to visit and index the site which has pinged it, or it can post a comment to the blog. This is exactly how trackbacks or pingbacks work.

There's more...

Knowing how to ping third party services is a good thing, but it is obviously totally useless if you don't know which third party service you should ping.

Services to ping

Actually, many web sites accept pings from blogs to stay tuned with their activity. Not all of these are useful, therefore here is a list of what I consider would be good to ping:

- `http://blogsearch.google.com/ping/RPC2`
- `http://ping.bitacoras.com`
- `http://topicexchange.com/RPC2`
- `http://www.blogdigger.com/RPC2`
- `http://www.blogoole.com/ping/`
- `http://api.moreover.com/ping`
- `http://api.my.yahoo.com/rss/ping`
- `http://www.popdex.com/addsite.php`
- `http://ping.feedburner.com`
- `http://ping.syndic8.com/xmlrpc.php`
- `http://www.wasalive.com/ping/`
- `http://www.weblogues.com/RPC/`
- `http://blogping.unidatum.com/RPC2/`
- `http://rpc.blogrolling.com/pinger/`
- `http://rpc.icerocket.com:10080/`
- `http://rpc.technorati.com/rpc/ping`
- `http://rpc.weblogs.com/RPC2`
- `http://www.wasalive.com/ping/`
- `http://www.weblogues.com/RPC/`
- `http://blogping.unidatum.com/RPC2/`

Enhancing your WordPress blog SEO with the All in One SEO Pack plugin

As SEO is currently a very hot topic and many WordPress plugins dedicated to enhance your SEO are available. These aren't all that bad, and some of them are really good. All in One SEO Pack is one of these and has lots of features to help you with your blog SEO:

- Automatically optimizes your titles for search engines
- Generates META tags automatically
- Avoids the typical duplicate content found on WordPress blogs
- For WordPress 2.7 you don't even have to look at the options, it works out-of-the-box; just install.
- You can override any title and set any META description and any META keywords you want
- You can fine-tune everything
- Backward-compatibility with many other plugins, such as Auto Meta, Ultimate Tag Warrior, and others

Getting ready

The All in One SEO Pack plugin can be downloaded from `http://wordpress.org/extend/plugins/all-in-one-seo-pack/`. It is currently, one of the most downloaded WordPress plugins ever.

Once you have downloaded it, install it on your blog by using the standard plugin installation procedure as described in Chapter 4.

How to do it...

After you have successfully installed the All in One SEO Pack, you have to configure it a bit. To do so, follow these simple steps:

1. Login to your WordPress dashboard and navigate to **Settings | All in One SEO** to go to the general configuration page of the plugin.
2. You now have to complete the form.

   - **Home Title**: The title of your homepage. For example, on my blog `WpRecipes.com`, the homepage title is **WpRecipes.com : daily recipes to cook with WordPress**.
   - **Home Description**: Describe your blog in less than 250 words. This will appear on search engines result pages, so try to do your best.
   - **Home Keywords**: Enter keywords that describe your blog. Separate each keyword by a comma.
   - **Rewrite Titles**: Uncheck this box if you have followed the **Optimize your title tag for SEO**. Otherwise, let it remain checked. You can leave the default format for all fields, except the **Post Title Format**. Use the following for this one:

     ```
     %post_title%
     ```

This way, it ensures that only your blog post title will be displayed on search engines results pages, as seen in the **Optimize your title tag for SEO** recipe.

▸ **Use categories for META keywords**: Check this if you want to use your categories name in Meta keywords.

▸ **Use noindex for Categories**: Prevent search engine indexing on categories and avoid duplicate content. You should leave this checked.

▸ **Use noindex for Tag Archives**: Same as above, but for tags pages. You should check it.

▸ **Autogenerate Descriptions**: Check this if you want All in One SEO Pack to automatically create description from post excerpts. Uncheck this if you have followed the *Create a Meta description* recipe.

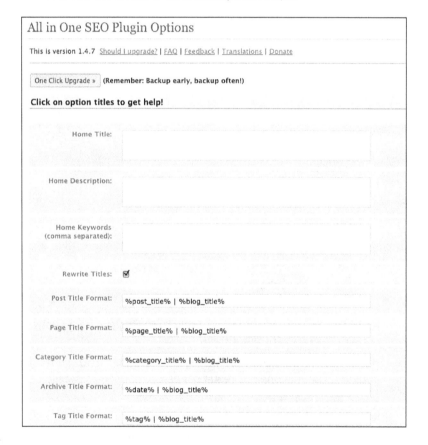

▸ **Additional Post Headers**: You can enter additional Meta tags here. You can even call stylesheets or JavaScripts.

▸ **Additional Page Headers**: Same as above with pages.

▶ **Log important events**: Check this and the SEO pack will create a log of important events (`all_in_one_seo_pack.log`) in its plugin directory which might help debugging it. Make sure this directory is writable.

There's more...

Another very good feature of the All in One SEO Pack is that it gives you the privilege to manually define post specific information as such as title (which will appear on the browser status bar as well as in search engines results), the Meta descriptions, and keywords.

You can also disable search engines on this post, simply by checking the checkbox.

All in One SEO Pack	
Click here for Support	
Title:	
Description:	
	0 characters. Most search engines use a maximum of 160 chars for the description.
Keywords (comma separated):	
Disable on this page/post:	☐

Five more tips for a better SEO

In this chapter, we saw many tips and tools to enhance a blog SEO and get more traffic from search engines. SEO is a big subject and there are many other things that you can do to improve your blog SEO. Here are five quick tips to help you get better rankings.

Get backlinks

In terms of SEO, the number of backlinks is the most important factor. Basically, the more backlinks you have, the better you'll be ranked by Google.

Getting a number of backlinks isn't always easy. If you produce good content, many other blogs will link you and make trackbacks to your blog. A good idea is to always link to your older posts when writing a blog post.

Use the proper h tags structure

It is very important that your WordPress theme use the proper h tag structure. Most themes do, but sadly I came across a few themes that use SEO non-friendly titles.

An example of a bad title is:

```
<strong><font color="#00FF00" size="24px">My blog post
    title</font></strong>
```

Instead, it should be:

```
<h1>My blog post title</h1>
```

With the following in your `style.css` file:

```
H1 {font-family: Arial; size: 24px;
color: #00FF00; font-weight: bold;}
```

Both of these code examples look the same, but the second is much better for SEO purposes. Do not hesitate to check your theme file and verify that they're using a proper h tag structure.

Make sure your blog is XHTML valid

Search engines love valid XHTML web sites. Having a valid XHTML blog means that it is coded according to the W3C recommendations.

To check if your blog is valid in terms of XHTML, go to `http://validator.w3.org/` and type your blog URL.

The results of the validation will appear as shown in the following screenshot. If you have any errors, the validator will tell you where they're located and why it is a problem.

	This document was successfully checked as XHTML 1.0 Strict!	
Result:	Passed	
Address :	http://www.wprecipes.com	
Encoding :	iso-8859-1	(detect automatically)
Doctype :	XHTML 1.0 Strict	(detect automatically)
Root Element:	html	
Root Namespace:	http://www.w3.org/1999/xhtml	

Make good use of keywords

A very important point for displaying your blog on the first page of search engines results is the use of keywords density. Let's say you wrote a post about SEO for WordPress blogs. You'll probably want your post to be featured in search engines results pages when someone searches keywords as such as 'WordPress SEO', or 'blog SEO'.

You have to make a keyword-rich title first. A good example would be SEO for WordPress blogs or Tips and tricks for a better WordPress SEO, which are concise, descriptive and contain the keywords you chose. Once done, it is also important that your post content contains the keywords. You don't need to repeat them on each paragraph of course, but make sure to use your keywords frequently.

Think about your permalinks twice

And last, but not least, a very important aspect of good SEO is your permalinks. Earlier in this chapter, I had shown you how to use a clean permalink structure to get more traffic. But even a good permalink structure can be further optimized.

When you're writing a post or page, WordPress allows you to edit the permalink for the current article. The idea is to have a good keyword density as well as getting rid of unnecessary words in your permalinks.

For example, if you have written a post entitled "Introducing my first WordPress theme", the default permalink will be

```
introducing-my-first-wordpress-theme
```

This permalink is bad because it contains unnecessary words, and not enough keywords. Think about the keywords people will search on Google. A really better permalink would be:

```
free-wordpress-theme-yourthemename
```

This way, you ensure that people will be able to find your post on search engines while searching for your theme. The fact of adding the "free" keyword is also important because many people will look for a **free** WordPress theme.

9
Making Money with WordPress

When you are reading blogs, you have probably come across at least one blog where the author says that he or she is making a lot of money online. In fact, many bloggers are making money with their blogs. Some people, who blog as a hobby, make enough money to pay their hosting. On the other hand, some Pro Bloggers make something like $3000 to $6000 a month online with their blog.

If you want to make money online, you've got to put in a lot of work, produce quality content, and promote your blog effectively. I'm not saying that the recipes contained in this chapter will make you a rich man or woman, but it can definitely improve your results with affiliate marketing, Adsense, or direct link sales.

In this chapter, you will learn:

- Integrating Adsense to your WordPress blog
- Displaying ads anywhere in your posts by using WordPress shortcodes
- Displaying Adsense ads to search engines visitors only
- Managing who sees ads
- Inserting ads in your RSS feeds
- Redirecting your WordPress RSS feeds to Feedburner
- Showing your blog stats to find advertisers
- Enhancing your Advertise page by adding Paypal subscriptions

Integrating Adsense to your WordPress blog

Many people already know Adsense, which is a Google advertising service. Google Adsense has many good points:

- Any sites, even the smallest, can signup and use Adsense on their pages
- You just have to copy and paste a code on your blog and then wait for money
- Google can send you a cheque or they can send money to your bank account directly, which is good for non-US residents

Google Adsense has its bad points as well:

- You'll have to wait to have earned at least $100 to get your first cheque.
- Most of the time, **CPC** (**Cost Per Click**) isn't very high.
- If you get a low CPM (**Cost Per 1000 Impressions**) you'll be "Smart Priced" which means less money for you. Later in this chapter I'll show you how to avoid this.

That's three good points as well as three bad points. You have nothing to lose and Adsense is easy to integrate. If you're looking to make money online, this is definitely a solution to consider, especially for a small or young blog.

Getting ready

The first thing to do is to get the Adsense code to display ads on your blog. To get the code, connect to `https://www.google.com/adsense` by using your Google account. If you don't have a Google account, creating one is necessary to take part in the Adsense program.

Once you're connected to Google Adsense you have to create a banner advertisement. To do so, click on the **Adsense Configuration** tab and select **Adsense for content**.

Then you'll be prompted to choose an ad size. Generally, people say that they have gotten better results by using the 300*250 or 250*250 ads, but it depends a lot on your blog layout. Integrating the 120*600 skyscraper on your blog sidebar sounds like a good idea too.

The last thing to choose is your ad's colors. There are no rules for this. Personally, I like to have ads which compliment my blog's color scheme, but some people like to use different colors in order to make their ads stand out.

Click on the **Continue** button when you're done choosing your ad style. As shown in the following screenshot, the next page will display your Adsense code. You will now have to paste somewhere in your blog theme files.

How to do it...

We can use the Adsense code in the following two ways:

Method 1: Using your Adsense code in your theme files

Now that you have your Adsense code, you can use it in your theme. To do so, follow these simple steps:

1. Open the file where you'd like the ads to be displayed, for example, `index.php` (your homepage), `sidebar.php` (your blog sidebar), or `single.php` (single posts pages).

2. Paste your Adsense code. Make sure that you're not inserting your Google Adsense code within PHP tags,(`<?php` and `?>`) as you'll probably get a parsing error.

3. Save the file. Your Adsense ads are now displayed on your blog. Please note that sometimes it can take up to 15 minutes until the first ads are displayed.

The second method is to use a text widget to display your Adsense ads.

Text widgets can't display PHP code, but they can display the JavaScript code used by Google Adsense.

1. Login to your WordPress dashboard and then go to **Appearance | Widgets**.

2. Add a **Text** widget to your sidebar and paste your Adsense code in the widget body.

3. You can also give a title to the widget, but this isn't recommended. Google Adsense terms and conditions don't allow text such as **Please visit** or **Recommended** above Adsense ads. You shouldn't give any title to the widget.

4. Click on the **Done** button of the widget to record your changes in this widget.

5. Don't forget to save your changes by clicking on the **Save Changes** button located below the widget list.

How it works...

Integrating Adsense into a WordPress blog is a simple operation. As I stated before, you only have to make sure not to insert your Adsense code with PHP tags in order to avoid the risk of PHP parsing errors.

Once the code is successfully inserted in your blog, Google will be able to display ads related to your blog's content.

Displaying ads anywhere in your posts by using WordPress shortcodes

In the previous recipe, I have shown you how to add Google Adsense ads to your blog by pasting them in your theme files, or by using a text widget. However, there's another really interesting option—being able to display ads anywhere on your posts by using a WordPress shortcode.

Getting ready

Introduced in WordPress 2.5, shortcodes are powerful, but yet are quite unknown WordPress functions. If you use forums such as phpBB or Vbulletin, you're probably familiar with the use of shortcodes, for example, to display an image. A basic shortcode looks like this:

```
[img]http://www.wprecipes.com/wp-content/themes/wprecipes
    /images/cat.png[/img]
```

As you can see in the preceding example, shortcodes let you use features such as inserting an image without having to use any HTML.

While this is very useful for people who don't know the HTML language, shortcodes can be used to achieve much more. In WordPress, they can be used, for example, to display an image gallery.

The most awesome thing with WordPress shortcodes is that you are able to create your own shortcodes. In this recipe, you'll learn to create a WordPress shortcode dedicated to inserting Adsense ads anywhere in your posts.

To execute this recipe, you'll need an Adsense code, as described in the previous recipe.

How to do it...

Shortcodes have to be created in the `functions.php` file from your theme. Follow these simple steps to get started:

1. Open your `functions.php` file.
2. Enter the following code. Don't forget to replace the Adsense code provided here by yours!

```
function showads() {
    return '<script type="text/javascript"><!--
    google_ad_client = "pub-XXXXXXXXXXXXXXXX";
    google_ad_slot = "4668915978";
    google_ad_width = 468;
    google_ad_height = 60;
```

```
//-->
</script>
<script type="text/javascript"
   src="http://pagead2.googlesyndication.com/pagead/show_ads.js">
</script>
';
}
add_shortcode('adsense', 'showads');
```

3. Save your `functions.php` file.

4. Edit any of your published posts. Switch the editor to HTML mode and insert the following shortcode anywhere in the post code, where you'd like Adsense to be displayed:

   `[adsense]`

5. Save your post and visit your blog. An Adsense ad is displayed where you inserted the `[adsense]` shortcode!

How it works...

Shortcodes are handled by a set of functions introduced in WordPress 2.5 called the "shortcode API". When a post is saved, post content is parsed and the shortcode API automatically transforms shortcodes into what they're supposed to be.

In this recipe, I started by creating a very simple PHP function, called `showads()`, to return my Adsense code. Then, I had to use the `add_shortcode()` function to create a shortcode by using the `showads()` function.

There's more...

Shortcodes are a very interesting and powerful WordPress function that can, for example, be used to display Google Adsense ads anywhere on your blog posts and pages. If you have read the first recipe of this chapter, you are probably thinking, 'What about pasting this WordPress shortcode directly in a sidebar widget?'

Inserting shortcodes into sidebar widgets

Using a custom WordPress shortcode to display your Adsense ads code is a lot quicker, and simpler, than pasting the whole code provided by Google. But sadly, by default, shortcodes can't be inserted into text widgets.

To change this, simply edit your `functions.php` file and paste the following code:

```
add_filter('widget_text', 'do_shortcode');
```

Now, you can insert WordPress shortcodes into sidebar widgets.

Displaying Adsense ads to search engines visitors only

In the first recipe of this chapter, when I described the pros and cons of using Google Adsense, I talked about a thing called "Smart Pricing", which basically causes you earn less money. In this recipe, I'm going to tell you what exactly "Smart Pricing" is and how to avoid being Smart Priced by Google.

Some blogs, or web sites, have a low **CTR** (**Click Through Rate**). CTR means the average clicks on your ads. For example, your CTR is 1% if your ads are displayed to 100 visitors and only one of them clicked on it.

The higher your CTR is, the more money Google earns from your ads. If they display some ads on your web site but no-one clicks on them, they don't earn any money and that space is a waste for them.

Due to the culture of secrecy that Google has, it is almost impossible to be sure on how **Smart Pricing** applies. Though, many Adsense users who have a CTR below 1 or 2 percent saw their Adsense earnings dramatically decrease. It appears that if you are "Smart Priced", clicks on your ads will only get about 10% of what they are worth.

The one thing that is sure is that **Smart Pricing** is definitely not smart at all. Since we can't do anything to fight it, the best thing to do is to try and avoid being Smart Priced.

Many search engine specialists agree on the point that it's mostly people coming from search engines who click on the ads. Your readership (such as RSS subscribers) don't often click on your ads—or they do it in order to make you earn money—because they are interested in your content, not the advertisements. People coming from search engines click on ads if they were looking for something they didn't find (or need more details) on your blog.

Getting ready

To execute this recipe, you'll need Google Adsense code like the one we had in the first recipe of this chapter.

How to do it...

In order to complete this recipe, we need to detect if the visitor comes from a search engine or not. I got these tips from my friend Stephen Cronin. You can read Stephen's blog at `http://www.scratch99.com/`.

1. Open your `functions.php` file for editing.

2. Enter the following function:

```php
function scratch99_fromasearchengine(){
  $ref = $_SERVER['HTTP_REFERER'];
  $SE = array('/search?', 'images.google.',
     'web.info.com','search.', 'del.icio.us/search', 'soso.com',
     '/search/', '.yahoo.');
     foreach ($SE as $source) {
  if (strpos($ref,$source)!==false) return true;
}


  return false;
}
```

3. Save functions.php and open the file where you want you Adsense ads to be displayed. Enter the following code:

```php
if (function_exists('scratch99_fromasearchengine')) {
  if (scratch99_fromasearchengine()) {
    echo '<script type="text/javascript"><!--
      google_ad_client = "pub-XXXXXXXXXXXXXXXX";
      google_ad_slot = "4668915978";
      google_ad_width = 468;
      google_ad_height = 60;
      //-->
      </script>
      <script type="text/javascript"
      src="http://pagead2.googlesyndication.com/
                        pagead/show_ads.js">
      </script>';
  }
}
```

4. Save your file and visit your blog. No ads are displayed because you aren't coming from search engine results pages. Now, Google your blog and ads are displayed!

How it works...

In this recipe, we first created a function called `scratch99_fromasearchengine()`, which is dedicated to look for the referrer. If the referrer is a search engine, this function returns `true`. Otherwise, it returns a `false`. Note that you can specify more search engines or sites by editing the `$SE` variable.

Then, we simply have to verify if the `scratch99_fromasearchengine()` function exists and if it returns `true`. If the answer is yes, then we can display our Adsense ads.

There's more...

With a bit of tweaking, we can modify this code to transform it into a shortcode and thus able to paste it everywhere in the posts. Follow these simple steps to do it:

1. Open your `functions.php` file for editing.

2. Paste the `scratch99_fromasearchengine()` function, which remains unchanged from the previous code:

```
function scratch99_fromasearchengine(){
  $ref = $_SERVER['HTTP_REFERER'];
  $SE = array('/search?', 'images.google.',
   'web.info.com','search.', 'del.icio.us/search', 'soso.com',
   '/search/', '.yahoo.');
  foreach ($SE as $source) {
    if (strpos($ref,$source)!==false) return true;
  }

  return false;
}
```

3. In the `functions.php` file, paste the `showadsSE()` function:

```
function showads() {
  if (function_exists('scratch99_fromasearchengine')) {
    if (scratch99_fromasearchengine()) {
    return '<script type="text/javascript"><!--
      google_ad_client = "pub-XXXXXXXXXXXXXXXX";
      google_ad_slot = "4668915978";
      google_ad_width = 468;
      google_ad_height = 60;
    //-->
```

```
    </script>
    <script type="text/javascript"
      src="http://pagead2.googlesyndication.com/pagead/
          show_ads.js">
    </script>
    ';
    }
  }
}
```

4. Finally, use the `add_shortcode` function to transform the `showadsSE()` function into a WordPress shortcode:

```
add_shortcode('adsenseSE', 'showadsSE');
```

5. Save the `functions.php` file and edit one of your published posts. Insert the following shortcode in it after changing the editor to HTML mode:

```
[adsenseSE]
```

6. You now have a WordPress shortcode to display Adsense ads to search engines visitors only!

Managing who Sees Ads

The previous recipe is a very good solution to try and avoid Google "Smart Pricing" by hiding Adsense to regular visitors and displaying it to search engine visitors only. Although this hack is good for achieving this goal, it is possible to have even more control over your ads and who sees these ads.

In this recipe, I'll show you a very interesting plugin for anyone who'd like to make money by blogging. It is called Who Sees Ads.

Getting ready

The principle of the Who Sees Ads plugin is exactly the same as the previous recipe. It allows you to make blogging money by displaying ads, but you can control who should see ads, and who shouldn't.

Unlike the hack, the Who Sees Ads plugin allows many different rules that define who can see ads and who cannot. For example, you can define that you should display ads only on posts older than 10 days, or only if the reader comes from a search engine.

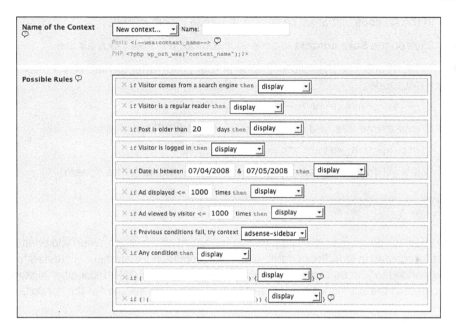

How to do it...

Simply follow these steps to install, configure, and use the "Who sees ads" plugin:

1. Grab a copy of the plugin at `http://planetozh.com/blog/my-projects/wordpress-plugin-who-sees-ads-control-adsense-display/`. Notice that a demo is available.

2. Install the plugin by following the standard plugin installation procedure, as described in Chapter 4.

3. Once the plugin is installed, you'll find a **Who sees ads** tab under **Settings** in your WordPress dashboard.

4. As the "Who sees ads" plugin is an advanced ad manager, you may be a bit disappointed by its numerous options as well as its specific jargon (contexts, and so on). Don't worry, it is easier than it looks!

5. The first thing you have to do is to create a context. A context can be posted as 'If the visitor comes from a search engine and the post is older than 10 days, then display ads'. As the two most popular contexts are 'If the visitor is a regular reader, don't display ads, otherwise do' and 'If the visitor comes from a search engine, display, otherwise don't display except if the post is older than 15 days', you can click on the related button on the top of the page, to create the context.

6. If none of the context fits your needs, you have to create your own context. Name it in the **Name of the Context** field and then drag and drop the available conditions (possible rules) to the **Active rules** container.

7. In the **Ad code** text area, paste your Adsense (or other) code.

8. Click on the **Save context** to save your context. It is now ready for use.

9. To insert ads, use the following code in your posts (after turning WordPress editor to HTML mode):

```
<!--wsa:context_name-->
```

10. In your theme files, you have to use the related PHP function :

```
<?php wp_ozh_wsa("context_name");?>
```

11. That's all! You can now manage who sees your ads, and who doesn't!

How it works...

The Who Sees Ads plugin is a very complex and advanced ad manager. When you create a context, it is recorded in WordPress database. A PHP conditional statement is created "on the fly" and appended to your theme files and posts. This code contains PHP conditional statements to make sure that the current visitor matches the conditions established in the context.

There's more...

Like any other very advanced plugin, Who Sees Ads has a lot of options created to fit any particular need. Now that you have learned how to install and configure this powerful plugin, let's have a look at the available option, from the basics to the advanced ones.

Global options

The Who Sees Ads plugin also allows you to set up global options such as what defines a regular reader, what is an old post, and so on.

Here are the possible options:

- **Old post**: The number of days after which a post is considered old
- **Regular reader**: How many pages a visitor must have seen in the last X days to be considered as a regular reader
- **Click safety**: If enabled, this option will not display any Adsense or Yahoo ads to the blog administrator
- **Date format**: You can choose to use two different date formats—the English mm/dd/yyyy or the French jj/mm/yyyy.

Once you're done with the global options, simply click on the **Update Options** button to save it.

Advanced conditions

You must have probably noticed that the last two lines of the context rules form are empty. This is due to the fact that you can define your own conditions, using PHP built-in functions, WordPress specific PHP functions, or even your own functions.

To use this part, you obviously have to know at least a bit of PHP. By default, it isn't possible to define your own conditions. You have to enable it first.

To do it, simply edit the plugin file and verify this line:

```
$wp_ozh_wsa['iknowphp'] = true;
```

If the previous variable is set to `false`, you have to set it to `true` before being able to create your own conditions.

Here are some examples of custom conditions, created by the "Who sees ads" plugin author. As you're gong to see, you can really do what you want with this tool.

- Inserting ads on all pages except the homepage using WordPress conditional tag `is_home()`:

- Displaying ads 30% of the time using the PHP built-in function `mt_rand()`:

- Displaying ads only to US readers using the "IP to Nation" plugin:

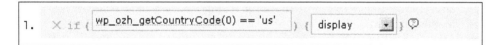

Inserting ads in your RSS feeds

When monetizing a blog, RSS feeds are definitely something to consider due to their current popularity. If you're using Feedburner, Google allows you to insert Adsense ads on your feed items if you have more than 500 RSS readers.

I see two bad points here—the first is obvious, if a blog is too young, or too small, and has less than 500 RSS readers, the blog owner simply cannot display any Adsense in his feed. The second bad point is that this system allows you to display only Adsense ads and not any other kind of ads such as affiliate marketing banners or direct sales ads.

Getting ready

Indeed, inserting ads on your RSS feed is a good way to get more affiliate sales, but this recipe can also be used if you have an important announcement to make to your readers. As an example, my blog `WpRecipes.com` currently has more than 2000 readers, so making an announcement on my RSS feed gets a lot of traffic.

In this recipe, you'll learn two ways to insert ads (or anything else) in your RSS feeds—the first is a hack, and the second is done by using a plugin.

How to do it...

As I mentioned, inserting ads in your RSS feed can be done by using a hack as well as using a plugin. Both solutions work exactly in the same manner, so just choose between either of these depending on whether you feel more comfortable with installing another plugin or inserting some lines of code in your theme `functions.php` file.

Let's try inserting ads into our RSS feeds using a hack.

Open your `function.php` file and insert the following code:

```
function insertRss($content) {
    if(is_feed()){
        $content = 'text before content'.$content.'<hr /><a
        href="http://www.wprecipes.com">Did you visited WpRecipes
        today?</a><hr />';
    }
```

```
       return $content;
}
add_filter('the_content', 'insertRss');
```

The simple hack consists of adding a filter to the `the_content()` function. The filter then checks if the current content is a RSS feed, and if it is, some content is appended to the `$content` variable that contains the post content.

Let's try inserting ads into our RSS feeds using a plugin.

Some people prefer using hacks while some others prefer using plugins.

The plugin we're going to use here is called RSS Footer and has been created by Joost de Valk, a well known developer in the WordPress community.

Follow these simple steps to install and use Joost's RSS Footer plugin:

1. Go to `http://yoast.com/wordpress/rss-footer/` and grab a copy of the plugin.

2. Install it following the standard plugin installation procedure, as described in Chapter 4.

3. Once the plugin has been successfully installed and activated, you'll find a RSS Footer option under **Settings**.

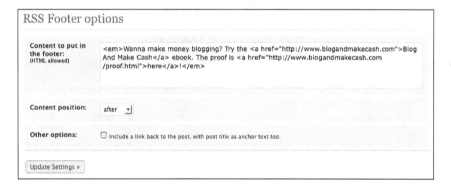

4. Simply type your message in the **Content to put in the footer** field. Of course, you can use HTML if you like.

5. Define where your custom message/advertisement should appear— on the top or bottom.

6. Click on **Update Settings**, and you're done!

How it works...

In this recipe, both the hack and the plugin work in the same manner.

After making sure that the visitor is on a RSS feed page by using the `is_feed()` conditional tag, the hack concatenates the `$content` variable (which contains your post content) to a custom prefix and suffix.

As a result, your `$content` variable now contains your blog post content and your custom text ad.

The plugin does the same thing as the hack, but with an easy installation and a nice form to define your ad title and link.

There's more...

Say if 95% of the bloggers are using Feedburner, it is possible that your RSS advertisement won't show up. In both the cases, using the hack or the "RSS Footer" plugin.

Solving problems with Feedburner

To solve this problem, just do the following:

1. First, ping Feedburner. To do so, point your browser at `http://www.Feedburner.com/fb/a/ping`. This should solve the problem.

2. If your RSS ad still doesn't appear, login to Feedburner.

3. Select the appropriate feed and click on the **Troubleshootize** tab.

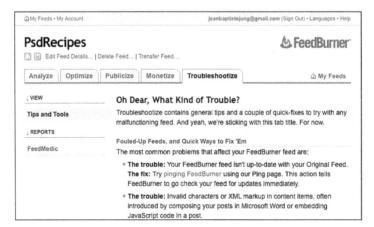

4. Scroll down the page until you see a button titled **Resync Now**. Click on it to re-synchronize your Feedburner feed.

> The Nuclear Option: "Resyncing" your feed
>
> As a last resort with a regular feed or a podcast, you can **resync** your feed. You should only resync if your feed is more than 1 hour out-of-date and pinging FeedBurner does not update it or your podcast files are not being turned into enclosures by our SmartCast service.
>
> Resync Now

Redirecting your WordPress RSS feeds to Feedburner

As I previously said, most bloggers use Feedburner for their RSS feeds. One of the good points of Feedburner is that you can display how many people are reading your blog daily, via RSS. This is, obviously, very good for finding potential advertisers because it gives the advertisers an idea about how popular your blog is.

Even if you edited your theme files and replaced WordPress feeds URL by your Feedburner URL, WordPress feeds are still active and you would be surprised to see how many people are subscribing to your "normal" feeds instead of your Feedburner feeds.

Getting ready

In this recipe, I'm going to show you how to make sure that all your RSS readers are tracked and counted by Feedburner by redirecting WordPress feeds to Feedburner. Like I did in the previous recipe, I'll show you both a hack and a plugin so you can choose the option that fits your blog the most.

How to do it...

As I said, redirecting your WordPress RSS feeds to your Feedburner account can be achieved both by using a hack or a plugin. There's no "better" solution, just choose the one you are the most comfortable with.

Let's lean how to redirect your WordPress RSS feeds to your Feedburner account using the first option, that is using a hack.

Proceed with the following steps to implement this hack on your blog:

1. Edit the `.htaccess` file, located at the root of your WordPress install. Make sure to **always backup** the `.htaccess` file before editing it.

2. Insert the following code in your `.htaccess` file. Don't forget to modify the last line with your own Feedburner URL.

```
<IfModule mod_rewrite.c>
  RewriteEngine on
  RewriteCond %{HTTP_USER_AGENT} !feedburner      [NC]
  RewriteCond %{HTTP_USER_AGENT} !FeedValidator [NC]
  RewriteRule ^feed/?([_0-9a-z-]+)?/?$ http://feeds2.feedburner.
    com/wprecipes [R=302,NC,L]
</IfModule>
```

3. Save the `.htaccess` file. And you're done!

Let's lean how to redirect your WordPress RSS feeds to your Feedburner account using the second option, that is using a plugin.

In this method, we redirect our feeds to Feedburner using the **Feedburner plugin**, by John Watson. Carry out the following steps to install and configure the plugin.

1. Download the plugin from `http://flagrantdisregard.com/Feedburner/`.

2. Install it as described in the standard plugin installation procedure in Chapter 4.

3. Once the plugin is installed, configure its option in the **Feedburner Configuration**, available under **Plugins**.

Feedburner Configuration

Redirect my feeds here:

http://feeds2.feedburner.com/Wprecipes

Redirect my comments feed here:

http://feeds2.feedburner.com/Wprecipes

Advanced Options

☐ Do not redirect category or tag feeds

☐ Append category/tag to URL for category/tag feeds (*http://url_category*)

Enregistrer »

4. In the **Redirect my feeds here**, type your Feedburner feed URL.

5. In the **Redirect my comments feed here**, you can specify a specific Feedburner URL for your comments feed, you can leave it blank to continue using WordPress feeds for comments, or type any other feed URL where you'd like your comments' feeds to be redirected.

6. You can also define if you'd like your tags or category feeds to be redirected to your Feedburner feed or not.

How it works...

To achieve this hack, I have used a rewrite rule to redirect anything which has feed in its URL to my Feedburner URL. On line 3 and 4, I have specified that this redirection should not be applied to Feedburner and Feedvalidators user agents. This ensures that Feedburner itself still can access my WordPress feed to update my Feedburner feed. With this hack, any WordPress feeds (posts, comments, category-specific feeds, and so on) are redirected to my unique Feedburner URL. Depending on the size of your blog and the number of subscribers, you can easily get 50 to 300 "new" subscribers to your Feedburner RSS feed.

John Watson's "Feedburner plugin" provide an easy to use interface designed to redirect your WordPress RSS feeds to your Feedburner feeds. When you submit your feed information, the plugin automatically creates 301 redirections for you.

There's more...

It's not easy to say if the hack is better than the plugin, or vice-versa. Personally, I try to avoid plugins whenever I can, but in this case, the Feedburner plugin offers more options than the hack.

Plugin versus hack

In fact, the plugin allows you to specify if you'd like to redirect comments, tags, and categories feeds while the hack automatically redirects it to your main Feedburner feed.

My advice is that if you plan to redirect all feeds to an unique Feedburner feed, you should use the hack. In any other cases, the plugin is probably what will give you the best results.

Showing your blog stats to find advertisers

In this chapter, I talked a lot about Google Adsense since it is a good way to make money using a blog. However, another way to make money is to sell ads directly from your blog. You can sell text links or banners. One of the most popular ad format in blogging is probably the 125*125 px ad, which are usually displayed in most blogs.

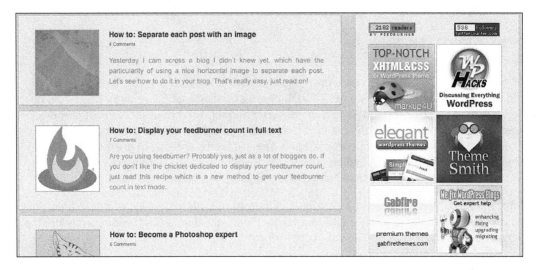

Getting ready

Selling ads directly from your blog isn't always easy because you have to find advertisers yourself. There are networks that sell ads, but they'll take up a lot of your profits so it isn't really the best idea.

In order to attract advertisers on your blog, a good idea is to publish your blogs stats; RSS readers, Pagerank, Number of comments, and so on.

In this recipe, you'll learn how to create a stunning "Advertise" page to proudly display your blog stats by using the "Automatic Blog Stats" plugin to attract new advertisers.

How to do it...

1. Get the Automatic Blog Stats plugin at the `http://www.improvingtheweb.com/automatic-blog-stats/`.

2. Install it by following the standard plugin installation procedure as described in Chapter 4.

3. Once the plugin is installed and activated, create a new page. Call it **Advertise**.

4. Turn the editor to HTML mode and insert the following code:

Thanks for your interest in advertising on XXXX.com. below, you'll find available spots, prices, as well as blog stats.

```
<h2>Spots availables/prices</h2>
```
We are currently selling text links as well as 6 125*125 px banner spots. Monthly prices are $25 for text links and $50 for banners.

```
<h2>Blog Stats</h2>
Google Pagerank: [pagerank]
Feedburner subscribers: [Feedburner_subscribers]
Alexa rank: [alexa_rank]
Technorati authority: [technorati_authority]
Technorati rank: [technorati_rank]
Users: [user_count]
Published posts: [post_count]
Published pages: [page_count]
Comments: [comment_count]
Trackbacks: [trackback_count]
Average comments per post: [avg_comments_per_post]
Categories: [category_count]
Tags: [tag_count]
Links: [link_count]
Google backlinks: [google_backlinks]
Yahoo backlinks: [yahoo_backlinks]
Delicious bookmarks: [delicious_bookmarks]
```

5. Save and publish the page. Your **Advertise** page is now available and advertisers can have a clear view of your blog potential.

Some stats...

- Google PageRank: 5 / 10
- Technorati authority: 5
- Technorati rank: 985,111
- Alexa rank: 493,820
- Compete stats
- Quantcast stats
- Newsletter + RSS feed subscribers: 30
- Google backlinks: 28
- Yahoo backlinks: 976
- Del.icio.us bookmarks: 7
- Posts: 131
- Pages: 4
- Comments: 498
- Trackbacks: 66
- Average comments per post: 4
- Tags: 274

How it works...

As you have probably noticed, the "Automatic Blog Stats" plugin makes an intensive use of WordPress shortcodes to allow you to display your stats in the easiest possible way.

One of the best features of this plugin is the fact that it auto updates on a daily basis so you will never have to manually check or modify the stats provided by the plugin.

There's more...

Now that I shown you a very effective way to convince advertisers to advertise on your blog, you'll quickly have to display their ads. The most common ad format nowadays is the 125*125 px squares.

Managing your 125*125 px ad spots

Most of the time, 125*125 px banners ads are displayed in the sidebar so the best way to manage and display them is a WordPress Widget. In Chapter 4, I have talked about "ISIS Ads Management", a WordPress Widget written by Michael Pierard and dedicated to managing and displaying 125*125 px banners ads.

Enhancing your Advertise page by adding Paypal subscriptions

If you have applied the previous recipe to your blog, you now have a stunning **Advertise** page with your blog stats. That's great, but how can the advertisers pay you? Sure, you can use a contact form and ask advertisers to email you and then send them your paypal ID. But going ahead with this procedure has a few cons:

- **Long and boring procedure**: The advertiser must send you an email, then you have to send him your paypal ID, get the payment, and finally put the link/banner online.

- **Can turn off some potential advertisers**: The long procedure described above can turn off advertisers. Most of them are busy and don't have any time to lose. They want their banner up quickly.

- **No reminder when paid time is passed**: If your advertiser paid for one month advertising on your blog, neither you nor him will be reminded when the time has passed. The result could be that you forget the date and leave the ad online longer than scheduled.

Getting ready

The solution to the problem described is Paypal subscriptions. Basically, when an advertiser subscribes to your Paypal subscription, he'll pay the subscription sum each month until he cancels it. This means that you'll never miss a payment date, and the advertiser just has to subscribe one time. Of course, the advertiser can stop his subscription whenever he wants.

To allow Paypal subscriptions on your WordPress blog, you need a Paypal account. If you don't already have a Paypal account, just go to `www.paypal.com` and create one.

How to do it...

Once you have your Paypal account ready, follow these steps to create a subscription for your ads.

1. First, login to Paypal. Once there, click on the **Merchant Services** that you can see on the horizontal menu.

2. In the **Merchant Tools** page, look for the **PayPal Website Payments Standard** title. There's a box below entitled **key features**. Click on the **Subscriptions & Recurring Payments** button.

3. Now, you have to fill a form to specify your subscription options.

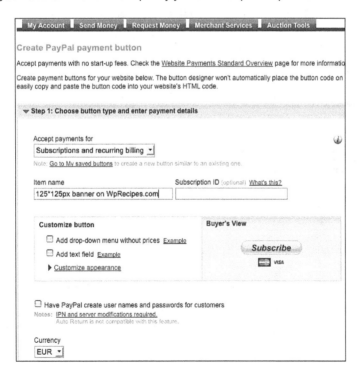

4. You need to fill in the following details:

- ❏ **Accept payments for**: Leave the default, **Subscriptions and recurring billing**.

- ❏ **Item name**: Give a name to the subscription, as shown in the preceding example.

- ❏ **Subscription ID**: You can leave this field blank.

- ❏ **Customize button**: Only useful if you wish to allow the advertiser to define the ads own price.

- ❏ **Currency**: The currency you'd like to display your prices in. You should choose USD, as US dollars are a de facto standard on the Internet, except if your blog is in any other language than English.

- ❏ **Recurring amount to be billed**: The sum you'd like to get each month.

- ❏ **Billing cycle**: Choose the time period for the subscription. On most blogs, 1 month is the default.

- ❏ **After how many cycles should billing stop**: You should leave the field as is, however you can decide that the subscription should be cancelled automatically after X cycles.

5. You should leave all of the other options as default.

6. Once done, click on the **Create button** button. The next page will provide your custom subscription code as seen in the following screenshot:

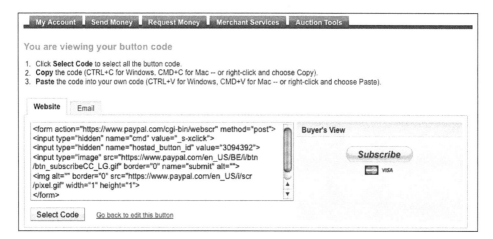

7. Copy the given code and login to your WordPress dashboard.

8. Edit your **Advertise** page and paste the code and you are done! Your advertisers can now subscribe to your blog and automatically pay on a monthly basis for their ads.

There's more...

If you followed this recipe, your blog will now have a Paypal button allowing advertisers to subscribe for advertising on your blog. This is great, but how can they unsubscribe?

Telling advertisers how to unsubscribe

Obviously, you don't want your advertisers to unsubscribe, but it is only fair to let them know how they can do it should they want to. Also, specifying how to cancel a subscription will leave a positive impression on the advertiser. Of course, he or she wouldn't want to do business with a dishonest person that may want to fool him.

Here is the quick "How to unsuscribe" text I use on my blogs. Feel free to use it on your own blog:

```
<h2>How To View/Cancel a Paypal Subscription</h2>

<ol>
<li>Login in to your Paypal account where the subscription
    was made.</li>
<li>Click <strong>Basic Search</strong> in
    the <b>History</b> drop-down menu.</li>
<li>Select <strong>Subscriptions</strong> in the
    <strong>View:</strong> drop-down menu.</li>
<li>Click <strong>Search</strong>.</li>
<li>Select the <strong>Details</strong> link next to the
    subscription you want to cancel.</li>
<li>Scroll down and click the <strong>Cancel
    Subscription</strong> button.</li>
</ol>
```

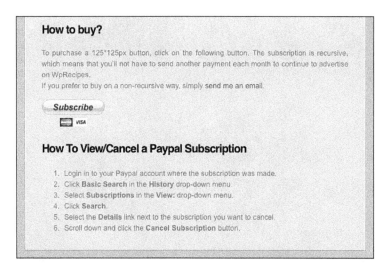

10
Enhancing User Experience

As a blogger, I read loads of blog posts every day, on many different blogs. Very often, I'm scared to see how many blogs have a non user-friendly interface.

How often does it happen that you can't click on the logo to go back to the blog homepage, or can't find what you're looking for by using the search engine? It is a well known fact that in blogging the content is king, but a nice, user friendly interface makes your blog look a lot more professional, and much easier to navigate.

In this chapter, I'll show you what can be done for enhancing user experience and makeing your blog a better place.

In this chapter, you will learn:

- ▶ Replacing the Next and Previous links by a paginator
- ▶ Highlighting searched text in search results
- ▶ Using the CSS sliding doors technique within WordPress
- ▶ Creating a dropdown menu for your categories
- ▶ Adding a breadcrumb to your theme
- ▶ Displaying related posts
- ▶ Displaying tabs on your sidebar

Replacing the Next and Previous links by a paginator

When a web site, or blog, publishes lots of articles on a single page, the list can quickly become very long and hard to read. To solve this problem, paginations were created. Pagination allows displaying 10 articles (for example) on a page. If the user wants, then he or she can go to the next page, or click on a page number to directly go to the related page.

I definitely don't understand why WordPress still doesn't have a built-in pagination system. Instead, at the bottom of each page you'll find a **Next** link to go to the next page, and a **Previous** link to go back. This works fine when you're on page two and would like to go to page three, but what if you're on page one, and remember a very interesting article which was located on page eight? Are you going to browse page per page until you find your article? The answer is yes, because you don't have the choice. You can't jump from page one to page eight.

In this recipe, I'll show you how to integrate a pagination plugin in your WordPress blog theme. One very good point of this recipe is that the plugin file is embedded in your theme, so if you're a theme designer, you can distribute a theme which has a built-in pagination system.

Getting ready

To execute this recipe you need to grab a copy of the WP-PageNavi plugin, which can be found at `http://wordpress.org/extend/plugins/wp-pagenavi/`. I have used version 2.40 of the Wp-PageNavi plugin in this example.

Once you have downloaded it, unzip the zip file but don't install the plugin yet.

How to do it...

1. Open the WP-PageNavi directory and copy the following files into your WordPress theme directory (For example, `http://www.yourblog.com/wp-content/theme/yourtheme`).

    ▸ `wp-pagenavi.php`
    ▸ `wp-pagenavi.css`

2. Once done, edit the `index.php` file

You can do the same with other files, such as `categories.php` or `search.php` as well.

3. Find the following code (or similar) in your `index.php` file:

```
<div class="navigation">
<div class="alignleft"><?php next_posts_link('Previous
    entries') ?></div>
<div class="alignright"><?php previous_posts_link('Next
    entries') ?></div>
</div>
```

4. Replace that with the following code:

```
<?php
include('wp-pagenavi.php');
if(function_exists('wp_pagenavi')) { wp_pagenavi(); }
?>
```

5. Save the `index.php` file. If you visit your blog now, you'll see that nothing has changed. This is because we have to call a function in the `wp-pagenavi.php` file.

6.. Open this file and find the following code (line 61):

```
function wp_pagenavi($before = '', $after = '') {
global $wpdb, $wp_query;
```

7. We have to call the `pagenavi_init()` function, so let's do this in the following way:

```
function wp_pagenavi($before = '', $after = '') {
global $wpdb, $wp_query;
pagenavi_init(); //Calling the pagenavi_init() function
```

8. Now, save the file and refresh your blog. The pagination is now displayed! This is great news, but the pagination doesn't look good.

9. To solve this problem, you simply have to integrate the `wp-pagenavi.css` file that you copied earlier in your theme directory. To do so, open the `header.php` file from your theme and paste the following line between the `<head>` and `</head>` tags:

```
<link rel="stylesheet" href="<?php echo TEMPLATEPATH.'/pagenavi.
    css';?>" type="text/css" media="screen" />
```

10. Visit your blog homepage one more time. The pagination looks a lot better. You may have to edit the `wp-pagenavi.css` file in order to make your pagination look and feel fit your blog style.

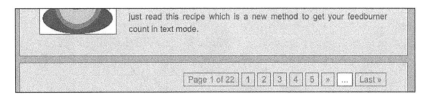

just read this recipe which is a new method to get your feedburner count in text mode.

Page 1 of 22 | 1 | 2 | 3 | 4 | 5 | » | ... | Last »

How it works...

In this recipe, you have discovered a very useful technique that I often use on my blogs, or in the themes that I distribute—the integration of a WordPress plugin into a theme.

When the plugin is integrated into your theme as I have shown you in this example, there's no activation process needed. All of the work is done directly from the theme.

The WP-PageNavi plugin itself works by using two values—the number of posts to be displayed per page and the first post to be displayed. Then, it executes the relevant query to WordPress database to get the posts.

The pagination bar is calculated by using the total number of posts from your blog, and then dividing this value by the number of posts per page.

One good point of this technique is that the plugin is integrated in your blog and you can redistribute the theme if you want. The end user will not have to install or configure anything.

Highlighting searched text in search results

I must admit that I'm not a big fan of the WordPress built-in search engine. One of its weakest features is the fact that searched text aren't highlighted in the results, so the visitor is unable to see the searched text in the context of your article.

Getting ready

Luckily, there's a nice hack using regular expressions to automatically highlight searched text in search results. This code has been created by Joost de Valk who blogs at www.yoast.com.

How to do it...

This useful code is definitely easy to use on your own blog:

1. Open your search.php file and find the following:

```
echo $title;
```

2. Replace it with the following code:

```php
<?php
$title = get_the_title();
$keys= explode(" ",$s);
$title = preg_replace('/('.implode('|', $keys) .')/iu',
    '<strong class="search-excerpt">\0</strong>',$title);
?>
```

3. Save the `search.php` file and open the `style.css` file. Append the following line to it:

```
strong.search-excerpt { background: yellow; }
```

4. You're done. Now, the searched text will be highlighted in your search results.

How it works...

This code is using PHP regular expressions to find the searched terms in the text returned by WordPress. When an occurrence has been found, it is wrapped in a `<strong>` HTML element.

Then, I simply used CSS to define a yellow background to this element.

Search Results for: wordpress

« Older posts

Seemore is the new Less

Less, my small but perfectly formed **WordPress** plugin, has changed its name and is now called Seemore. A different plugin called Less has been added to the **WordPress** Plugin Directory, so I finally decided to change my plugin's name to something marginally less confusing.

14 February 2009 | *By Bennett* | *Topics: WordPress* | *Comments*

Seemore: a WordPress plugin

Latest version is 1.1, released on 14 February 2009.
Seemore is a **WordPress** plugin that makes reading posts more intuitive for your many readers. With Seemore, when readers click a (more...) link they see the full article on the screen, not just the part after the (more...).

I write these **WordPress** plugins because I enjoy doing it, [...]

14 February 2009 | *By Bennett* | *Topics: General* | *Comments (1)*

Using the CSS sliding doors technique within WordPress

The CSS "sliding doors" technique allows you to create sophisticated tabs for your menus. Sadly, WordPress doesn't allow you to use a `<span>` element in the `wp_list_pages()` and `wp_list_categories()` functions.

Getting ready

In order to achieve this very cool menu, you first need to have a bit of knowledge about the CSS sliding doors technique, and the necessary images.

If you need to know more about this technique, you should consider reading this article: http://www.alistapart.com/articles/slidingdoors/

If you don't already know this awesome technique here's a quick example to get you started:

Let's start by building a typical navigation list:

```
<ul id="nav">
<li><a href="#">link n°1</a></li>
<li><a href="#">link n°2</a></li>
<li><a href="#">link n°3</a></li>
</ul>
```

If we use CSS to apply background images to our links in order to make this menu look prettier, we'll quickly come across a big problem. We must add a fixed width to the links otherwise, the image will be truncated for a very short link, or the link will overflow the image if its width is too long.

That's why sliding doors are very useful. We just have to add a span element inside the link. Then, in our CSS, assign a different background image to both the span element and the link.

```
<ul id="nav">
<li><a href="#"><span>link n°1</span></a></li>
<li><a href="#"><span>link n°2</span></a></li>
<li><a href="#"><span>link n°3</span></a></li>
</ul>
```

Our CSS should look like this:

```
#nav a, #nav a:visited {
    display:block;
}
#nav a:hover, #nav a:active {
    background:url(images/tab-right.jpg) no-repeat 100% 1px;
    float:left;
}
#nav a span {
    float:left;
```

```
    display:block;
}
#nav a:hover span {
    float:left;
    display:block;
    background: url(images/tab-left.jpg) no-repeat 0 1px;
}
```

Please note, as this is only an example, the preceding CSS isn't complete and only shows how to apply the sliding doors hack.

How to do it...

I have read many WordPress users who modified their WordPress core files to achieve this technique. I have already talked about how modifying core files is a bad idea. Instead, let's use some regular expressions (as we did in the previous recipe!) to obtain the desired effect.

Carry out the following steps to apply this hack to pages:

1. Open your `header.php` file (or any file you'd like to apply this technique).

2. Look up for the following function:
   ```
   <ul>
   wp_list_pages();
   </ul>
   ```

3. Replace it by the following code:
   ```
   <ul id="nav">
   <li><a href="<?php echo get_option('home');
       ?>/"><span>Home</span></a></li>
   <?php echo preg_replace('@\<li([^>]*)>\<a([^>]*)>(.*?)\<\/a>@i',
       '<li$1><a$2><span>$3</span></a>', wp_list_pages('echo=
       0&orderby=name&exlude=181&title_li=&depth=1')); ?>
   </ul>
   ```

4. Save the `header.php` file and open the `style.css` file. Finally append the following styles:
   ```
   #nav a, #nav a:visited {
   display:block;
   }
   #nav a:hover, #nav a:active {
   background:url(images/tab-right.jpg) no-repeat 100% 1px;
   float:left;
   }
   #nav a span {
   ```

```
float:left;
display:block;
}
#nav a:hover span {
float:left;
display:block;
background: url(images/tab-left.jpg) no-repeat 0 1px;
}
```

You may have to style it a bit more in order to make it compatible with your blog's look and feel, but basically, you're done.

Of course, you can easily apply the previous hack to categories. Follow these simple steps:

1. Open your `header.php` or `sidebar.php` file, depending on where your categories are listed.

2. Look up for the following function:

```
<ul>
wp_list_categories();
</ul>
```

3. Replace it by this code:

```
<ul id="nav">
<li><a href="<?php echo get_option('home');
    ?>/"><span>Home</span></a></li>
<?php echo preg_replace('@\<li([^>]*)>\<a([^>]*)>(.*?)\<\/a>@i',
    '<li$1><a$2><span>$3</span></a>', wp_list_categories('echo=
    0&orderby=name&exlude=181&title_li=&depth=1')); ?>
</ul>
```

4. Save the file and paste these styles to your `style.css` file:

```
#nav a, #nav a:visited {
    display:block;
}
#nav a:hover, #nav a:active {
    background:url(images/tab-right.jpg) no-repeat 100% 1px;
    float:left;
}
#nav a span {
    float:left;
    display:block;
}
```

```
#nav a:hover span {
    float:left;
    display:block;
    background: url(images/tab-left.jpg) no-repeat 0 1px;
}
```

How it works...

As you can see, applying this hack to categories or pages is almost the same. Basically, you just have to change the `wp_list_categories()` function for categories and `wp_list_pages()` for pages.

To embed `<span>` elements in the list, this code uses the PHP `preg_replace()` function with the `wp_list_categories()` function as a second argument. In the `wp_list_categories()` function, the `echo=0` parameter is specified, which means that the function doesn't print the result on screen but instead returns the result to be used in PHP.

Creating a drop-down menu for your categories

Do you use a lot of categories along with their sub-categories? If so, using a drop-down menu is a nice way to categorize content, especially on larger sites. However, giving a quick access to the categories or sub-categories to readers can become a pain.

Over the years, the drop-down menu has become very popular on the Internet. In this recipe, I'm going to show you how to create your own drop-down menu for your WordPress blog categories.

Getting ready

The menu you are going to create will first list your pages, and then at last a tab called **Categories** will obviously list your categories.

This menu is achieved only with XHTML and CSS. No JavaScript is needed (unless you want to maintain compatibility with it commonly referred to as IE6) to ensure the best SEO possible for your WordPress blog.

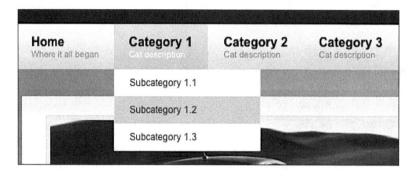

How to do it...

In order to make this recipe more readable, I have divided it in 3 steps—the PHP and the HTML, the CSS, and the JavaScript for IE6 compatibility.

Let's start with the first step, that is PHP and HTML.

Open the `header.php` file from your theme and paste the following code where you'd like your drop-down menu to be displayed:

```
<ul id="nav" class="clearfloat">
<li><a href="<?php echo get_option('home'); ?>/"
    class="on">Home</a></li>
<?php wp_list_pages('title_li='); ?>
<li class="cat-item"><a href="#">Categories</a>
<ul class="children">
<?php wp_list_categories('orderby=name&title_li=');
$this_category = get_category($cat);
if (get_category_children($this_category->cat_ID) != "") {
    echo "<ul>";
    wp_list_categories('orderby=id&show_count=0&title_li=
    &use_desc_for_title=1&child_of='.$this_category->cat_ID);
    echo "</ul>";
    }
?>
</ul>
</li>
</ul>
```

The purpose of this code is to make a list of all our pages and subpages, as well as a last list element named **Categories**. When a reader hovers on one of the top-level menu, the subpages (or categories) are displayed.

Let's go ahead with step two, that is the CSS.

Open the `style.css` file from your theme and paste the following styles:

```css
#nav{
    background:#222;
    font-size:1.1em;
}
#nav, #nav ul {
    list-style: none;
    line-height: 1;
}
#nav a, #nav a:hover {
    display: block;
    text-decoration: none;
    border:none;
}
#nav li {
    float: left;
    list-style:none;
    border-right:1px solid #a9a9a9;
}
#nav a, #nav a:visited {
    display:block;
    font-weight:bold;
    color: #f5f5f4;
    padding:6px 12px;
}
#nav a:hover, #nav a:active, .current_page_item a, #home .on {
    background:#000;
    text-decoration:none
}
#nav li ul {
    position: absolute;
    left: -999em;
    height: auto;
    width: 174px;
    border-bottom: 1px solid #a9a9a9;
}
#nav li li {
    width: 172px;
```

```
    border-top: 1px solid #a9a9a9;
    border-right: 1px solid #a9a9a9;
    border-left: 1px solid #a9a9a9;
    background: #777;
}
#nav li li a, #nav li li a:visited {
    font-weight:normal;
    font-size:0.9em;
    color:#FFF;
}
#nav li li a:hover, #nav li li a:active {
    background:#000;
}
#nav li:hover ul, #nav li li:hover ul, #nav li li li:hover ul, #nav
li.sfhover ul, #nav li li.sfhover ul, #nav li li li.sfhover ul {
    left: auto;
}
a.main:hover {
    background:none;
}
```

You may have to tweak this code a bit to match up to your blog's look and feel, for example, by adjusting colors. Once you are finished, simply save the file.

Let's go ahead with step three, that is JavaScript (optional).

I'm not going to teach you something new here since, Internet Explorer 6 is a totally obsolete, crappy, and buggy browser. Sadly, many peoples are still using it and you may want to make sure that your blog is IE6 compliant.

Modern browsers as such as Safari, Firefox, Opera, and even Internet Explorer 7 will not have any problem with the :hover pseudo-class on li elements. But you guessed it, it is asking too much from the IE6.

1. To ensure backward compatibility on your WordPress blog, create a new file and call it dropdown.js.

2. Put this code in the dropdown.js file:

```
<![CDATA[//><!--
sfHover = function() {
var sfEls = document.getElementById("nav").
    getElementsByTagName("LI");
for (var i=0; i<sfEls.length; i++) {
    sfEls[i].onmouseover=function() {
        this.className+=" sfhover";
    }
```

```
sfEls[i].onmouseout=function() {
    this.className=this.className.replace(new
        RegExp(" sfhover\\b"), "");
    }
}
}
if (window.attachEvent) window.attachEvent("onload", sfHover);
//--><!]]>
```

3. Save the `dropdown.js` file and upload it to your `wp-content/themes/yourtheme` directory.

4. Open `header.php` and add the following line within the `<head>` and `</head>` HTML tags:

```
<!--[if lte IE 6]>
<script type="text/javascript" src="<?php bloginfo(
    'template_url');?>/dropdown.js"></script>
<![endif]-->
```

That's all! Your blog now has a very professional looking drop-down menu.

How it works...

As IE6 cannot deal with `:hover` pseudo-classes on `<li>` elements, this small piece of code automatically ads a new CSS class, named `sfhover` to `<li>` elements when they are hovered over. When the mouse goes out of the top level element, a new function is executed, using a regular expression to remove the `sfhover` class.

There's more...

Now that I have shown you're the principle of creating a drop-down menu, you can use what you have just learned to create various kinds of menus. As an example, let's see how to re-use the previous code and create a very nice horizontal drop-down menu.

Creating a horizontal drop-down menu

As you'll notice by observing the code, there's a lot of similar things between this code and the one that you saw earlier.

Part 1: PHP and HTML

Simply copy this code where you want the menu to be displayed, for example, in your `header.php` file:

```
<ul id="nav2" class="clearfloat">
<li><a href="<?php echo get_option('home'); ?>/"
    class="on">Home</a></li>
```

```php
<?php wp_list_categories('orderby=name&exlude=181&title_li=');
$this_category = get_category($cat);
if (get_category_children($this_category->cat_ID) != "") {
    echo "<ul>";
    wp_list_categories('orderby=id&show_count=0&title_li=
    &use_desc_for_title=1&child_of='.$this_category->cat_ID);
    echo "</ul>";
    }
?>
</ul>
```

Part 2: The CSS

In modern drop-down menus, CSS are a very important part. Indeed, in this example it is CSS that display our menus horizontally.

Paste the following code in your `style.css` file:

```css
#nav2{
    background-color: #202020;
    display: block;
    font-size:1.1em;
    height:50px;
    width:100%;
}

#nav2, #nav2 ul {
    line-height: 1;
    list-style: none;
}

#nav2 a ,#nav2 a:hover{
    border:none;
    display: block;
    text-decoration: none;
}

#nav2 li {
    float: left;
    list-style:none;
}

#nav2 a,#nav2 a:visited {
    color:#109dd0;
    display:block;
    font-weight:bold;
```

```
        padding:6px 12px;
    }


#nav2 a:hover, #nav2 a:active {
    color:#fff;
    text-decoration:none
}


#nav2 li ul {
    border-bottom: 1px solid #a9a9a9;
    height: auto;
    left: -999em;
    position: absolute;
    width: 900px;
    z-index:999;
}


#nav2 li li {
    width: auto;
}


#nav2 li li a,#nav2 li li a:visited {
    color:#109dd0;
    font-weight:normal;
    font-size:0.9em;
}


#nav2 li li a:hover,#nav2 li li a:active {
    color:#fff;
}


#nav2 li:hover ul, #nav2 li li:hover ul, #nav2 li li li:hover ul,
    #nav2 li.sfhover ul, #nav2 li li.sfhover ul, #nav2 li li li.
    sfhover ul {
    left: 30px;
}
```

Once you have added theses lines to your `style.css` file and saved it, your WordPress blog will feature a very cool horizontal menu for displaying your categories.

Part 3: (Optional) JavaScript

As usual, if you want to maintain backward compatibility with Internet Explorer 6, you'll have to use the Javascript code that you have already seen in the previous example.

Adding a breadcrumb to your theme

When you're looking for a way to improve your blog's usability, a breadcrumb is definitely an option to consider.

According to Wikipedia,

> *Breadcrumbs typically appear horizontally across the top of a webpage, usually below any title bars or headers. They provide links back to each previous page that the user navigated through in order to get to the current page, for hierarchical structures usually the parent pages of the current one. Breadcrumbs provide a trail for the user to follow back to the starting/entry point of a website. Generally, a greater than (>) is used as hierarchy separator, although other glyphs can be used to represent this.*

Getting ready

There are many different solutions available in order to implement a breadcrumb on your WordPress blog, such as hacks and plugins. In this recipe, I'm going to show you how to use the Yoast Breadcrumb plugin, that in my opinion, is the best solution available. But don't worry if you're a hack fanatic, or if you're just curious to know about how breadcrumbs work; I'll also be explaining how to create a breadcrumb without using a plugin.

How to do it...

Using Yoast Breadcrumbs is definitely easy. Follow these simple steps to install and configure it on your own blog:

1. Go to `http://yoast.com/wordpress/breadcrumbs/` and download the plugin. In this example, I have used the 0.7.4 version of the plugin.

2. Follow the standard plugin installation procedure, as described in Chapter 4, to install and activate the Yoast Breadcrumb plugin.

3. Once the plugin is activated, you have to insert a code snippet on your blog. Open the files where you want your Breadcrumb to appear (in my opinion, it is a good thing to enable the breadcrumb at least in `single.php`, `page.php`, `search.php`; but you can also enable it in some custom pages that you may have on your blog, such as your archive page or author pages).

4. Paste the following code where you want the breadcrumb to be displayed:

```php
<?php if ( function_exists('yoast_breadcrumb') ) {
    yoast_breadcrumb('<p id="breadcrumbs">','</p>');
} ?>
```

5. Save the files and visit your blog. Breadcrumbs are now displayed. Looks very nice, doesn't it? Note that if you want to style your breadcrumb with CSS, you can do so by using the p#breadcrumb ID.

The Yoast Breadcrumb plugin allows you to print your breadcrumb directly on your blog page or post. You may also want to get the result only as a PHP variable for further tweaking.

The following code will create a $breadcrumb variable that will contain your breadcrumb:

```php
<?php if ( function_exists('yoast_breadcrumb') ) {
    $breadcrumbs = yoast_breadcrumb("","",false);
} ?>
```

How it works...

The Yoast Breadcrumb plugin takes three arguments. Let's see in detail what these are:

- $prefix: The code that your breadcrumb should be prefixed with. Defaults to an empty string.

- $suffix: The code that should be added on the back of your breadcrumb. Defaults to an empty string.

- $display: If set to false, will return the breadcrumb path instead of echoing it. Defaults to true.

The Yoast Breadcrumbs plugin works by getting information from your blog, such as the post (or page) name, the category where the post belongs to, and the blog homepage URL. This can be seen in the following example:

```
Home > Category name > Sub-Category name (if any) > Post name
```

The Yoast Breadcrumbs plugin will then dynamically create a clickable breadcrumb, which allows visitors to click on any of the links to go on to the selected section of your blog.

For example, if a visitor clicks on the **Category name** link in the above Breadcrumb, he or she will be redirected to that category page. Clicking on **Home** will lead him or her to your blog homepage.

There's more...

As we have already discussed, it can sometimes be better to use a hack instead of a plugin. Now that we saw how to easily add a breadcrumb to your WordPress blog by using the excellent "Yoast breadcrumbs" plugin by Joost de Valk, let's see how we can create a breadcrumb on our own.

Using a hack to display breadcrumbs

One more time, WordPress conditional tags will be very useful. With them, we'll be able to know easily if the page displayed by a visitor is an article, a page, or a category archive.

Then, we'll have to use the right functions to show the site's hierarchy. Nothing difficult here, WordPress has all of the functions that we need to get links to the homepage, articles, and single pages.

Simply paste this code in the `functions.php` file of your theme:

```php
function the_breadcrumb() {
    if (!is_home()) {
        echo '<a href="';
        echo get_option('home');
        echo '">';
        bloginfo('name');
        echo "</a> » ";
        if (is_category() || is_single()) {
            the_category('title_li=');
            if (is_single()) {
                echo " » ";
                the_title();
            }
        } elseif (is_page()) {
            echo the_title();
        }
    }
}
```

Now, when you'll want to display breadcrumbs, simply use `the_breadcrumb()` function:

```php
<?php the_breadcrumb(); ?>
```

Displaying related posts

Guess what your readers will do when they finish reading one of your posts? 90% of them simply leave without even trying to see if you have any interesting related articles. It is a well known fact that the typical Internet user doesn't spend a lot of time on a web site: however, a few tips can increase your chance to have longer visits and maybe new RSS subscriptions. One of them is to display related posts at the end of your articles.

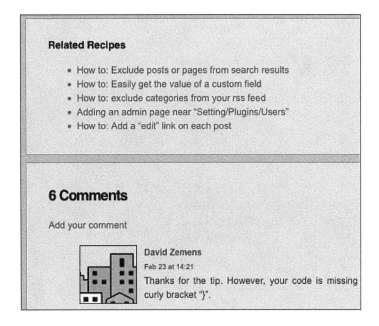

Getting ready

The easiest way to display related posts on your WordPress blog is to use the "WordPress Related Posts" plugin (Version 1.0). This plugin is compatible with WordPress 2.3 and later versions. You can use it with any theme.

How to do it...

To display related posts, follow these simple steps:

1. Get your copy of the "WordPress Related Posts" at the following URL `http://wordpress.org/extend/plugins/wordpress-23-related-posts-plugin/`.

2. Install the plugin by following the standard plugin installation procedure as described in Chapter 4.

3. Once the plugin is installed successfully, login to your WordPress dashboard and go to **Settings | WordPress Related Posts** to configure the plugin.

Related Posts Options...

WordPress Related Posts Plugin will generate a related posts via WordPress tags, and add the related posts to feed.

Related Posts Preference

Related Posts Title:	Related recipes
When No Related Posts, Dispaly:	Text: 'No Related Posts' ▾
No Related Post's Title or Text:	
Limit:	
Exclude(category IDs):	
Other Setting:	☐ Auto Insert Related Posts ☐ Related Posts for RSS ☐ Display Comments Count ☐ Display Post Date

(Update Preferences »)

Available options are:

▸ **Related Posts Title**: Enter **Related posts** or any other title in this tab

▸ **No Related Posts, Display**: What to display if no related posts are found

▸ **No Related Post's Title or Text**: Text to be displayed if no related posts are found

---

> ▸ **Limit**: Limit of posts to be displayed simultaneously

> ▸ **Exclude (category IDs)**: Categories to be excluded

> ▸ **Other Setting**:

>> ❑ **Auto Insert Related Posts**: Automatic insertion of related posts

>> ❑ **Related Posts for RSS feeds**: Display related posts in your RSS feed

>> ❑ **Display Comments Count**: Display the number of comments

>> ❑ **Display Posts Date**: Display the date of the posts

4. After you have configured the plugin to work the way you want, simply open your `single.php` file and insert the following line of code where you want your related posts to be displayed:

```php
<?php wp_related_posts(); ?>
```

How it works...

The "WordPress Related Posts" plugin executes some SQL queries based on tags. For example, if you tag a post with the `cats` tag and have two other posts tagged with `cats`, you can be sure that these two posts will be shown as **related** in the first post.

 If the plugin doesn't seem to work properly, the first thing to check would be to make sure that your posts are tagged.

Displaying tabs on your sidebar

There are a lot of things that you can add in your blog sidebar such as Blogroll, Feedburner suscribers, categories, 125*125 pixels ads, and more. The problem is, your sidebar becomes quite lengthy which isn't visually appealing. And to make it worse, not too many people will scroll down your blog to see what is available at the very bottom of your sidebar.

Getting ready

You can create a tabbed sidebar by using some custom HTML, CSS, and JavaScript codes. But the easiest solution is to use the "Fun With Sidebar Tabs" plugin, by Andrew Rickmann. The latest version of the plugin is 0.5.4. The plugin author has stopped maintaining it, but the plugin has been tested for its compatibility with WordPress versions up to 2.8. So, there's no particular reason that the plugin will stop working properly for higher versions, but there's no guarantee either.

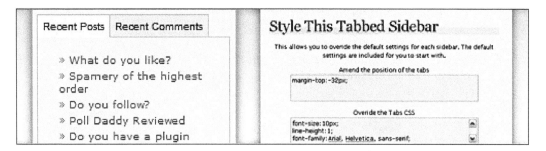

How to do it...

The "Fun With Sidebar Tabs" plugin can be installed easily. Just follow these steps to get started.

1. Go to `http://wordpress.org/extend/plugins/fun-with-sidebar-tabs/` and download your copy of the plugin.

2. Install it on your blog by following the standard plugin installation procedure as described in Chapter 4.

3. Once the plugin is installed and activated, go to **Appearance | Widgets** on your WordPress dashboard. You can then use either the **Fun with Sidebars** widget (by adding each **Tabbed Sidebar** widget into your main sidebar) or you can simply insert the following tag anywhere in your theme files:

   ```
   <?php the_tabbed_sidebar(1); ?>
   ```

How it works...

The "Fun With Sidebar Tabs" plugin adds a new widget-ready sidebar which displays the widgets in it as tabs, instead of a list. It adds a widget and a template tag, so that it can be inserted wherever it needs to be.

11
Make your Blog Stand Out

This is the last chapter of the book. In the previous chapters, we have learned about a lot of plugins, hacks, and tips to help us get a very professional blog that has almost every ingredient to succeed.

In this last chapter, we are going to learn some tips and tricks which I have learned since I started blogging.

In this chapter, you will learn:

- Rewarding your commentators to get more comments
- Adding a print stylesheet to your blog
- Using WordPress as a photoblog
- Creating an iPhone-friendly version of your blog
- Integrating a forum in your WordPress blog

The number of comments is definitely a proof of a blog's popularity. When a blog has an average of 25 to 30 comments per post, we tag the blog to be popular. Most bloggers like to receive comments. However, this is also a quality that most advertisers look at before buying advertising spots.

To get comments, of course, you have to provide good and valuable content—nobody can help you with that but yourself. However, there's also something you can do to get more comments, for example, rewarding your commentators.

Rewarding your commentators to get more comments

By default, the links left in the comments have a `rel="nofollow"` attribute automatically added by WordPress. According to Wikipedia, `nofollow` is an HTML attribute value used to instruct some search engines that a hyperlink should not influence the link's target ranking in the search engine's index. It is intended to reduce the effectiveness of certain types of search engine spam, thereby improving the quality of search engine results and preventing spamdexing from occurring.

In other words, any link pointing to a site provides a **PageRank** to the site. PageRank is used by Google to assign a numerical weight to each element of a hyperlinked set of documents—such as the World Wide Web—with the purpose of **measuring** its relative importance within the set. If a link has a `rel="nofollow"` attribute, it will not provide any PageRank to the linked site.

How to do it...

In order to reward commentators it is, in my opinion, a good idea to get rid of this `rel="nofollow"` attribute on links. This way, your commentators will gain some PageRank when they'll leave comments on your blog. This is a good reason for them to comment, because a lot of web site or blog owners are trying to enhance their site SEO that way.

Let's use the NoFollow Free pugin in order reward your commentators to get more comments.

In order to remove the `rel="nofollow"` attribute on comments links; the Nofollow Free plugin does a good job. The `rel="nofollow"` attribute can be easily removed by editing the WordPress core files—but as I previously said, editing any file from WordPress core isn't generally a good idea.

Carry out the following steps to install the NoFollow Free plugin and get rid of the `rel="nofollow"` attribute:

- Visit the link, `http://wordpress.org/extend/plugins/nofollow-free/` and download your copy of the NoFollow Free plugin.
- Install the plugin by following the standard installation procedure for plugins, as described in Chapter 4.
- Once the plugin has been activated, log in to your WordPress **Dashboard**, and go to **Settings | NOFF**—in order to customize the nofollow Free plugin settings.

NoFollow Free

If you would like to use the Top Commenters widget you can find it in Presentation -> Widgets menu

Select NOFF language

English ▾

Select if you want to remove "nofollow" attribute from comment author and/or comment body text link and/or registered users link

Do you want to remove nofollow from: (default Author | Registered Author | Registered Comment)

☑ Author Link

☐ Comment text Link

☑ Registered Author Link

☐ Registered Comment text Link

Set how many comments the author must have written before I remove the nofollow. (default 10)

Set 0 to always remove the nofollow. | 0 |

Set how many comments the REGISTERED author must have written before I remove the nofollow. (default 5)

Set 0 to always remove the nofollow. | |

Here you can set some comma separated words. If one or more of these words are found in the text comment I put b spammers.

The following settings can be edited about the NoFollow Free plugin, as shown in the preceding screenshot:

- Language: The NoFollow Free plugin is a multilingual plugin. It supports English, Spanish, Italian, German, Turkish, Swedish, French, Portuguese, Romanian, Russian, Danish, Arabic, Croatian, Norwegian, Indonesian, Dutch, Hungarian, Chinese, Japanese, Polish, and Finnish languages.

- Remove nofollow: The `rel="nofollow"` attribute can be removed from various locations. I'd recommend you to remove it from **Author Link** and **Registered Author Link**.

- Number of comments before the nofollow to be removed: Sets the number of required comments before the links became dofollow for the commentator. This can be very useful in avoiding spam and unwanted comments.

- Number of comments before the nofollow is removed for registered author: Performs the same action like the previous activity, the only difference being that you can set a different number for registered users.

- ▸ Word blacklist: This text area allows you to specify some words used by spammers. If any of these words are found in the comment, the links will be nofollow.

- ▸ Top band: The NoFollow Free plugin can automatically add an image on your blog, in order to tell your visitors that your blog is dofollow. If you choose to display this image, you can select its position.

Once you have defined your settings and updated it, your blog is now dofollow.

Let's use the Top Commentators widget in order reward your commentators to get more comments.

Another good way to reward commentators is to use the Top Commentators widget. This widget displays the list of people who have left the maximum number of comments on your blog—with an optional link to their blog or web site. As the widget is usually displayed on all your blog pages, including the homepage, a commentator has much to gain in terms of SEO if he or she gets featured on it.

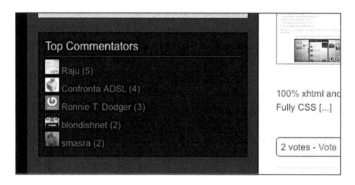

Carry out the following steps to install the Top Commentators widget:

1. Get your copy of the plugin from the link, `http://wordpress.org/extend/plugins/top-commentators-widget/`

2. Install the plugin by following the standard plugin installation procedure as described in Chapter 4.

3. Once the widget is installed, go to **Appearance | Widgets** and add the Top Commentators widget to one of your widget zones.

4. Click on the **Edit** link of the Top Commentators widget in order to define the widget settings.

The following settings can be edited:

- ▸ **Change widget title**: A title to be displayed.

- ▸ **Add description below the title**: An optional description related to the title.

- ▸ **Exclude these users**: You can exclude users by entering their usernames. Excluding yourself is, in my opinion, a good idea.

- ▸ **Reset list every**: Choose to reset the list of top commentators hourly, daily, weekly, monthly, yearly, or never.

- ▸ **Limit number of names to**: How much names you'd like to display. Should be between 5 and 10.

- ▸ **Limit characters in names to**: Limit the display of usernames to X characters.

- ▸ **Remarks for blank list**: A text to be displayed if there are no commentators.

- ▸ **Filter the following full/partial URLs**: Allows you to restrict the display of one or more specific URLs.

- ▸ **Filter the following full/partial e-mail**: Similar to the previous point, but for email addresses.

- ▶ **Display list type as**: Choose between bulleted and numbered display of list. This can be overwritten by using CSS.

- ▶ **Hyperlink each name**: Specify is you'd like the Top Commentators Usernames to have a hyperlink to their site or blog. In my opinion, you should definitely set **Yes** to this option.

- ▶ **Nofollow each name if hyperlinked**: Add `rel="nofollow"` attributes in the top commentators names. You should select the **No** option.

- ▶ **Show number of comments for each commenter**: Allows you to display the number of comments posted by a specific user.

- ▶ **(Hijack-proof?) Group commenters based on**: This option is to eliminate Username stealing. Choose between Usernames and email addresses. Email addresses are a bit more safer.

- ▶ **Show in home page only**: Define if you'd like to display the widget only on your homepage, or on all your blog pages and posts.

- ▶ **Display only commenters with URL**: Allows you to only display the commentators who have a blog or web site.

- ▶ **Display Gravatar**: Allows you to define whether to display gravatars or not.

- ▶ **Gravatar Size**: Size of the gravatar—in pixels

- ▶ Once you are done with the settings, click on the **Done** button and don't forget to save your changes. The Top Commentators widget is now active on your blog!

How it works...

In this recipe, we have learned how to remove the `rel="nofollow"` attribute from our blog as well as to reward our commentators with the help of Top Commentators widget. Of course, don't expect to get a lot of comments if your content isn't interesting or if you're not promoting your blog enough. Personally this technique helped me to get more readers. These readers first visited my blog in order to gain some PageRank by leaving comments, however, they enjoyed the content and became regular readers.

Adding a print stylesheet to your blog

While creating web sites for my company, most of our clients ask us to create print functions for the web site which we're designing for them. Yes, it can seem a little obsolete in a technically advanced world and it isn't green at all, but the fact is that many Internet users still print pages for offline consultation.

In this recipe, we shall learn how to create a print button and add it to your blog, as well as creating an efficient print stylesheet..

Getting ready

To achieve this recipe we need to perform two actions. The first action is to create a print button and add it to your `single.php` file. The second action is to create a CSS stylesheet specially designed for printing so that we can hide the useless parts of the page (while being read offline) such as site footer or sidebar.

How to do it...

Let us start with adding a print button to our blog.

1. Open the `single.php` file from your theme.

2. Add the following code anywhere in the file (though it is better to add it below the post title):

```
<a href="javascript:window.print();" id="print">Print
     this page</a>
```

3. Save the file, and you're done. In case you want, you can give a special look to the link by using the `#print` CSS id.

4. Now, let' create a print stylesheet. First, open your `header.php` file and insert the following line of code within the `<head>` and `</head>` tags:

```
<link rel="stylesheet" type="text/css" href="<?php
bloginfo('template_url'); ?>/print.css" media="print" />
```

5. Save the changes and create a new file on your computer. Name it `print.css` and enter the following code in to it:

```
html
{
    width:100%
}
body
{
    background-color: #fff;
    color: #000;
    font-size: 12pt;
}
a
{
    color: #000;
}
img
{
    border: 0;
```

```
}
.noprint, #footer, #sidebar
{
    d isplay: none;
}
h1, h2
{
    page-break-before: auto;
}
p
{
    page-break-inside: avoid;
}
```

6. Upload the `print.css` file in your server—in the `wp-content/themes/yourtheme` directory.

7. You just created a print button as well as the related print stylesheet.

How it works...

Print button:

The print button uses the JavaScript `window.print()` method that automatically opens the printer dialog for printing the page.

Print stylesheet inclusion and selection:

We include the print stylesheet in the `header.php` file by using the following code:

```
<link rel="stylesheet" type="text/css" href="
<?php bloginfo('template_url'); ?>/print.css" media="print" />
```

You must have noticed the `media="print"` attribute. This attribute tells your computer the case in which that stylesheet has to be used. As this is a print stylesheet, your computer will only use it while printing the page.

Carry out the following steps to print a stylesheet:

1. The biggest part of this work is probably creating the print stylesheet itself. Let's first take a look at the first part of the CSS stylesheet:

```
html
{
    width:100%
}
body
{
```

```
        background-color: #fff;
        color: #000;
        font-size: 12pt;
}
a
{
        color: #000;
}
img
{
        border: 0;
}
```

2. Set the width to 100%. This will allow the printer to use the full length available on the sheet. We should not forget to specify the background color is white—the user will save money and ink.

3. For the text, we will print in black with a size of 12 points. This ensures good visibility on the paper. Personally, I do not see the point in applying a different color to the links. I defined links color to be the same as the rest of the text.

4. The second part concerns hiding the page elements which we don't need in the printed version, with the help of the following code:

```
.noprint, #footer, #sidebar
{
        display: none;
}
```

We have also added a .noprint class. This way, you can hide any element of your page for printing by simply adding the noprint class to the element.

5. The last part of the print stylesheet controls the display of elements on the paper sheet. The page-break-inside, page-break-before, and page-break-after css properties are not known to many developers. It's a bad thing in my opinion. Even though you're not going to use it, they are very useful during the set up of the print stylesheet.

6. The css properties, control page breaks and allow you to define the location where it is possible to jump to the next page.

Let's talk a bit about the `page-break-inside` property. Its role is to specify whether it's possible to split an element in two different pages, or not. There are 3 different values available—`avoid`, `auto`, and `inherit`.

Let's continue to analyze our print stylesheet. It is obvious that we do not want, for example, to have a `<h2>` title at the very bottom of the page and the text printed on the next page. This is where the `page-break-before` property will be very useful.

Also, we'll define that we don't want any paragraphs to be split and printed on two different pages by using the `page-break-inside` CSS property:

```
h1, h2
{
    page-break-before: auto;
}


p
{
    page-break-inside: avoid;
}
```

There's more...

As we have seen in the earlier chapters of this book, WordPress is very extensible. In fact, WordPress isn't only a blog platform as it can be used to perform a lot more things such as creating an online store, a social bookmarking site, or a photoblog.

Using WordPress as a photoblog

A photoblog is a blog—but here you post pictures instead of text. In this recipe, Let's check out a few ready-to-use photoblog themes, and you'll also learn how to create a theme of your own.

Let's start with a list of beautiful photoblog themes. Due to the nature of a photoblog, most themes end up looking like the others—so I felt that it was a good idea to list a lot of themes. The following list of themes is my personal favorite

Installing these themes is easy since you install them as **normal** themes. Just follow the theme specific instructions to get the most out of it.

Photoblog

This theme can be downloaded for free by visiting the following link,
`http://www.blogohblog.com/wordpress-theme-photo-blog/`.

The preceding screenshot depicts the Photoblog theme.

Nishita

This theme can be downloaded for free by visiting the following link,
`http://code.google.com/p/nishita-theme/downloads/list`

The preceding screenshot depicts the Nishita theme.

Fotolog

This theme can be downloaded by visiting the following link,
`http://www.flisterz.com/wordpress-themes/`.

The preceding screenshot depicts the Fotolog theme.

Creating your own Photoblog theme

Now that you have seen some great photoblog themes, how about creating your own
theme? In fact, due to WordPress' flexibility, we can easily transform any existing theme
into a photoblog theme. In this example, I'll transform the default WordPress theme into a
photoblog theme.

Getting ready

The first thing we need to do is to identify the needs for the purpose of achieving the goal of
transforming a classic theme into a photoblog theme.

We need to:

- Be able to post pictures
- Display only one picture at the time
- Have **next** and **previous** links for the visitor to see more pictures
- Have the possibility of inserting a caption for each picture

How to do it...

Carry out the following steps in order to display one picture at a time:

1. Open the `index.php` file and find the loop:

```php
<?php while (have_posts()) : the_post(); ?>

    <div <?php post_class() ?> id="post-<?php the_ID(); ?>">
    <h2><a href="<?php the_permalink() ?>" rel="bookmark"
    title="Permanent Link to <?php the_title_attribute(); ?>">
    <?php the_title(); ?></a></h2>
    <small><?php the_time('F jS, Y') ?><!-- by
    <?php the_author() ?> --></small>

    <div class="entry">
      <?php the_content('Read the rest of this entry &raquo;'); ?>
    </div>

    <p class="postmetadata"><?php the_tags('Tags: ', ', ', ' '
    <br />'); ?> Posted in <?php the_category(', ') ?> |
    <?php edit_post_link('Edit', '', ' | '); ?>
    <?php comments_popup_link('No Comments &#187;', '1
    Comment &#187;', '% Comments &#187;'); ?></p>
    </div>

<?php endwhile; ?>
```

2. Just before the preceding code, add the following line:

```php
<?php query_posts('showposts=1'); ?>
```

3. Save the file and check out the theme—only one post is displayed at a time.

Carry out the following steps in order to remove the useless parts:

1. In the preceding code, you probably must have noticed that we do not need the `meta` part in case of a photoblog as we're not going to use categories and tags. Of course, you can use it if you want. Just skip this step.

2. Simply remove the following part from the code:

```php
<p class="postmetadata"><?php the_tags('Tags: ', ', ', '<br />');
?>
Posted in <?php the_category(', ') ?> |
<?php edit_post_link('Edit', '', ' | '); ?>
<?php comments_popup_link('No Comments &#187;', '1
Comment &#187;', '% Comments &#187;'); ?></p>
```

Carry out the following steps in order to retrieve the picture:

As we are creating a photoblog, we need to retrieve the picture for each post. To do so we're going to use a custom field named `image`.

1. If you have followed the first two steps, the loop on your `index.php` file should look like this:

```php
<?php query_posts('showposts=1'); ?>
<?php while (have_posts()) : the_post(); ?>
        <div <?php post_class() ?> id="post-<?php the_ID(); ?>">
        <h2><a href="<?php the_permalink() ?>" rel="bookmark"
        title="Permanent Link to <?php the_title_attribute(); ?>">
        <?php the_title(); ?></a></h2>
        <small><?php the_time('F jS, Y') ?><!-- by
        <?php the_author() ?> --></small>

        <div class="entry">
          <?php the_content('Read the rest of this entry &raquo;');
             ?>
        </div>

        </div>
<?php endwhile; ?>
```

2. You now have to use the following code in order to get the value of the `image` custom field and display it:

```php
<div class="entry">
<?php $customField = get_post_custom_values("image");
      if (isset($customField[0]))
      {
        the_title(); ?>
        <img src="<?php echo $customField[0];?>" alt="
        <?php the_title();?>" />
        the_content();
      } ?>
</div>
```

3. Now, the theme will automatically retrieve the picture, the title, and eventually a caption (the post content).

4. Here is what your code should look like:

```php
<?php query_posts('showposts=1'); ?>
<?php while (have_posts()) : the_post(); ?>
        <div <?php post_class() ?> id="post-<?php the_ID(); ?>">
        <h2><a href="<?php the_permalink() ?>" rel="bookmark"
        title="Permanent Link to <?php the_title_attribute(); ?>">
        <?php the_title(); ?></a></h2>
        <small><?php the_time('F jS, Y') ?><!-- by
        <?php the_author() ?> --></small>

        <div class="entry">
<?php $customField = get_post_custom_values("image");
```

```
    if (isset($customField[0]))
    {
      the_title(); ?>
      <img src="<?php echo $customField[0];?>" alt="
      <?php the_title();?>" />
      the_content();
    } ?>
    </div>
    </div>
<?php endwhile; ?>
```

Carry out the following steps in order to remove the side bar:

1. In a photoblog, you may want to get the maximum width for your pictures. For this purpose, we need to get rid of the theme sidebar. To do so, edit the `index.php` and `single.php` files. Find and remove the following line from the code:

```
<?php get_sidebar();?>
```

2. If you have a look at the theme now you will find that the sidebar is not displayed, but the content doesn't fill the entire space available. To correct this problem, simply open the `style.css` file and append the following piece of code with it:

```
#content
{
    width:680px;
}
```

Once done, you have your basic photoblog ready!

The following screenshot depicts the photoblog theme which we have created:

If you have followed the earlier stated instructions, you should have a nice photoblog. Sure, some more tweaking can be done to enhance it—for example, disabling links to single posts, or displaying the picture in single posts.

How it works...

In this recipe, we have learned how to easily modify an existing theme in order to create a blog that really fits all your needs.

Custom WordPress queries and loops have been used to grab the information needed from WordPress database. And also, the custom fields are used to display the pictures.

Creating an iPhone-friendly version of your blog

Apple iPhone is very good at displaying web site. However, due to the small size of the screen it isn't always easy to read on—particularly on blogs which have a **magazine** layout.

In order to help people read your blog, even on their iPhone, you should create a mobile version of your web site.

Getting ready

Creating a mobile version of your web site requires you to create a second theme for your blog. If the visitor is using a regular browser, you display your normal theme. If you detect that the visitor is using the iPhone (or any other mobile device) then you display the **made for iPhone** theme.

Lot of work, isn't it? Luckily, a great WordPress plugin can handle all that for you. This plugin is called **iWPhone** and was released in 2008 by Content Robot. The following screenshot shows iWPhone plugin, in action, on an iPhone:

How to do it...

Installing and using the iWPhone plugin is very easy. Carry out the following steps to get started:

1. Grab your copy of the plugin on the ContentRobot web site, by visiting the following link: `http://iwphone.contentrobot.com/2007/07/04/iwphone-wordpress-plugin-and-theme/#download`

2. Unzip the `iwphone-wordpress-plugin-and-theme` directory on your computer's hard drive.

3. Find the `iwphone.php` file inside the `iwphone-wordpress-plugin-and-theme` folder and upload it into your `wp-content/plugins/` directory.

4. Locate and upload the entire `iwphone-by-contentrobot` directory into your `wp-content/themes/` directory.

5. Log in to your WordPress **Administration** area, click on **Plugins,** and activate the iWPhone plugin.

> Do not make the iWPhone-by-ContentRobot theme the current theme.

6. Visit your blog with an iPhone or iPod Touch, and you shall now see your content in the iPhone or iPod touch-optimized theme.

How it works...

The iWPhone plugin consists of a plugin (the `iwphone.php` file) and a specially designed theme for iPhone users. Once the plugin is activated, it will recognize an iPhone user by its user agent and automatically switches to the iWPhone theme.

There's more...

Great, your blog is now optimized for the iPhone and other mobile devices. The problem is that it doesn't use your colors at all. What about a bit of customization to make your blog iPhone version looking like your **real** web site?

Using an header image

In my opinion, the required steps for customizing the iWPhone plugin are to create and use a header image—using your blog logo, for example. Carry out the following steps to customize the iWPhone plugin:

1. Open the theme images directory. You'll find an image named `header.jpg`.

2. Create your image. The width of the image must be 320 pixels and the height must be 60 pixels. Save this image as `header.jpg` in the image directory, replacing the default `header.jpg` image.

3. Open the theme `style.css` file and go to line 54 of the code. Uncomment the line (but don't forget to comment the beginning of the line, which follows), save the file, and you're done. Your header image will now be displayed!

Eventually, get rid of the automatically inserted title and slogan by reading the upcoming paragraph.

Modify the title and slogan

By default, similar to the well known Kubrick theme, the iWPhone plugin shows your blog name and slogan as a text header. Although this will be useful for most blogs, you may want to display, for example, the iPhone or iPod version as the slogan..

If you want to have a slogan of your choice, you just have to follow a few simple steps. Open the `header.php` and go to line 42 of the code. The function on that particular line is the function which displays your blog name. The function located on the following line will display your blog slogan. You've guessed it right; you simply have to replace the function with the text you want to display, like the blog name and slogan. The following screenshot shows an iPhone displaying my blog with its custom iPhone theme.

Integrating a forum in your WordPress blog

A blog is all about discussion. Sure, your readers can discuss your article in the comments, but they can't submit any ideas except by sending you an email.

A great way to make your visitors visit your blog again is to integrate a forum, so that they can have discussions—with you and other visitors about various topics.

Getting ready

Forums don't work for any kind of blog. For example, I launched a forum on my blog www.wprecipes.com and it is pretty busy. I launched the same forum on www.psdrecipes.com, but this one is absolutely empty! It depends of your blog topic and your visitors. A great way to make people post on your forum is to give free help and advice.

Many solutions are available to integrate a forum on your WordPress blog: PhpBB/Vbulletin integration, BBPress, and so on. In my opinion, the easiest, and best, forum solution for WordPress is definitely the WP-Forum plugin. This plugin is complete, powerful and easy to install, use and manage.

In this recipe, you're going to learn how to integrate a forum on your WordPress blog using the wp-forum plugin. The following screenshot shows the www.wprecipes.com forum.

How to do it...

1. As you can guess, the first thing to do is to get the plugin by visiting the following link: `http://www.fahlstad.se/wp-plugins/wp-forum/`

2. Once you have downloaded the plugin, install it on your blog like any other plugin (you can find the standard plugin installation procedure in Chapter 4)

3. Then, create a new page on your blog. Switch the editor to html or source mode and type the following line:

   `<!--WPFORUM-->`

4. To publish the page, go to **Settings | Wp-Forum** and customize the options according to your needs.

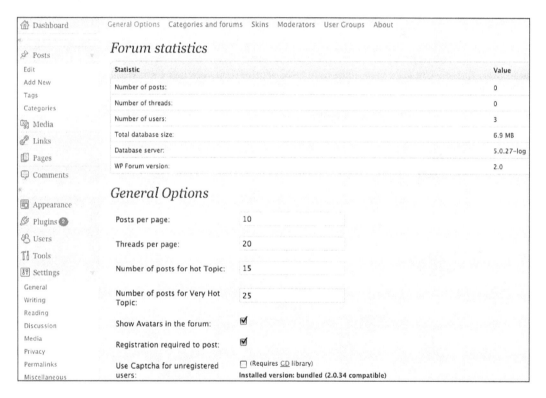

5. In the horizontal menu click on the **Categories and forums** option. Then, click on the **Add category** link. A category is a group of forums. For example, you can create a category named **Computers** with a **Mac** and **Pc** forum inside.

 Note that a forum must belong to a category.

6. Create categories and forums according to your needs.

7. That's all for the basics. Your forum is now up and running!

How it works...

When installed, the wp-forum plugin creates some new database tables in order to record threads and topics of your forum. For the rest, it is an advanced forum working the same way (but with less functionality) as popular solutions such as V-Bulletin or PhpBB.

There's more...

As you have seen in the wp-forum plugin option page, the horizontal menu is full of options that you can customize.

Skins

Skins are CSS files and images which can give a new look and feel to your forum. The idea is very good, but the most notable problem is the lack of available skins. Some can be downloaded from the link `http://www.fahlstad.se/wp-content/plugins/wp-forum/skins/`, and one more can be found at `http://dikma.web.id/2007/11/18/add-on-skin-wp-forum/`.

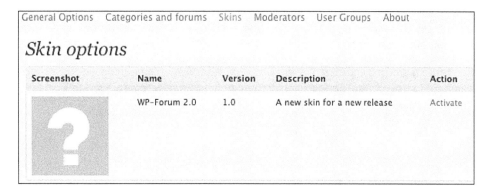

To activate a style, first upload it into your `wp-content/plugins/wp-forum/skins/` directory. Then, got to **WP-Forum** option page in your **Dashboard**, select **Skins** on the horizontal menu, and activate the skin you want.

Moderators

This part is very useful if you're running a multi author blog or if your forum has a lot of traffic.

On this page, you can select one of your registered users (who must have the right to edit posts) and allow him to moderate your forum. You can create a global moderator (who can moderate all forums) or a normal moderator (who moderates one forum). Once you have chosen the user to be the moderator, just click on the **Add moderator** button to give him or her moderation rights.

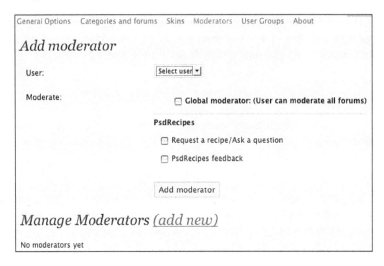

User groups

User groups allow you to group a few users together. I know this is a very common feature in lot of forums, but I never really found it useful .

You can create a group by naming it and giving it a description. Once done, you can add members to the group. The following screenshot shows how to add a group in the WordPress forum.

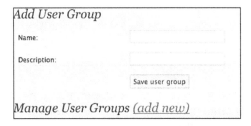

Congratulations, you have just arrived to the last page of the WordPress Cookbook. At this point, if you have read and understood all the recipes from this book you are known as an advanced WordPress user. A user who knows how to enhance an existing theme, secure his or her WordPress blog, add plugins, and use hacks to unleash the power of WordPress and much more.

I really hope this book helped you!

Index

time saving, WordPress shortcodes used 126, 127
two different loops, using without duplicate posts 114-116

premium themes
citrus theme 38
fresh news 39
Mimbo Pro theme 35
open air theme 37
WP Vybe theme 36

print stylesheet
about 264-266
adding, steps 263, 264
adding, to blog 263
inclusion and exclusion 264
print button 264
starting 263
working 264

Q

query_posts() function 111, 112

R

read_private_pages 144
read_private_posts 144
Rebel Magazine theme, advanced themes 32
Redirection plugin
installing 88
simple redirection, creating 88
using, for affiliate marketing and cloaking 89
register_sidebar() function 98, 100
register_sidebars() function 99, 100, 104
rel="nofollow" attribute, removing 258
related posts plugin
displaying, steps 254, 255
working 255
Revolution 2 theme, advanced themes 33
Rio theme, classic themes 25
robot.txt file
used, for avoiding duplicate content 191
role manager plugin
about 141
URL 141
working 142
RSS feed
ads, inserting 221, 223

displaying, on blog 119
plugin versus hack 227
redirecting to Feedburner, hack used 226
redirecting to Feedburner, plugin used 226, 227
redirecting to Feedburner, steps 226

S

search results
searched text highlighting, steps 238, 239
Search Unleashed plugin
installing 93
search extending, steps 93, 94
search extending, working 94
SEO
permalinks optimizing, steps 182
permalinks optimizing, working 183
title tag, optimizing 187, 188
title tag optimizing, steps 188
title tag optimizing, working 189
SEO, enhancing tips
backlinks, getting 205
blog, checking for XHTML valid 206
keywords, using 206
permalinks, optimizing 207
proper h tags structure, using 205
shell script
using, to create automatic files 164, 165
using, to create database backups 164, 165
sidebar.php file
about 135, 136
code, adding 139, 140
show_fullname parameter 157
sidebar widget-ready
preparing, steps 97, 98
working 98
sitemap
adding, to blog 192
article priority 196
basic options 195
basic options, advanced options 196
basic options, construction mode 195
basic options, file types 195
basic options, notifications 195
content 196
data, to exclude 196

working 201
title tag
optimizing, steps 188
working 189
to_ping 117
Top Commentators widget
about 260
installing 260
settings 261
Twitter Tools plugin
twitter integrating, steps 59
twitter integrating, working 59
used, twitter integrating 58

U

unfiltered_html 144
unfiltered_upload 144
update_plugins 145
upload_files 144
user access, controlling
current_user_can() function, arguments
144, 145
current_user_can() function used 143
user groups 278
User Manager
authors and users, managing 12
users deleting, steps 13
users details editing, steps 14
working 14
user roles 142
user roles, capabilities
administrator 142
author 142
contributor 142
editor 142
subscriber 143

V

visitors, Adsense ads managing 218-220

W

web site, for WordPress theme download
100 excellent WordPress themes 40
best WP theme 40

free magazine style WordPress theme gallery
40
premium WordPress themes gallery 40
ThemeLab free themes 41
WordPress.org theme gallery 40
WPVote WordPress themes 41
Who sees ads plugin
advanced conditions 221
configuring 219
global options 220
global options, click safety 220
global options, date format 220
global options, old post 220
global options, regular reader 220
installing 219
starting 218
working 220
widget-ready zones
creating, steps 99, 100
two (or more) creating, steps 99
working 100
widget_test($args) function 104
widgets
adding to theme, steps 96
complete widget code 104
core widgets, modifying 101
downloaded widgets, installing 97
installing, steps 96
own widget, creating 102, 103
own widget, working 104
pre-installation steps 95
two (or more) different widget-ready zones,
creating 99, 100
versus plugins 95
working 96
WordPress
Adsense ads, displaying to search engine
visitors 215, 216
Adsense ads, inserting in RSS feed 222-224
authors and users managing, User Manager
used 12-14
content exporting, Export tool used 18
content importing, Import tool used 15, 17
media files managing, media library used 6, 7
plugins editing, Plugin editor used 11, 12
RSS feeds, redirecting to Feedburner
225-227

Thank you for buying
WordPress 2.7 Cookbook

Packt Open Source Project Royalties

When we sell a book written on an Open Source project, we pay a royalty directly to that project. Therefore by purchasing WordPress 2.7 Cookbook, Packt will have given some of the money received to the WordPress project.

In the long term, we see ourselves and you—customers and readers of our books—as part of the Open Source ecosystem, providing sustainable revenue for the projects we publish on. Our aim at Packt is to establish publishing royalties as an essential part of the service and support a business model that sustains Open Source.

If you're working with an Open Source project that you would like us to publish on, and subsequently pay royalties to, please get in touch with us.

Writing for Packt

We welcome all inquiries from people who are interested in authoring. Book proposals should be sent to author@packtpub.com. If your book idea is still at an early stage and you would like to discuss it first before writing a formal book proposal, contact us; one of our commissioning editors will get in touch with you.

We're not just looking for published authors; if you have strong technical skills but no writing experience, our experienced editors can help you develop a writing career, or simply get some additional reward for your expertise.

About Packt Publishing

Packt, pronounced 'packed', published its first book "Mastering phpMyAdmin for Effective MySQL Management" in April 2004 and subsequently continued to specialize in publishing highly focused books on specific technologies and solutions.

Our books and publications share the experiences of your fellow IT professionals in adapting and customizing today's systems, applications, and frameworks. Our solution-based books give you the knowledge and power to customize the software and technologies you're using to get the job done. Packt books are more specific and less general than the IT books you have seen in the past. Our unique business model allows us to bring you more focused information, giving you more of what you need to know, and less of what you don't.

Packt is a modern, yet unique publishing company, which focuses on producing quality, cutting-edge books for communities of developers, administrators, and newbies alike. For more information, please visit our website: www.PacktPub.com.

WordPress 2.7 Complete

ISBN: 978-1-847196-56-9   Paperback: 296 pages

Create your own complete blog or web site from scratch with WordPress

1. Everything you need to set up your own feature-rich WordPress blog or web site

2. Clear and practical explanations of all aspects of WordPress

3. In-depth coverage of installation, themes, syndication, and podcasting

4. Explore WordPress as a fully functioning content management system

WordPress for Business Bloggers

ISBN: 978-1-847195-32-6   Paperback: 356 pages

Promote and grow your WordPress blog with advanced plug-ins, analytics, advertising, and SEO

1. Gain a competitive advantage with a well polished WordPress business blog

2. Develop and transform your blog with strategic goals

3. Create your own custom design using the Sandbox theme

4. Apply SEO (search engine optimization) to your blog

5. Market and measure the success of your blog

6. Integrate analytics and paid advertising into your WordPress blog

Please check **www.PacktPub.com** for information on our titles